THE PAINTINGS OF

Ken Howard.

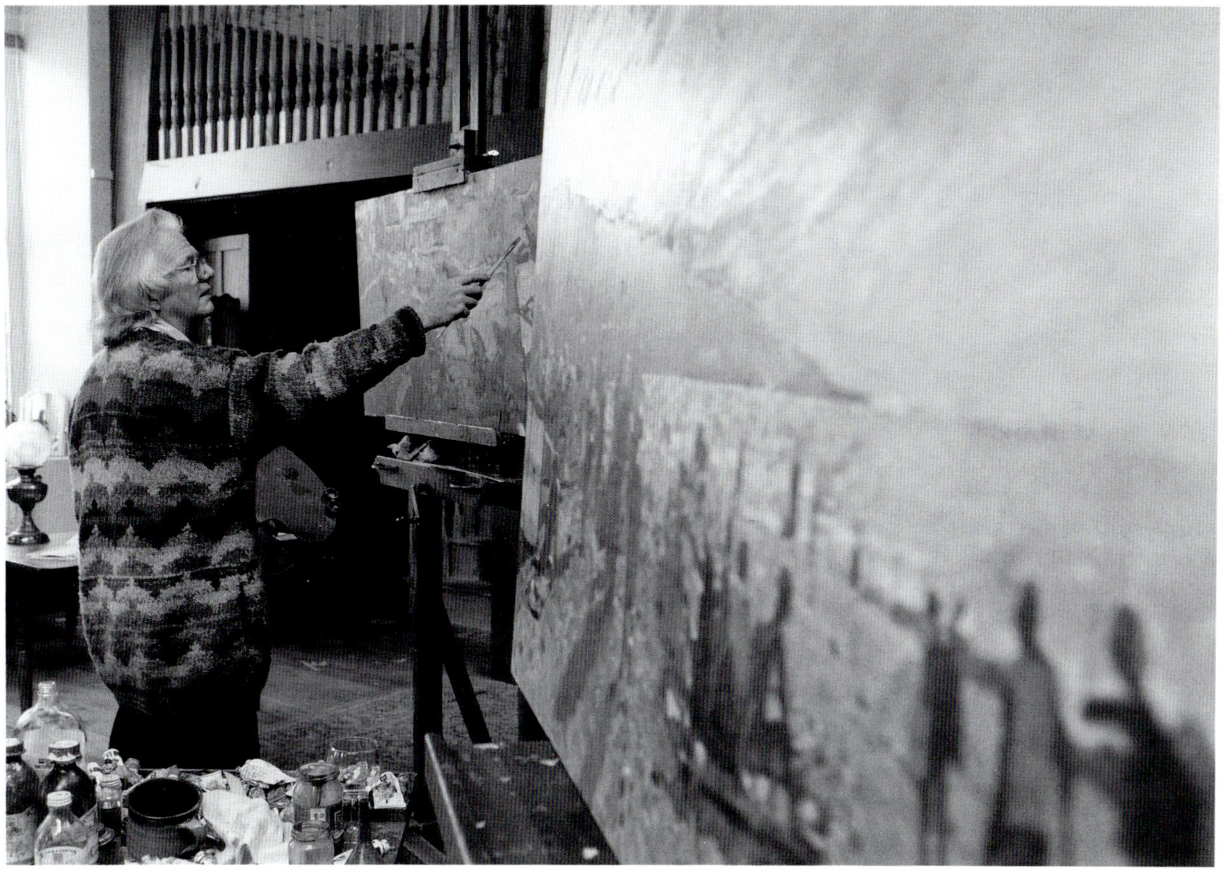

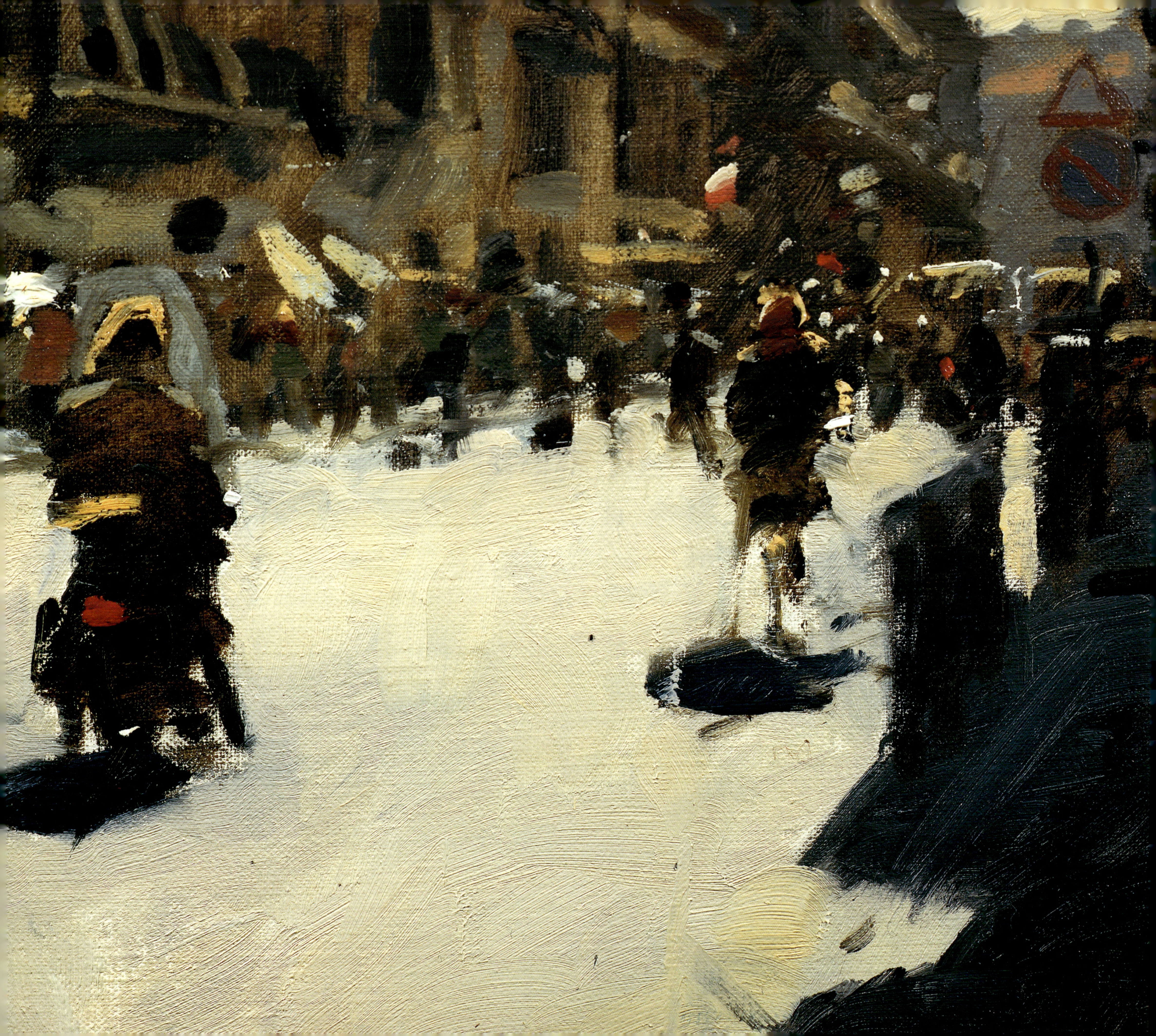

THE PAINTINGS OF
Ken Howard.

– DRAWN BY THE LIGHT –

MICHAEL SPENDER

To Carol & Alan
with very best wishes
Ken.

David & Charles

Acknowledgements

For Steve, Joanna, Edwin and Patrick

(Page 1) Ken Howard working on **'Charlotte and the Silk Shirt'** (p 94) in St Clement's Studio, Mousehole. In the foreground is **'Sennen Evening II'** (p 63).
Photograph, 1990.

Frontispiece: **September Light, Afternoon, Via Cavour, Florence** (detail) (see p 40).

British Library Cataloguing in Publication Data

Spender, Michael
The paintings of Ken Howard.
I. Title
759.42

ISBN 0 7153 9919 5

Typeset by Ace Filmsetting Ltd, Frome, Somerset
Book designed by Michael Head
and printed in Singapore by CS Graphics Pte Ltd
for David & Charles plc
Brunel House Newton Abbot Devon

I am greatly indebted to the artist for allowing me to indulge myself in his art. Ken has not only submitted himself to many hours of interviews and discussion about his work and life, but he has also been generous enough to accept without reservation what I wanted to write about him. During the preparations for the book Christa and Ken have been generous in entertaining me at their homes in Cornwall and London.

Without the many patrons who have collected Ken's work, he would not have been able to devote himself to his art and become the painter we admire today. We are both particularly grateful to all those private and corporate collectors, as well as the Imperial War Museum and Plymouth Art Gallery, who have allowed us to illustrate their paintings. The choice of work was difficult, and we only wish we could have included more.

A particular pleasure is that John Ward agreed to write the foreword. Both Ken and I would like to thank him, as well as the many friends in galleries, studios, classrooms, workshops and offices, who have encouraged us to produce the book and to mount the accompanying retrospective exhibition at the Bankside Gallery. While we would prefer to mention all these colleagues, space only permits us to name a few of them:

Peter Johnson and Sarah Sowerby, who have put in many hours collecting together paintings at the Lowndes Lodge Gallery and arranging for their photographing, as well as giving Ken their total support; David Wolfers and Sarah Russell-Walling, with whom Ken has been associated over many years of exhibitions at the New Grafton Gallery; Ken's long-suffering models, several of whom are referred to in the text; Alison Elks, my editor, and those at David and Charles who have made the book a reality; Charles Bartlett PRWS, who encouraged the staging of the exhibition; Sarah Hassall, Sandie Fillingham and the rest of the Bankside Gallery staff for their patience and fortitude; Maureen Connett, who conceived the subtitle; John Richardson and Michael Todd-White, who shouldered the burden of the photography; C.D. Soar, Ken's excellent framers.

Our chief acknowledgements go to those who have given us most support. Helen helped me with the text and the transcription of many hours of interview tapes. She also deserves my thanks for looking after Haddon, while I tapped away on the keyboard. Ken reserves his deepest thanks for Christa, who has come into the studio each evening to talk over the day's work, and who has in so many ways helped him try to find himself.

MICHAEL SPENDER
London, June 1991

Contents

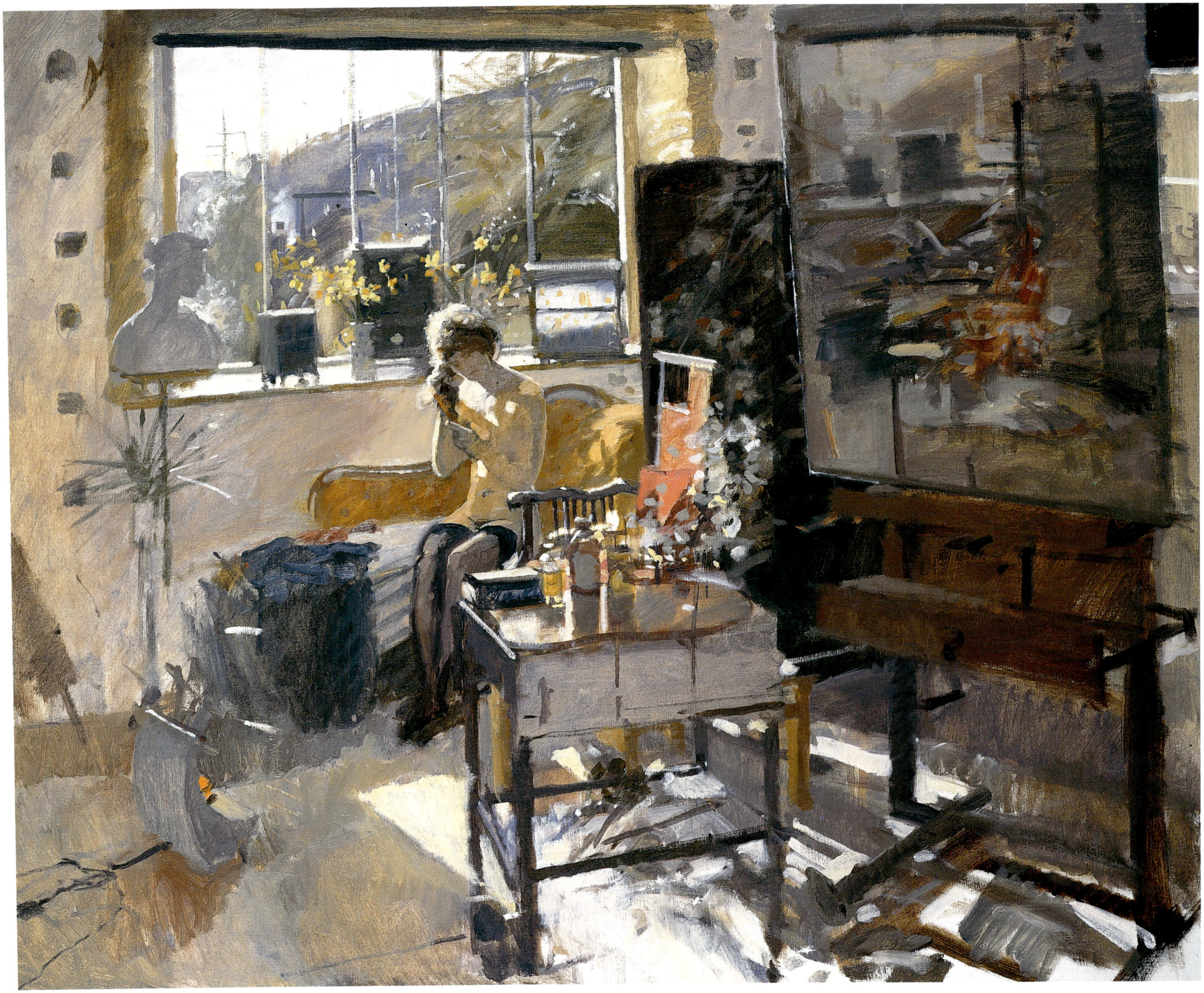

Valerie combing her hair to Vivaldi Oil on canvas, 1989. 40 × 48ins.

Foreword

I don't think there is a bushel which could hide Ken Howard's talents. From early student days he has shown energy, enterprise and intelligence about his skills which is outstanding. 'Many are called but few are chosen' can be said about the students of art schools; the energies of some evaporate in two or three years of hot air while many disappear comforted by the endless excuses and respectability of failure in the Arts. The 'steadies' will opt for teaching with a pension in prospect. There is something about Ken which will have none of this. The skills he so readily acquired he meant to use, this exercise was – and is – as necessary to him as drink to a drunkard. But he is also an awkward customer, a rough dealer with the notions of what's what in the fashionable art circles and possessing a more than adequate ability to argue his case.

And what, may we ask, is his case? It is that a painter should be able – and encouraged – to use to the full his particular talents. The disdain, often contempt, for the gifts of drawing and objective painting conveyed by the critics, who drag their weary eyes round exhibition after exhibition for twenty years or so before sinking into oblivion, should not be allowed to blight and destroy talents which could delight and fulfil. Certainly painting and drawing delight Ken, and about this he is refreshingly brash without any 'ivory tower' stuff. He has few illusions about either the art world or the real world, even enjoying the rough and tumble, having a lot to say and a lot to paint for time is precious.

When he accepted commissions in Northern Ireland to paint, he was not wheeled on and off a set piece guarded and cosseted as a privileged onlooker. He chose to live there depending on the nimbleness of mind and foot gained during his National Service with the Royal Marine Commandos. His common touch has a robustness – he wasn't a pupil and friend of Ruskin Spear for nothing – which found for him in the streets and back yards of Belfast inspiration and excitement in plenty. A large painting of a wall stays in my mind, a wall covered with graffiti and eloquent of the waste and sorrow of the Irish situation. For Ken this was the main force behind the picture, a still life of colossal sadness, yet the painter's eye is there noting the subtleties of colour – the orange and radiance of the bruise – and it is a beautiful picture.

His good, large appetite for work and for being used has taken him all over the world, giving him a capability and power of decision and a fund of experiences. He enjoys life but it is never of the refined, monastic, studio variety. He has forged a talent which is now in full spate and there just isn't any one else working in England at this time who has such a talent. This superb gift is at the moment exercised mostly either in pictures of his studio or of the beaches and harbours of Cornwall. Happy pictures of pleasant places? Yes, but more than that. In the studio sunlight fingers round the mess of paints, reduces the model to an object of secondary importance. It is a visitation of our fickle English summer, the impossible mixture of sharp garish glare and the everlasting echoes of light reverberating round the room, turning the dusty furniture into the perfect subject for this gifted man's brush. Here a grimy pot of turps will have the bloom of the rarest peach, and there the sticks of furniture will vibrate with the energy with which he seizes upon the shape. Here is no settling down to paint what is measureable but a breathless, fierce attempt to grasp at once a moment when all is fizz before flatness descends. And he does it. He bangs nails on the head with real gusto and with a wonderful touch of excitement.

On the beach in the kaleidoscope of humans and their litter of wind-breaks, chairs, games and towels which occupy for a summer's day, he nails down the same transient moment, mostly grandly in his large pictures and exquisitely in the little panels. Perhaps you need to turn one of these studies upside down to perceive the full excitement of touch and brush work scratch and scrawl, how again and again he achieves wonderful passages of colour. Nowhere do you find a tired moment, the falling back onto a stock formula.

Here is a show of gifts to make us rejoice and while he does paint to please it is only after he has first pleased himself. How few painters working today can have given so much pleasure and yet there will be much carping over such success and all the old cannon will be brought out to bombard him. 'Is he a "serious" painter? Can a man paint such pleasurable subjects and yet be worthy of critical acclaim? He brings nothing new to painting, it's all been said before, he churns out picture after picture of the same subject.' Art is marvellously unsentimental. While the desire to be a serious, respectable painter is indeed laudable, it provides no royal road to anything at all except perhaps dull conformism. Think for one moment of the ticks and measurements which have constipated the good and holy students of the Slade School over the past few decades. All that effort for such monumental dullness. The dubious practice of painting pleasurable subjects? This is a piece of puritanism, one of the props thought up by those devoid of talent who felt that it was safer to be in the ugly-ugly territory than that of the pretty-pretty, a herd instinct fostered in art schools to cover the high proportion of failures they produce. The question to be asked is not about subject matter but whether it is a good painting or a bad painting. To the accusation of 'it has all been done before' the answer is yes, but not by Ken Howard. His pictures don't disappear in mixed exhibitions, they sing out 'Ken Howard'. His work – his handling of paint and his eye – is unique. He won't have imitators, since what he does calls for gifts and skills of great rarity. No conscious labour will forge these gifts, it is just that unfair, unreasonable thing – great talent. 'He paints the same subject over and over again', but painters have always worked thus. Who carps when El Greco churns out another saint, or Monet another haystack?

This is a good moment to look back over Ken Howard's work, not only for the pleasure such a collection gives but also for the encouragement it extends to those who, sometimes overawed by the pretensions of those dominating the world in Art, may feel released and able to say, this I like, this pleases, this does me good.

And it leaves us with the lovely question – what lies ahead?

JOHN WARD

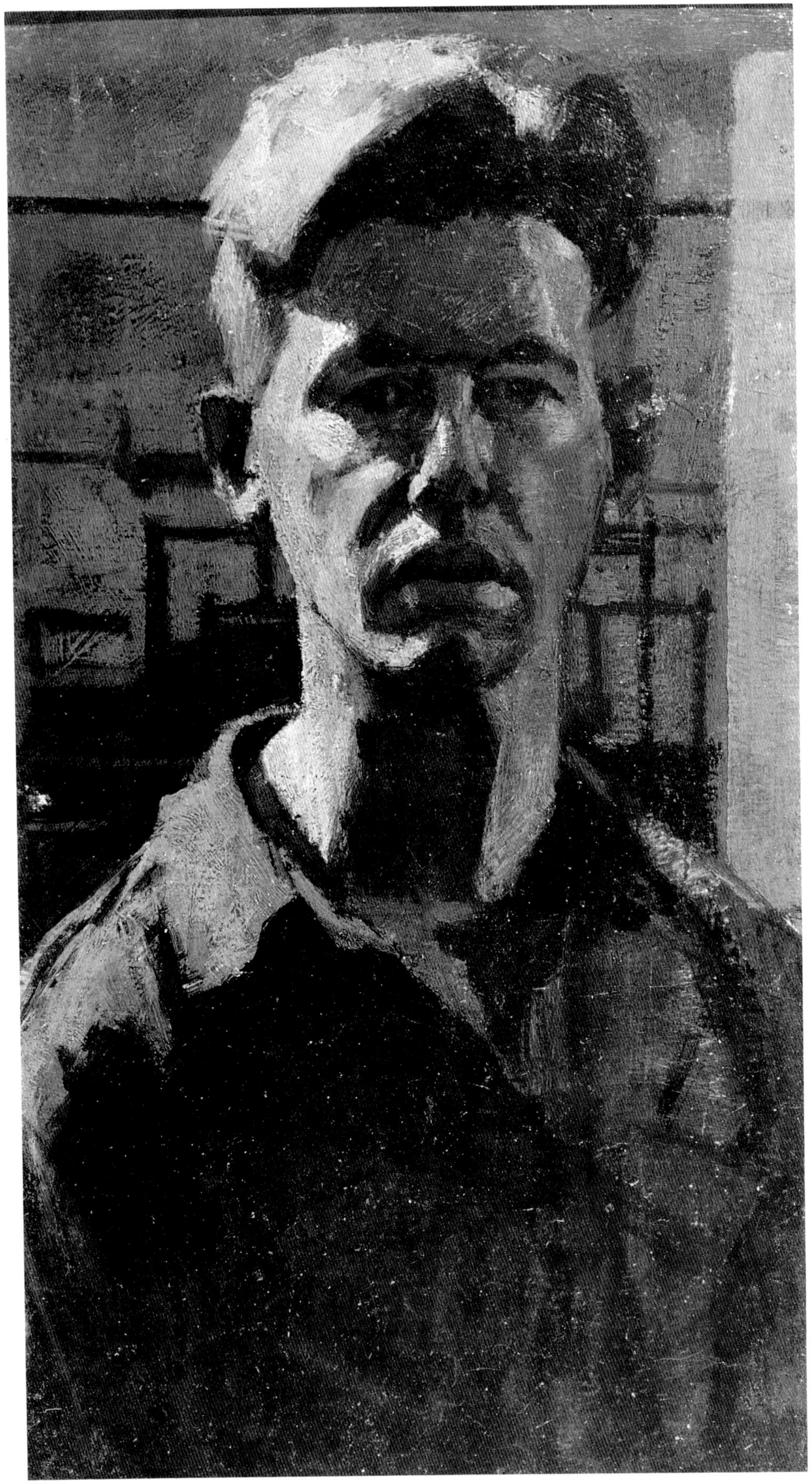

Self-Portrait
Oil on board, 1954. 17 × 9ins.

Marine Broadley
Oil on board, 1954. 17 × 13ins.

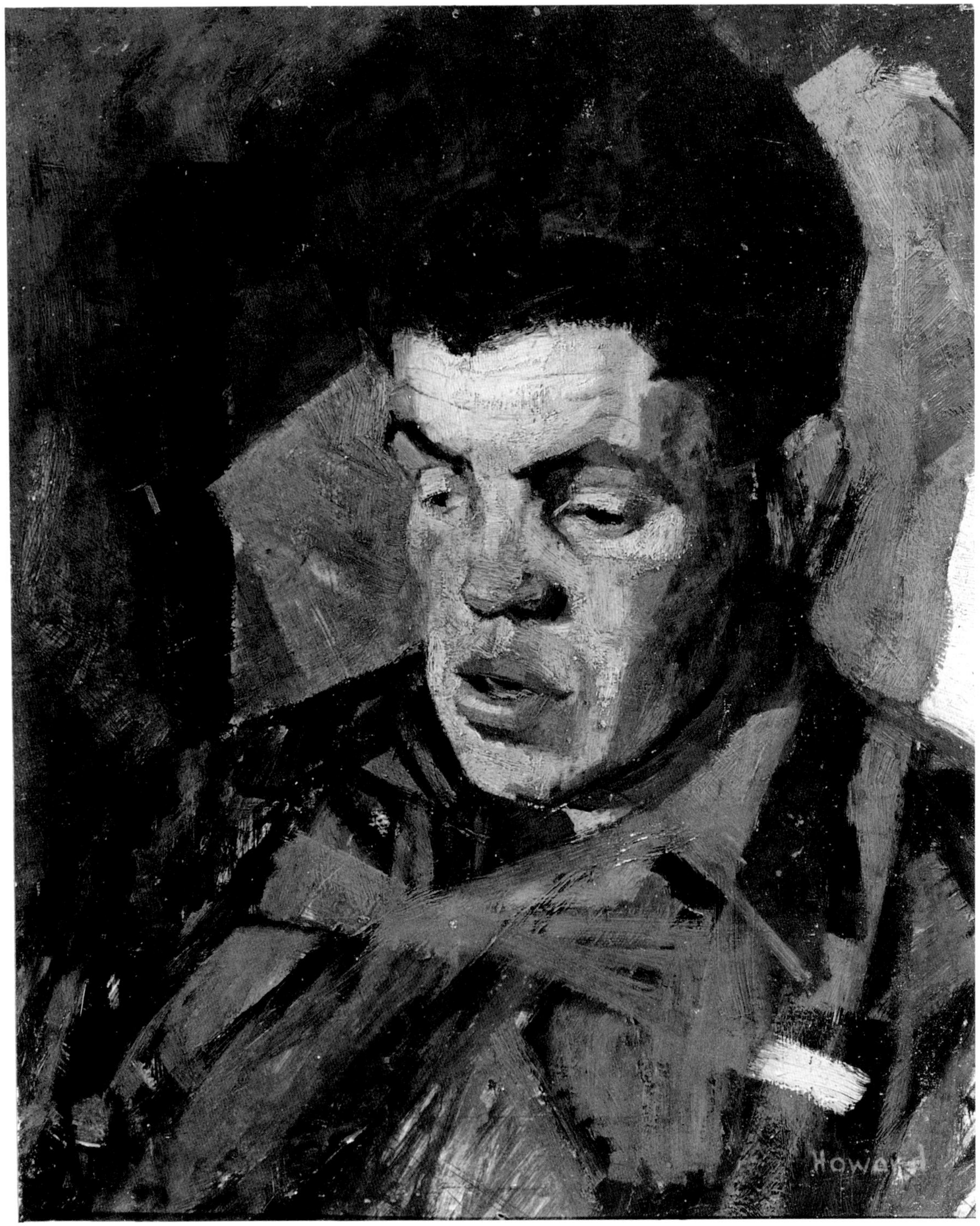

Life and Work

The eyes stare uncertainly from the shadowed face, his intense features sharply sculpted by the light from the window of a Plymouth barrack-room. This is the enquiring, but determined face of a youthful painter with a passionate will to establish himself as an artist of merit and recognition. This strength of purpose was to carry him through periods of disquiet and gloom towards what is, for those who enjoy his art, a light and airy world, in which lucid brushwork flows with apparent effortlessness from gifted hands.

For Ken Howard the effort remains intensive, however, and is exerted with the enthusiasm, energy and undisguised addiction to hard work which are characteristic of the man. He is perpetually driven onwards in search of an ever clearer and more truthful, yet less restrained, evocation of the world. Over the three and a half decades of his career to date, this search has led the artist to streamline his range of subject matter. Having settled on his subject, he has channelled his experiments through this subject, watching it, worrying it, exploring it from every angle. In the early 1990s he is to be seen concentrating on images of three types: the figure in a studio setting; Venice, the magical city of light; the beaches of the Cornish peninsula of West Penwith. In his hands each of these subjects provides infinite possibilities for picture-making, and each offers its own challenges and uncharted territory.

Through constant, but scarcely repetitive, reworking of his themes, Howard continues to explore the potential for, and approach the limits of, academic figurative painting. Like all truly remarkable painters, his art transcends his stylistic bed-rock, although this is of necessity solid. Many of the oil paintings and watercolours painted since the mid-1980s seem to reveal an artist in search of a quasi-religious affirmation of the power and meaning of light. Any painter who admires Turner and Monet as Howard does is likely to place great emphasis on the naturalistic and pictorial revelation of light in the world. But the manner in which he seeks to grasp the essential character not only of reflected light on objects in the world, but also the very light source itself, is perhaps peculiar to this artist among his contemporaries. So too is the way that in all his best pictures the light can be seen to sculpt the scene, to illuminate and describe life.

The selection of images reproduced here is a survey of the painter in mid-career. It also clearly demonstrates how he has increasingly, and with growing confidence, been drawn by the light towards a painterly world at the very edge of realism.

The young man doing his National Service with the Royal Marines was already certain he would be a painter. The *Self-Portrait* and the strong study of *Marine Broadley*, two of his earliest surviving works, reveal an interest in the effects of strong light. The journey from the chiaroscuro darkness of these pictures to the dazzling light and bright shadows of the large and ravishing painting of *Valerie combing her hair to Vivaldi* echoes, in half a lifetime, that from Caravaggio-inspired early Velázquez to the bright palette of Impressionism. This chapter will briefly outline the often difficult steps along this path of Ken Howard – painter.

He was brought up with his sister in a terraced house in the industrial North London suburb of Cricklewood, where he had been born in 1932. From the Depression into the War, times were hard and his family lived extremely modestly. The boy showed an early interest in drawing, which his parents encouraged to the remarkable extent of acquiring for him a coveted paint box, which cost three times his father's weekly wage. Many hours were spent sketching, often at home, while the other boys were out playing. He would copy the old masters – Frans Hals's *Laughing Cavalier*, the defeat of the Spanish Armada, jousting knights. At the Great Western Railway sidings at Old Oak Common, where he went train-spotting, he also started to draw the railway scene. Subjects were found even in the air-raid shelter under the factory where his father worked.

As time passed Howard received sufficient encouragement to pursue his passion for painting with uninterrupted determination. His father had no preconceived ambitions for him. When, at fifteen, the aspiring artist said he wished to go to art school, the only paternal comment was that he would have to earn his own living, for his father could not afford to keep him. Howard believes this was the best advice he could have been given and inherent in it is a philosophy which he has always stuck to as a professional painter.

At sixteen, he left Kilburn Grammar School and enrolled at Hornsey School of Art. Arriving at Hornsey he found the drawings of his fellow students impressed him, but the paintings – 'art school art' as he describes them – mostly did not. Abstract painting, particularly that inspired by Picasso and Braque, was becoming fashionable, but for his inspiration Howard turned back to early Velázquez, and to contemporaries casting new light on the objective world, such as Stanley Spencer, the young Victor Pasmore, the American illustrator Ben Shahn and, eventually, the 'Kitchen Sink' school.

Relying already on the still-held axiom that form and content should be one, Howard absorbed and drew from such influences in pursuit of a goal that was already clear – the depiction of the world in which he found himself. His own work was at first branded 'conscientious' by his teachers.

'I hated that. I felt it was almost an insult, as if they couldn't think of anything else to say about me. Later on, thank goodness, I began to get a little more said, but it is true that I have always had a tendency towards conscientiousness – in other words reworking and sometimes over-working a picture.'

Possibilities for exhibiting in galleries were few and far between for students at the beginning of the 1950s, but the Hampstead Open Air exhibitions did provide a regular opportunity to supplement a basic income. These were held along a wall near Whitestone Pond. Each Sunday students from Hornsey, the Slade and other colleges would take their previous week's paintings up to the Heath, hang their offerings in a place chosen by lot, then wander around to see what people from other colleges were doing. If, at the end of the day, Howard went home with his portfolio slightly lighter, he would be gratified. Not only had he earned a few pounds, but crucially it had been demonstrated that someone actually wanted some of his new work. The sense of elation when a buyer shows the wish to live with one of his paintings is still, it seems, a driving force behind the artist's prolific output.

At the end of his first year at Hornsey, Howard spent six weeks travelling in Spain. In Madrid he studied Velázquez and discovered Goya, whose Black paintings affected him deeply and, on a technical level, encouraged him to deepen his palette. He also produced a body of work and, on his return, had sufficient confidence to enter six paintings for an exhibition in Willesden. This foray proved encouraging, as the artist describes:

'Ruskin Spear was the judge, and he gave me first, second and third prize in oils and first and second prize in watercolours. They said "You can't do that, Mr Spear, we need a first, a second and a third in both categories". And he said "You told me to choose the best three pictures in oils and the best three pictures in watercolours, and that's what I have done". And he wouldn't change his mind.'

For further subject matter Howard did not need to travel any greater distance from home than the railway sidings at Neasden and Cricklewood, between which his parents' house stood. The oil paintings of these subjects which survive are often painted on small, but wide, panoramic boards, whose shapes mirror the essentially horizontal world of the shunting yards. They are typically dark in tone and serious of mood. The two paintings illustrated are intensively worked and convey understated, yet tangible emotion. They also contain an assured grasp of form and space that betrays the experience of many hours' hard graft with pencil and paper.

These beautiful panels indicate that by his early twenties Howard had achieved an adult vision and sense of direction, with a technique to match. Representing the first steps along his career path, they at once show how remarkably consistent and purposeful in its evolution that career has been. The artist recalls how he went about recording the railway yards:

'I'm an early starter, and I always feel I work best in the morning. In those days I used to go off to Neasden, draw or paint for an hour or so, from about seven-thirty to nine, and then cycle off to Hornsey to be there by ten. The railway workers used to come across the yard on their way to work, with cans of tea and boxes of sandwiches. I was sitting there one morning – doing this very painting of the sidings – and this old guy stopped and watched me paint. He said to me "Do you know, I've walked across this railway yard for the last thirty years, and I've never seen it was beautiful". That to me is one of the key things about painting – not only to communicate – but that it should open people's eyes, reveal the world to people.'

Both the Neasden panel, which so impressed the railway worker, and its slightly later companion of Cricklewood, convey a convincing feeling for the grim realities of the scene. It was presumably not any prettification of the subject that led the workman to wonder at its beauty, for these are not pretty paintings. Rather, Howard has expressed his own strong affection for and familiarity with the scene through believable realism. What also helps lift the paintings above the descriptive is the imaginative arrangement of horizontal and vertical elements. This rhythmical tableau of shapes forms a sort of urban version of Ivon Hitchens' rural idyll.

The much later painting of *Southall 2: Silver Morning* indicates that Howard retained his interest in the structures and shapes of the railways long after the age of steam had passed. Rather than the horizontal axis of the earlier paintings, this canvas centres around the strong vertical axis which is a hallmark of much of the artist's most impressive work of the late 1960s and early 1970s. At the

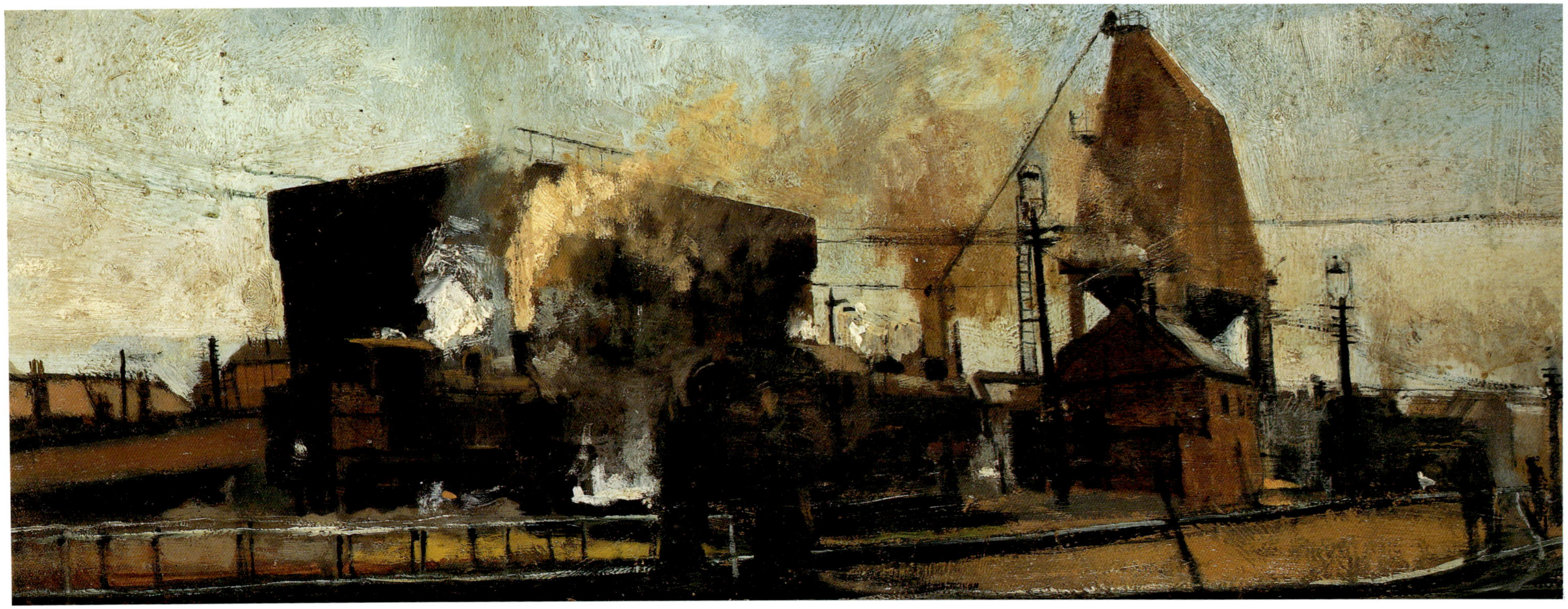

Neasden Sidings
Oil on board, c 1952. 10 × 27ins.

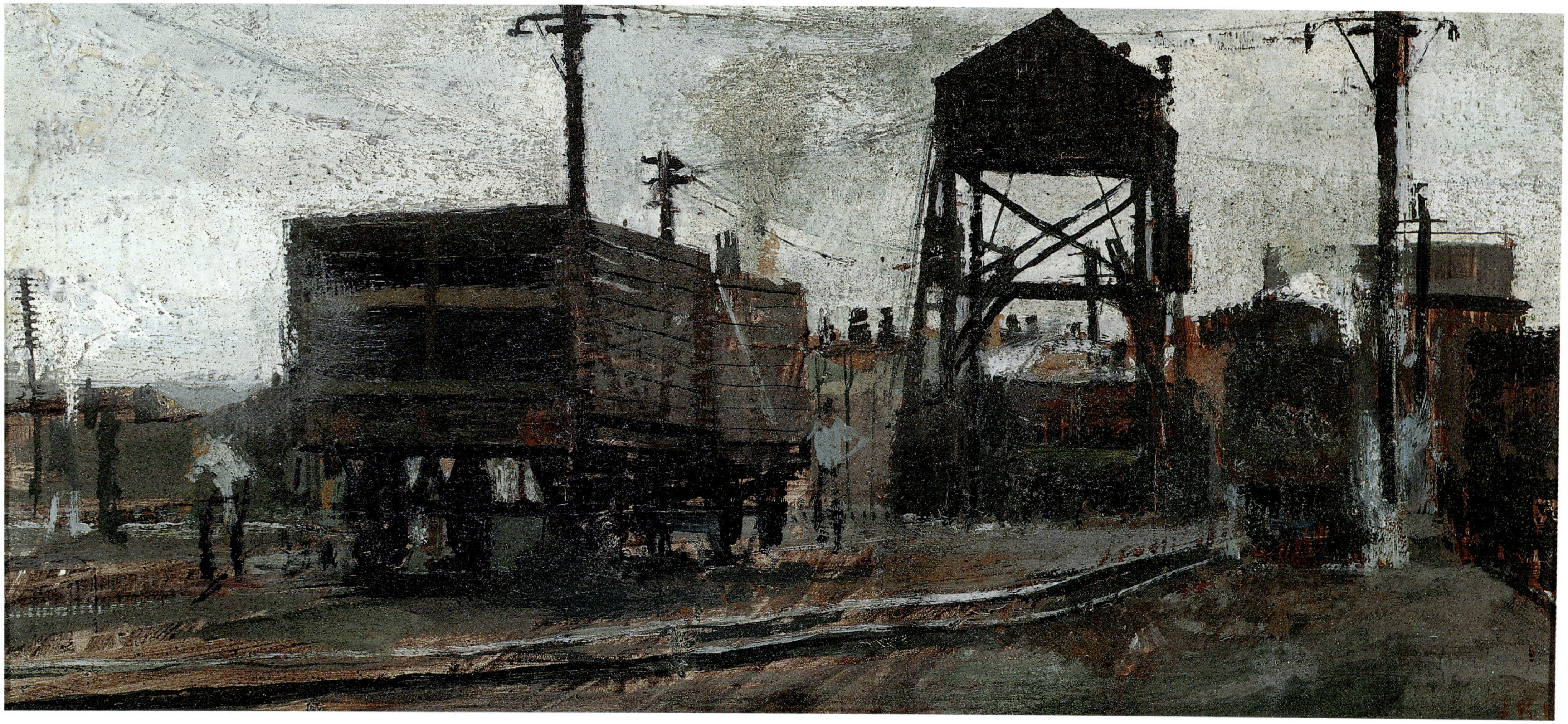

heart of the symmetrical composition is the crucifix-like presence of the telegraph pole, even more prominent than the similar shape of the lamp post we shall see in the slightly later *Ulster Crucifixion*. In many ways the strong designs and conscious shape-making of the early railway paintings resulted in 'abstract' arrangements equal to the non-figurative essays of fellow students. That what was in front of Howard's eyes was making these shapes – dictating the arrangement – provided an extra and vital dimension to his work. He thrived on the excitement he felt in the presence of the subject and expressed this in the tensions which abound between shapes on his panels. Such tensions are often lacking in the comfortable world of uncommitted 'abstraction' – pattern-making divorced from nature.

Howard's early railway yards are powerful, active places. Despite the lugubrious weight of the buildings, engines and trucks, these – like so many of the artist's later subjects – are animated scenes, feasts of visual excitement. The former train-spotter has responded to the activities of the steam locomotives, and the pillars of steam being emitted into fractured skies increase the drama. The varied bulks silhouetted against the sky give notice of an early interest in painting *contre-jour*: against the light. Both panels were painted with household undercoat – a cheaper substitute for zinc white. The undercoat dried quickly onto the panels and allowed for the painting of thin glazes in the skies, rather in the manner of watercolour, which Howard considered his principal medium in the early Hornsey days. Essential to any *contre-jour* effect is the skilful management of closely toned shapes with a limited palette. At this stage Howard was beginning to master this lesson and in the Cricklewood picture at least, tonal harmony is reinforced by the visible use of an additional burnt sienna ground reminiscent of Constable.

These serious and satisfying works are clearly indebted to the Impressionists, whose use of free brushwork to capture instants of light and action was already having an effect on the young painter.

The Coal Hopper, Cricklewood Sidings
Oil on board, c 1955. 10 × 17ins.

It is likely, indeed, that Howard was aware of Monet's series of paintings of the Gare Saint-Lazare. Consistent as Ken Howard's development as an artist has been, it is still perhaps a little unusual that the painter who helped inspire some of his earliest adult work should remain a major inspiration – albeit through other paintings and series – nearly forty years later.

At Hornsey, Howard's maturing vision and style singled him out and he ended up as one of the stars of his year. He applied to the Royal College of Art and was accepted, although National Service had to intervene before he could commence his studies. In 1952 he joined the Royal Marines, hoping he might travel extensively – there being no available places in the Royal Navy. His early experience in the Marines was not happy and he sought solace elsewhere:

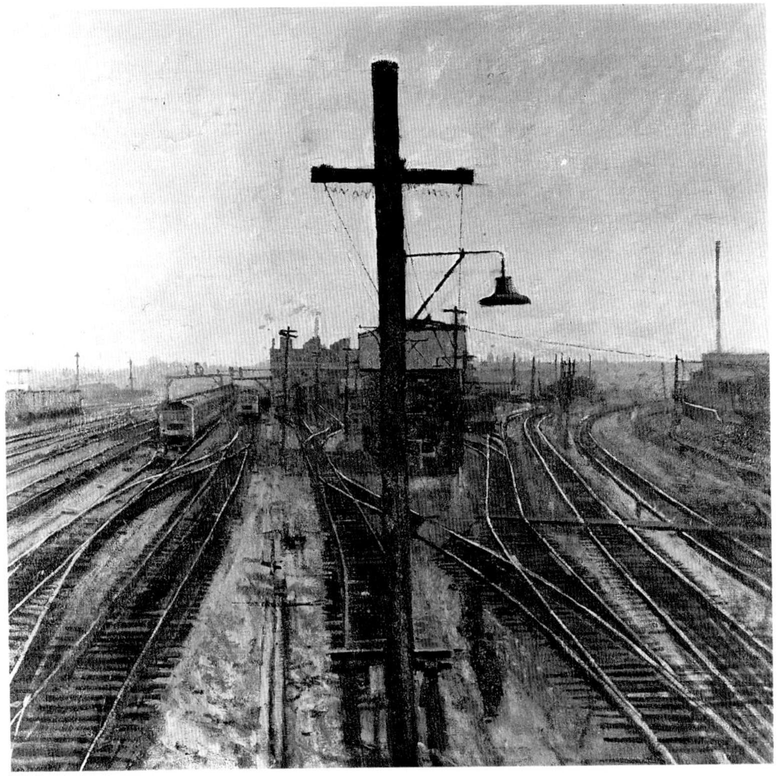

Southall 2: Silver Morning
Oil on canvas, 1975. 72 × 60ins (RA 1975, No 499).

'I think it is true to say I was the worst marine in the squad and was constantly criticised. I suppose that, having been a committed art student for four years, I went in very unfit. I started to attend the church and was confirmed. I remember feeling I had to find strength outside myself – or perhaps inside myself. I drew a lot of strength from my new-found religious belief.'

His position within the squad was transformed, for whatever reason, and he was eventually judged its most meritorious and fittest marine, being awarded the coveted Commando Medal. At the end of his training Howard was offered the opportunity to apply for a commission, but knowing this would interfere with his freedom to paint, he asked to be posted to the educational section as a teacher and soon found himself in Plymouth Barracks.

Promoted to lance-corporal, Howard was in charge of his dormitory, which included men of fifteen years' service. He found this responsibility difficult at first, but soon he settled in and was able, with the blessing of the authorities, to concentrate on his work. Every evening he painted – often powerful portraits of his eventually understanding colleagues, like Marine Broadley.

In time he was offered his first one-man exhibition at Plymouth Art Centre. The show, consisting mainly of barrack-room paintings, proved successful by all accounts. Plymouth Art Gallery purchased ten works for their schools collection, Howard was offered a London show, which sadly fell through, and he was besieged with commissions for paintings. Such commissions were later to sustain him for many years, but for the immediate future the sales proceeds were extremely valuable grant-aid as, in 1955, Howard left the Marines to take up his place at the Painting School at the Royal College of Art. Before starting there he took the opportunity to hitch-hike to Madrid again to renew his acquaintance with Velázquez and Goya. He was by this stage clear that here were his artistic roots.

Up to this point the artist had received little but encouragement. At the Royal College, brought together with some of the most talented young painters of that or any other time, as well as some of the most demanding tutors, Howard came down to earth with a rather cruel bump. His work was the subject of much criticism in the first year and his perhaps over-confident bearing took such a jolt that he stopped exhibiting and destroyed a lot of work. In despair, he was led to question his presence at the College:

'I was convinced I had got there through false pretences. At the end of the year I thought they would kick me out and that the best I could do was get a provisional pass. Rodrigo Moynihan was still Professor of Painting and didn't seem to like what I was doing, but he could see I was committed. Of course there were very good people in the year. I was all the time conscious of being very low down the rating – I was no longer the star.'

The stars were people like Graham Arnold, Ian Simpson and Robin Plummer. Most unusually, the year produced three eventual Royal Academicians, Olwen Bowey, Sonia Lawson and finally Howard himself. In retrospect Howard thinks the mental pummelling he was dealt was not entirely negative and was possibly even helpful to him: 'I gradually got my strength back and began to believe in myself again. By the end of my time at the College I recovered myself and got an upper second.'

If Howard's dedicated and sometimes over-intensive perseverance helped to get him through the Royal College of Art, it also produced at least one lighter moment there:

'I had been working for weeks on a figure painting, because once I'd begun to get my strength back I decided to go really deeply into things. So I'd been working on this picture for three weeks, whereas nearby a fellow student was scraping her picture off and redoing it every day. On the last day I think I was fiddling away with a fine sable brush and trying to get the last bit right, and Ruskin Spear came into the life room. It was Friday afternoon and everyone else had gone home, and he watched me work and eventually turned to me and said "Howard, I'm going down the staff room. If you make a mistake while I'm away will you come down and let me know".'

If some of the advice was on occasion ambiguous, Howard much admired tutors like Spear, Robert Buhler, Rodney Burn and Carel Weight. Even if he had at times thought of abandoning painting, there were certainly also times of encouragement. On the occasion of his Diploma Show in 1958, Jack Beddington of the Wildenstein Gallery visited the College and liked Howard's work. Learning that the student was graduating with a British Council Travel Scholarship to Italy, Beddington told him to look him up on his return, with a view to participating in an exhibition.

Howard reached Florence by scooter and stayed for eleven months, painting Impressionist-influenced landscapes in the surrounding hills. In the Uffizi he studied Caravaggio and the Venetian masters, finding Florentine *quattrocento* art a touch decorative, although he was affected by the struggle for significant form of Giotto and Masaccio and came under the spell of Piero della Francesca. The modern Italian painter, Giorgio Morandi, also had a powerful effect on the young artist, as he did upon many of his contemporaries. The British Council representative arranged for Howard to visit the great still-life painter in Bologna. Morandi received the young man with kindness, although the two did not have a language in common. Before leaving, Howard was offered a painting for the equivalent of £50. However good an investment such a treasure might represent, he knew its purchase would shorten his remaining time in Italy by six weeks and declined the offer.

At a party in Florence, Howard met a German girl called Christa Koehler. Their blossoming romance was rudely interrupted when, on her return home, Christa was informed in no uncertain terms that a penniless English art student was not a suitable marriage prospect. They lost contact.

On arriving back in London, Howard found a shop in a derelict part of Kentish Town that was awaiting redevelopment. For the payment of the rates he obtained a limited tenancy and set up his first London studio. He also took up part-time teaching posts at Harrow, Walthamstow and Ealing schools of art. Within two years of returning from Italy he had married a student in dress design at Harrow called Annie Popham, whose father taught silversmithing at the Royal College of Art. Howard wanted a steady income and at the beginning of the 1960s teaching was relatively well paid. But he desperately wanted to paint as much as possible and within two years had cut his four days' teaching per week to two.

'When I was teaching, people used to say how lucky I was, only teaching two days a week, and living by painting. I used to say I'm not living by painting, I'm living by teaching. This was despite the realisation that the recently-graduated painter is in the peculiarly privileged position of not actually needing any back-up to get started on his career. The writer obviously needs a publisher, the musician an orchestra, the actor a theatre, and indeed the sculptor a gallery. The young painter, who works on the spot, immediately has his audience. In my case those who saw me paint quickly developed into patrons, albeit on the small scale of wishing to purchase from the easel.

'Not for one minute would I deny the importance of the dealer and the gallery in furthering one's career, but one could at least get started this way. Neither would I deny how important it was to be able to have a small, but secure income from teaching at the beginning of my career. Those two days of teaching gave me the freedom to paint what I wanted and where I wanted, without considering a market for what I was doing.

'After fourteen years of teaching I gave it up altogether. So I have to admit I didn't have the nerve to really stick my neck out and trust to painting. Indeed in later years I often wished I had. I think people are more likely to be easy-going about their living when they've come from a secure background.'

Despite his commitments, Howard still managed to complete and exhibit oil paintings through the early 1960s – paintings with titles like *Mornington Crescent Café*, *Chiswick Road Construction* and *Willesden High Road*. He was taken up by Wildenstein's and participated with five other artists in three of their annual shows of *Some Contemporary British Painters*. His work sold well there and he had his first London one-man exhibition at the John Whibley Gallery in 1966. He was also being chosen on a regular basis for the Royal Academy Summer Exhibitions. He was elected a member of the New English Art Club in 1962, and of the Royal Institute of Oil Painters in 1966.

While the realist painters of the Kitchen Sink school had remained popular during Howard's time at the Royal College, in the 1960s he found himself less in sympathy with the American-inspired Abstract Expressionism that was beginning to cover vast canvases in the art colleges of Britain. The artists of what has been recently tagged the School of London were becoming known. Howard was aware of the work of Lucien Freud and Frank Auerbach, and of the thick impasto canvases Leon Kossoff was making at Willesden Junction. Howard's early, intense technique was in the spirit of this time. In the architectural paintings that were now to follow, his handling of paint was to become even more dense and sculptural.

'All of a sudden, I saw all these paintings, coming to me in flashes. One day I saw Westminster Abbey, and I painted the big north door picture. It was the first time I had attempted a really large painting. I think it was six by five feet and I couldn't get the stretched canvas into the room. It was painted entirely from drawings – sketch-books full of drawings. While I was a student I worked in one of two ways – from drawings or in front of the subject. During the past twenty years I would say 95 per cent of my work has been done in front of the subject, but I did the church and cathedral pictures principally from drawings.

'I filled sketch-books, and rushed home to paint. There is no point in trying to remember exactly what you saw on the spot, but that was what I was doing. I used to write myself letters in my sketch-book so I could conjure up what I was looking at.'

In choosing such an imposing subject and embarking on a series of cathedral pictures, Howard seems to have been intent on making a significant statement that would establish him as a painter of substance. In some senses this period might be seen to mark the beginning of the long and successful campaign to be fully recognised by the Royal Academy. Indeed this picture elicited a letter asking if Howard would be willing to be considered for election to its ranks, but there proved to be a long road ahead before this actually came about.

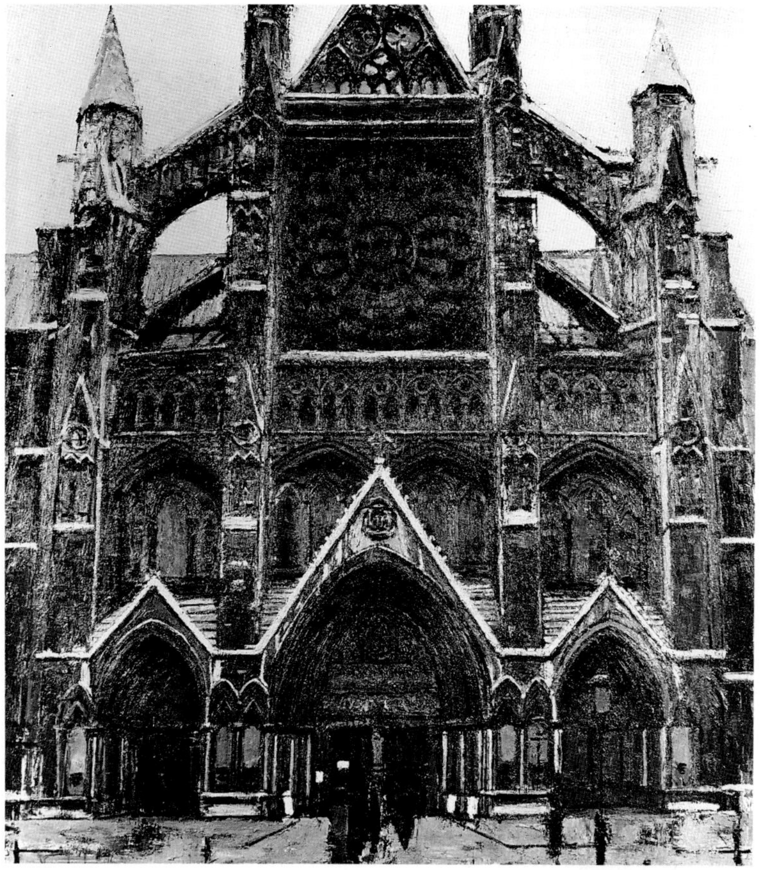

The North Door, Westminster Abbey
Oil on canvas, 1965. 72 × 60ins (RA 1965, No 158).

St Martin-within-Ludgate
St Edmund King and Martyr
St Magnus the Martyr
Oil on canvas, 1969. 72 × 72ins (RA 1969, Nos 801–803)

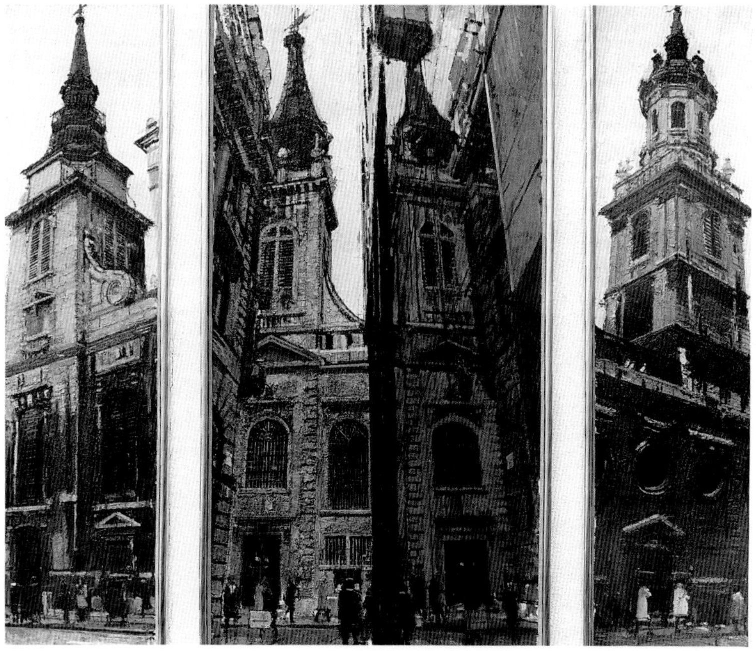

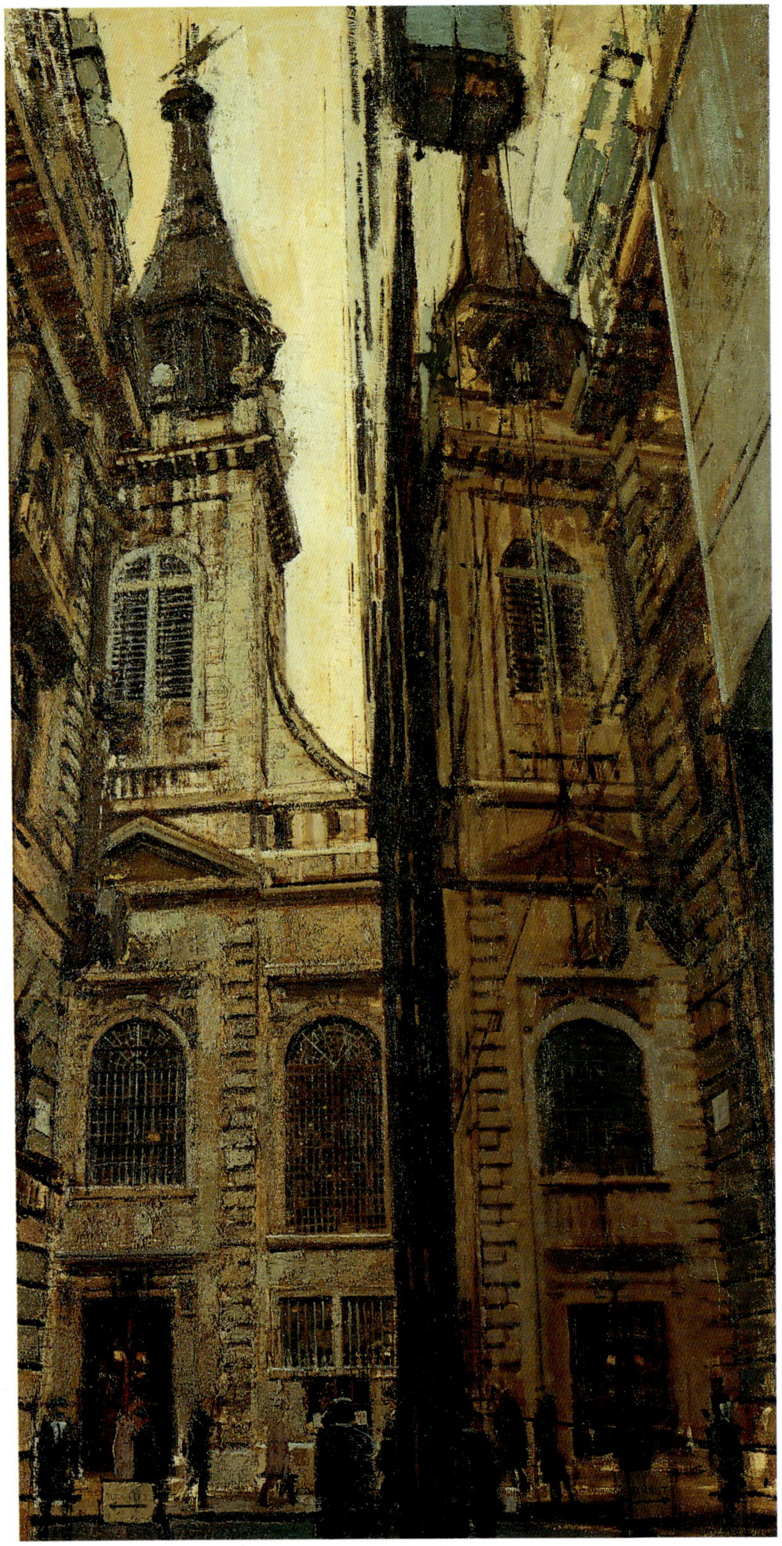

St Edmund King and Martyr
Oil on canvas, 1969. 72 × 36ins (RA 1969, No 802).

It is possible to imagine why the Westminster picture had impressed the Academicians. The subject matter was suitably grand and the artistic precedents – Monet's Rouen Cathedral façade series and the Parisian scenes of Utrillo – were appropriately ambitious. Like Monet's Rouen, the soot-encrusted Abbey transept is tangibly represented in impasto, much of it applied with the palette knife. Characteristically the drawing is masterly and the relationships of volumes and space, within an essentially flat picture-plane, quite convincing.

Howard's cathedral series became something of an obsession, and over a couple of years he travelled widely for subjects:

'I wanted to create a sense of the place. I used to go to the cathedral, and spend time just feeling the stones, and when I got home I did everything to re-create that sense. They were all very two-dimensional – there was never any perspective. I started to mix sand with the paint, and came under the influence of early Utrillo.

'It really did absorb me, until in the end I became mannered. The paint became too thick, too mixed with sand and plaster. I suppose I was moving more and more towards abstraction and I didn't really want to. I then began to get very concerned with drawing and perspective – vertical rather than horizontal perspective – and used a device I could actually measure distances through. In the end it got hold of me to such a degree that I couldn't see the subject any more.'

What seems to have been happening was that Howard was becoming too analytical, more concerned with science than aesthetics:

'When I was very young I read John Ruskin's *Stones of Venice*. That nearly stopped me painting, because it told me so much intellectually about what I was seeing, that I couldn't see anything at all. If I looked at the sky, I saw it in terms of cumulus clouds and what happens when the sun drops, and I was no longer getting the thrill of seeing. I think one must always be painting what one sees is there, not what one knows is there.'

In 1967 the artist turned his attention from cathedrals to City of London churches, and in the city streets he rediscovered *plein air* painting and a rather less congested technique. The culmination of the series which followed was his first major triptych, the central panel of which – *St Edmund King and Martyr* – is reproduced here (in colour). The church, jostling for air space among the finance houses of Lombard Street, was designed either by Sir Christopher Wren or by his assistant, Robert Hooke. A more spacious conception than the Westminster Abbey picture, this large canvas is nevertheless dominated by the sculptural painting of the strong architecture of St Edmund's narrow, three-bay front. The facade is offset and converted to a twin-towered structure by the reflection in the marble wall of a modern office block.

With the companion panels representing two other Wren churches, St Martin-within-Ludgate and St Magnus the Martyr, the completed triptych presents an imposing and dynamic, symmetrical composition. This arrangement echoes the formality of the cathedral paintings, but the image is perhaps less emblematic, more a visual idea, observed and recorded. This sense is confirmed when we learn that it was painted on the spot.

'In the end, returning all the time to paint in the studio killed the subject for me. But as often happens in life I find that one subject moves on to another, and the individual churches had moved me on to their reflected images. When I had decided on this image I went to the spot and worked on a large-scale drawing. One morning a businessman came by on his way to work, and he looked and said he liked the drawing. But he couldn't understand why I had drawn two churches – there was only one. I said of course there are two – look! And he looked and suddenly his eyes opened wide. He said he'd been walking down that road ever since that marble building was put up, and had never seen that reflection. Now he

The Children's Ward, Charing Cross Hospital
Ink and wash, 1972. 15 × 21ins.

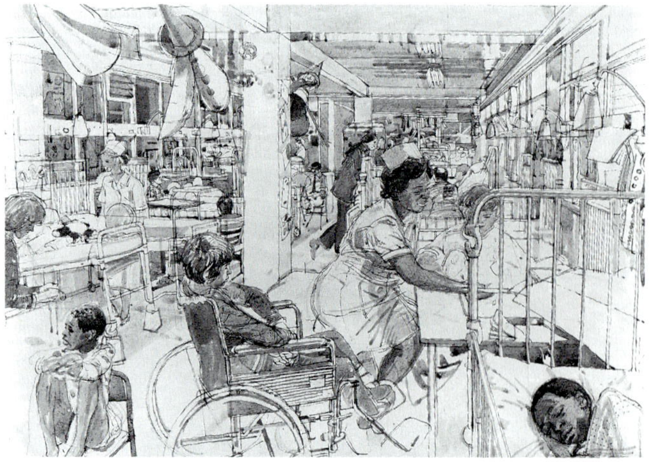

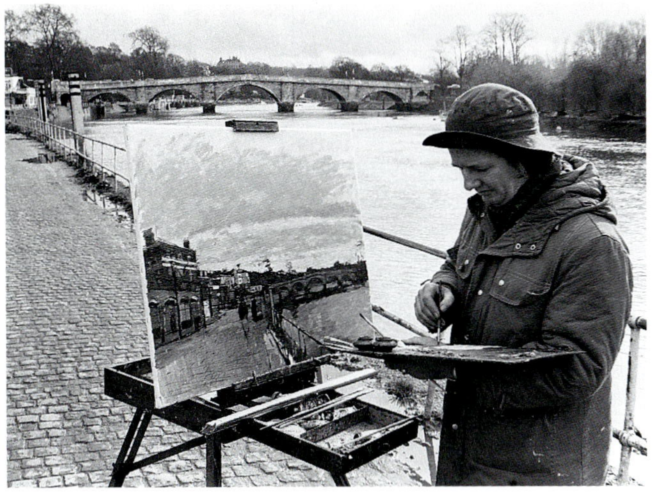

Ken Howard painting Richmond Bridge
Photograph, c 1973.

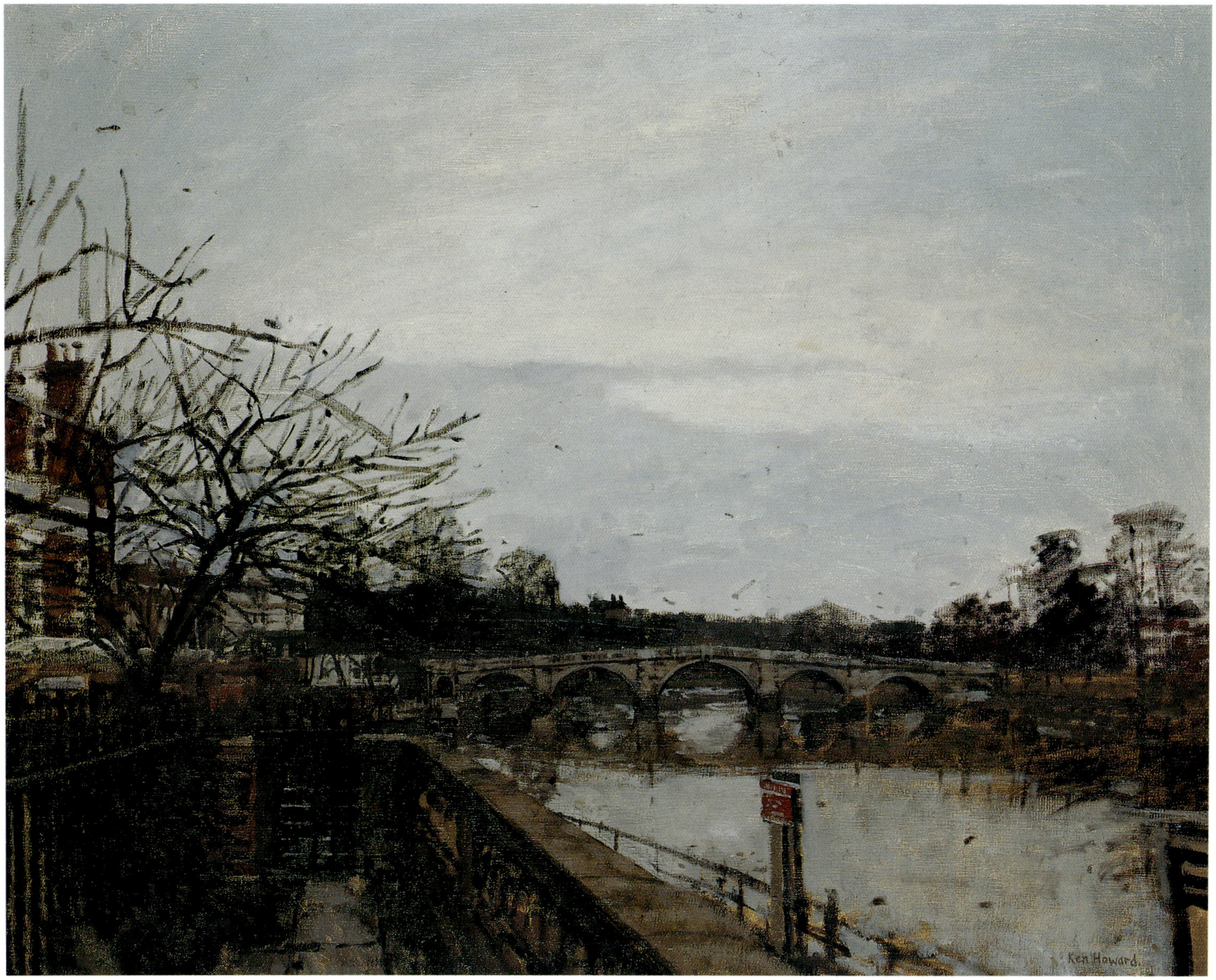

From St Helena Terrace, Richmond
Oil on canvas, c 1973. 25 × 30ins.

would never walk past again without being aware of it. That gave me a great feeling, making him see something for the first time.

'I used to go into the City on a Sunday, when it was quiet, and sit there painting with this huge canvas propped against the wall. It was only after I had finished the central canvas that I decided to add the two extra panels to make a foursome of City churches.'

By the early 1970s Howard was finding teaching to be an impediment to the development of his own work. Also rather discouraging was the fact that, however much he enjoyed working with the students, a lack of respect for good draughtsmanship was growing in the colleges. Teaching was not to be a long-term goal, but what he could do was to revive a prospect, which had surfaced during the Plymouth show, of earning his living through commissions.

He was already carrying out some illustration commissions. Through Olwen Bowey he had in 1965 met David Wolfers, who was then the editor of the two Shell house magazines, *Catalyst* and *Land*, and was commissioning drawings for these publications. Although Wolfers seemed cool about his work to begin with, Howard was given some commissions and soon settled into what became a moderately lucrative career, in which his drawing skills were in some demand. The man who had been charged with decorating the covers and introductory pages of the new GPO telephone books saw Howard's work and thus started a lengthy commission, involving some five directories a year, eventually covering most of England. This was an excellent way of getting to know the country and mastering the unforgiving discipline of pen-and-ink work. Doctors at Charing Cross Hospital noted this work and Howard was invited to produce a series of drawings to be reproduced and sold in aid of the hospital's fund-raising programme. It seemed like an interesting proposition.

'It was a strange stage in my life, a dark stage. My marriage was breaking down. We'd never been quite compatible – Annie finding it difficult to accept the full-time commitment necessary in a painter. Then my father died, and I had been very close to him. It was a pretty dark stage. I had to draw in the operating theatre when they were doing operations, and in the Out-Patients when they were bringing drug addicts in. There was a very beautiful young girl brought in one night, dying from an overdose. This shocked me deeply and instilled in me a totally uncompromising attitude against the use of drugs.

'They weren't all grim drawings. Some were quite innocuous studies of the canteen and kitchens and others were of the wards, like this one of the children's ward. By this time I was drawing much more than I was painting because of all these commissions, and I could put something down very quickly and directly.'

The drawing of the children's ward does indeed show how developed Howard's mastery of line now was. Using a free and sweeping pen line he could embrace a complex and ever-shifting scene with both accuracy of perspective and a feeling for the noisy bustle of the subject. Essential to this was the innate, but determinedly nurtured, ability to lay down the telling line with speed and confidence. Carel Weight saw these drawings and, although Howard believes that his former teacher generally found his work too comfortable, these often sharp and poignant drawings clearly struck the great man.

Having forgone studio-based painting for the time being, between commissions Howard turned his attention to the River Thames near his home at Hampton, west of London. For a period of four or five years he worked on a series of river paintings and, not for the only time in his life, became a landscape painter. According to the artist this was not for any great love of straightforward landscape painting, for the concept was anathema to his sense of human life and activity in his subject:

'It's like asking me to paint an empty studio. For me a landscape comes to life when the figure becomes part of it. It's possibly because the figure moves, is alive, and is constantly making you reassess. The figure makes the landscape much more exciting for me.'

At first he had difficulty adjusting the large scale of his recent work to the demands of working on the river bank. He started using unwieldy canvases, but tended to find the light would change too much between painting sessions to achieve any real truth to his subject.

'I could never do them in a day because I didn't have the practice in those days. So I started making small boards – about six by eight inches – that I could crack in one session of two or three hours. In other words the oil would never dry as I was working – they were painted in one wet. That may seem a little obvious, but it made all the difference to me, because for years I'd been going onto the spot day after day and returning to work in the studio, instead of completing the thing in front of the subject.'

In 1970 he had by chance met David Wolfers again. Wolfers had opened his own gallery, the New Grafton, and the next year Howard had the first of many one-man shows there. The artist came to have great faith in the dealer's judgment of his work. He recalls Wolfers selecting an exhibition from the assembled works in his studio, including one of Richmond Bridge:

'It was one I had laboured over. The more I worked on a picture in those days, the more I loved it. He came and took this and that, and said "Have you got any that you think I've left out, that I shouldn't have?" I said "Yes – that one", and he said "No – you're wrong Ken". And I said "No – I'm right David, I want that one in". I went to the Private View and there was one picture in that exhibition that was completely wrong, and that was the one.'

The view of the bridge from St Helena Terrace is, by contrast, freshly painted. Unusually, Howard had found himself able to resolve the sizeable canvas in one session. His natural ability, reinforced by diligent practice and years of on-the-spot drawing, was at last translating itself into a more spontaneous attitude to the process of painting. In one 'wet' he has caught not only the subtle architecture of the eighteenth-century bridge, but also the soft English river light.

The paint-handling itself – probably with a small household brush – is altogether broader and more relaxed than before. In several passages, thin strokes of the brush barely conceal the buff ground, which itself helps unify the whole canvas. Here, at the beginning of the 1970s, Howard was taking his first tentative steps on the road to the pure, uninhibited painting and diaphanous glazes of the early 1990s.

Despite this significant step forward, Howard's painting was still overshadowed by his teaching, and there seemed little likelihood that it would continue to develop without his taking some action. It was becoming clear to him that he had to reorganise his life. By 1973 his marriage was finally ending in separation, to be followed four years later by divorce. His heavy work-load had aggravated an ulcer that had bothered him since his time in the Marines and an operation had ensued. Teaching, which had sustained him for so long, was becoming a less satisfying profession – due in great part to the decline of interest in drawing in art schools.

He was asked to take on a full-time teaching post at Harrow, or face the possibility of losing his part-time position. His reaction was to accept a half-lectureship, which did not involve any increase in his hours. Soon, however, he found he was spending most of his time in meetings and realised he had made the wrong decision. In the year of his separation he decided not only to quit teaching, but also to cut back on the amount of illustration work he was accepting. As he gave up these commitments, a new challenge appeared.

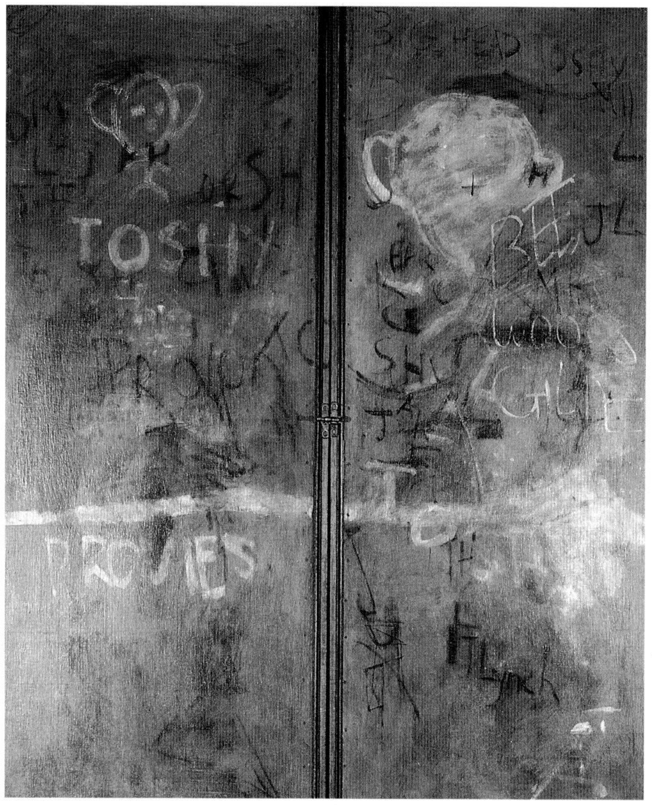

Ulster Crucifixion, the doors closed
Oil on canvas, 1978. 48 × 36ins main panels, 9 × 36ins predella (RA 1978, No 1009).

Through a recommendation by Carel Weight, who had remembered the Charing Cross Hospital drawings, Howard was in 1973 commissioned as official artist in Northern Ireland by the Imperial War Museum, initially for a five-week stint. Depicting the life of the province and the troops who served there was to be a part of the next seven years of his life.

Finding a rapport with the troops, Howard worked easily in the tense environment. His ink and wash drawings of life under the threat of fire form one of the most comprehensive and objective artistic records of modern soldiery and of civilians accustomed to its presence in their midst:

'All the work I was doing was simply recording Northern Ireland. I could draw until I dropped, because of the stimulus of the subject matter. I didn't look upon myself as anything other than a visual journalist, but as long as you didn't have a camera in your hand, the people had no suspicion. They had a pride that you were drawing in their street, especially when they knew it was for a museum in England. I never had any problem relating to the Protestants or the Catholics. If I'd ever allowed myself to feel fear – except for once or twice, when I really was threatened – I couldn't have done it.

'Once I was working for the Welsh Guards, who were on patrol in the Divis Flats, which are solid IRA. Two heavies came up to me and accused me of being SAS, collecting information. I said, if I was in the SAS and I had been sitting in the middle of the Divis Flats for four hours, I would have to be some sort of nutter. They agreed. That sort of thing happened a lot – once I had to show a woman the cover of her telephone directory, with my signature on it, to prove I was a bona fide artist.'

The more the soldiers of the various regiments stationed in the province got to know Howard's work, the more they liked the objectivity and pictorial realism of the drawings and paintings he made for the War Museum. He was repeatedly invited back to make drawings for regiments on their tours of duty. A large number of commissions followed, bringing valuable income and taking Howard with the forces to a wide range of destinations – Belize, Brunei, Canada, Cyprus, Hong Kong, Nepal, Norway and Oman among them.

Much as this period in his life broadened the artist's horizons and gave respite to his restless spirit, the role of army artist-in-residence threatened to take over from the career of the painter. Much of the work had become tailored to the nature of the commissions, which often had to please a broad section of the regiment, and Howard found himself producing montages of army activity which, although well drawn, were really pure illustration.

By 1983, the painter in him could be stifled no longer. The travels on commission pleased the bank manager, but were stunting Howard's career as a painter. They had to become a less dominant part of his life. This was the right time for a change. Howard was sure he had a lot to say as an artist, but that he was not really giving himself the space in which to make his mark. He needed to settle down to paint his world, not someone else's. It took another two years before he was finally able to abandon commissioned work and concentrate exclusively on the development of his painting career. At least the artist now had a stable environment from which to launch this process, for in 1980 Christa Gaa – formerly Koehler – came to England to set up home with Howard in Cornwall and London. They had re-established contact in 1974, some fifteen years after their Italian romance had been unceremoniously truncated. On 13 October 1990 they were married at Chelsea Register Office.

Despite his activities with commissioned work in Northern Ireland and elsewhere, Howard had not at any stage in the 1970s relaxed his pace in producing paintings for exhibition, particularly at the Royal Academy, where he enjoyed a remarkable string of successful submissions. Indeed, in the ten years from 1964 he exhibited usually two or three works in each Summer Exhibition. From 1975 until his election as ARA in 1983, three paintings were hung on every occasion.

Several important Northern Ireland paintings were among the Academy exhibits, including some 'difficult' pictures, such as *Ulster Crucifixion*. This triptych went on to win the artist an unexpected award at the prestigious and predominantly avant-garde John Moores Exhibition of 1978. In 1982 the *Self-Portrait at Oriel* brought him first prize in the Hunting Group Awards. Such recognition for his ever-maturing standing as an oil painter increased in its turn the artist's faith in his ability to continue to earn a living as a professional artist.

During the 1980s Howard's painting was truly to mature and his prolific output to strengthen into one of the richest of any contemporary figurative painter. In addition to the group exhibitions came an astounding succession of one-man shows. One of his last commissions had been to paint the Tite Street, London studio of John Singer Sargent, which was owned by Sir Gordon, now Lord, White. Through this commission he met Peter Johnson and from the mid-1980s he alternated annual one-man exhibitions in Johnson's Lowndes Lodge Gallery with the New Grafton.

Within his developing *oeuvre*, Howard was becoming associated with a limited number of subject types, which he continues to explore and enrich with characteristic ambition. Out of doors he has notably concentrated on images of Venice and scenes on the beaches of West Penwith, where he has a home in the fishing village of Mousehole. Perhaps he is most closely identified with the great series of studio paintings, which started in earnest around the beginning of the 1980s. The majority of these have been painted in the Cornish house and studio, acquired in 1984, or the fine studio in South Bolton Gardens, Kensington, where he had moved in 1975. This latter space, in which for many years had been conducted the celebrated portrait practice of Sir William Orpen, was to become as much the subject as the setting of many of the studio canvases.

Howard recalls how his move to South Bolton Gardens sowed the seed of the studio paintings:

'After my separation I came to live here. Fifteen years later, through the kindness and co-operation of my landlady, Mavis Millns, and her solicitor, Gerald Kidd, I was able to fulfil my dream of own-

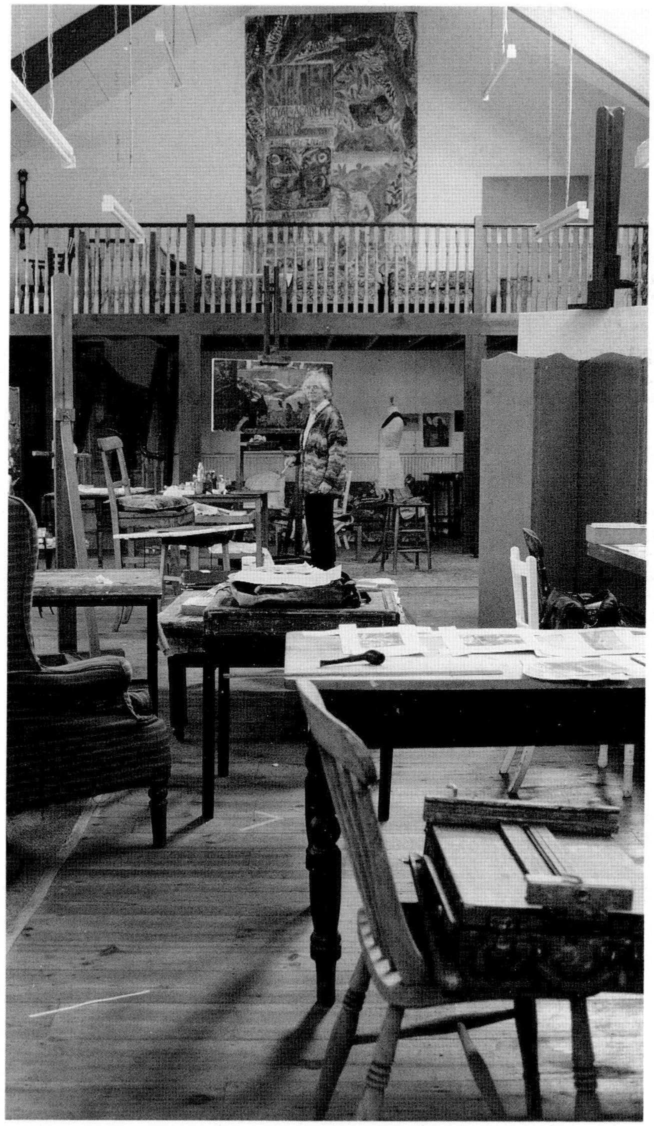

Ken Howard in St Clement's Studio
Photograph, 1990.

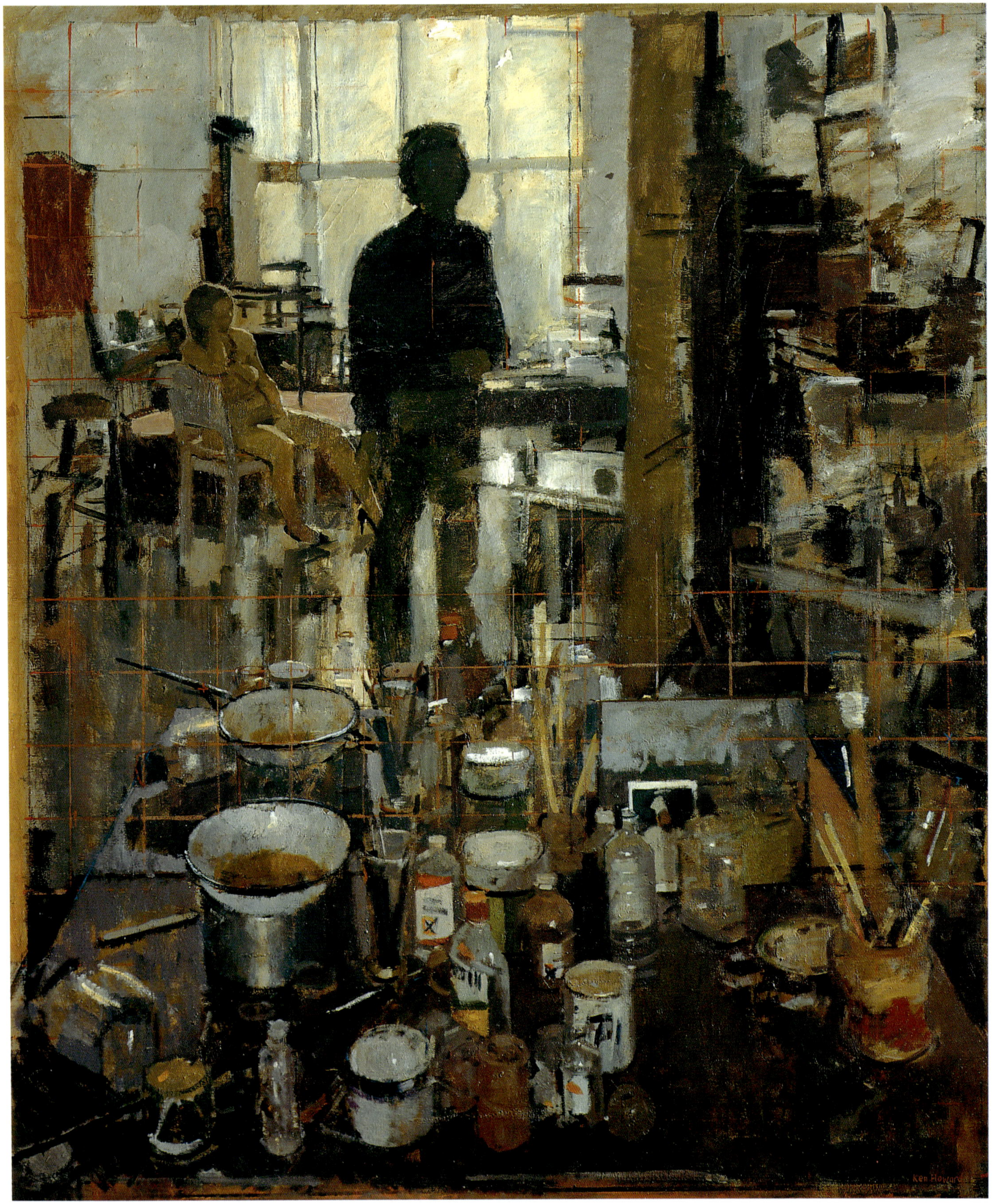

ing a London studio. At that time I was up to my neck in commissions and couldn't do any of my own work. Mavis used to have a group of friends here to paint with her every Wednesday, and sometimes I'd draw with them. That set me off on the figure again, and I started getting models on Thursdays for a day's drawing. But it was only the figure, not the studio. After I'd lived here for four years, I suddenly realised what a fantastic subject there was here – right on, or rather inside, my doorstep.'

The self-portrait, *Le Chef de l'Hotel Chatham, Paris* – known as such after the postcard of Orpen's painting of that title, which is to be seen within the foreground 'tablescape' – shows the painter silhouetted in a mirror image of the studio's north-facing window. In the middle-ground of the studio landscape his model sits, resting. This is a visually complex painting, in which the expected subject of the picture is sidelined in favour of the painter. This happens to an extent in Velázquez's great *Las Meninas*, another ambiguous composition which was undoubtedly an influence on this fine and dramatic work.

Attached to Howard's home in Mousehole, Cornwall, is the former village hall, now known as St Clement's Studio. At sixty feet by thirty feet it presents a considerably more voluminous space than the London studio. Before he converted the hall to his liking as an appropriate working-space, the artist would work in the large and often sun-drenched living-room of the school house. In front of the south-facing window, which looks down over the village to the Atlantic Ocean he would arrange a still-life, or pose a model – as with *Valerie and the Chaise Longue*. Bringing the sunlight inside the room, Howard had a complete subject. There was no need to consider the requirements for preliminary drawing, as the scene could be painted directly from the easel.

This St Clement's Hall picture, of the model wearing black stockings that set off her light skin, is one of the more luxuriant of Howard's depictions of the female nude. The question inevitably arises whether such paintings of the scantily-clad female figure are provocative. The answer is yes, they are, but they are not prurient. The provocation is a largely painterly experience, which conveys not so much sexual excitement as the artist's passionate response to the forms, colours and light

Le Chef de l'Hotel Chatham, Paris
Oil on canvas, 1984/5. 68 × 56ins (RA 1985, No 574).

of the wonderful, ravishing world that he sees, and is able to depict.

Despite the appreciation lavished on his recent work in oils, Howard did not abandon the more discreet language of pencil and watercolour. In fact the 1980s saw a strengthening in his confidence and skill with the medium, following – and perhaps in part as a result of – his election as an Associate Member of the Royal Watercolour Society in 1979.

He uses watercolour principally to get down information rapidly before the subject, often because no other medium is capable of doing the job. It is therefore no surprise that most of his work on paper is on a small scale. Indeed, there are relatively few watercolours that one would describe as substantial exhibition pictures. Even if he therefore uses the medium as an oil painter and not as a watercolourist, it would be wrong to say that the watercolours are not, in the main, independent works. The handling characteristics of watercolour suit his painterly style, and as he draws with the oil-painting brush, so he does with sable. An example is the portrait of Gerald Durrell.

Valerie and the Chaise Longue
Oil on canvas, 1979. 20 × 24ins.

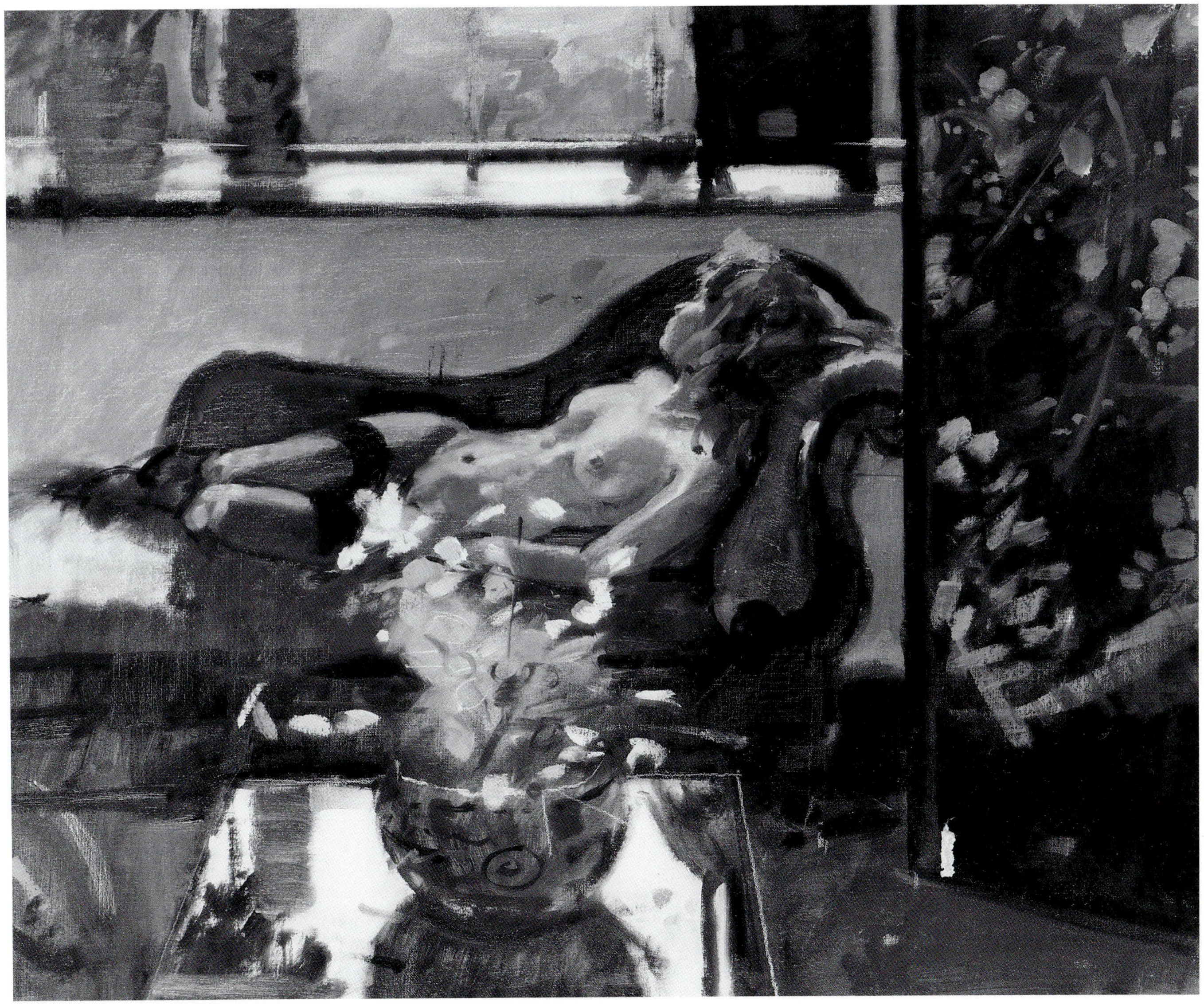

Howard had gone to Jersey to undertake a commissioned painting of the Queen opening the Parliament. As a result of attendant publicity and following an exhibition at the St Helier Gallery, he was asked by the Jersey Wildlife Preservation Trust to make an oil portrait of Durrell.

'One of the problems with painting him was how was I going to get the two sides to his character?

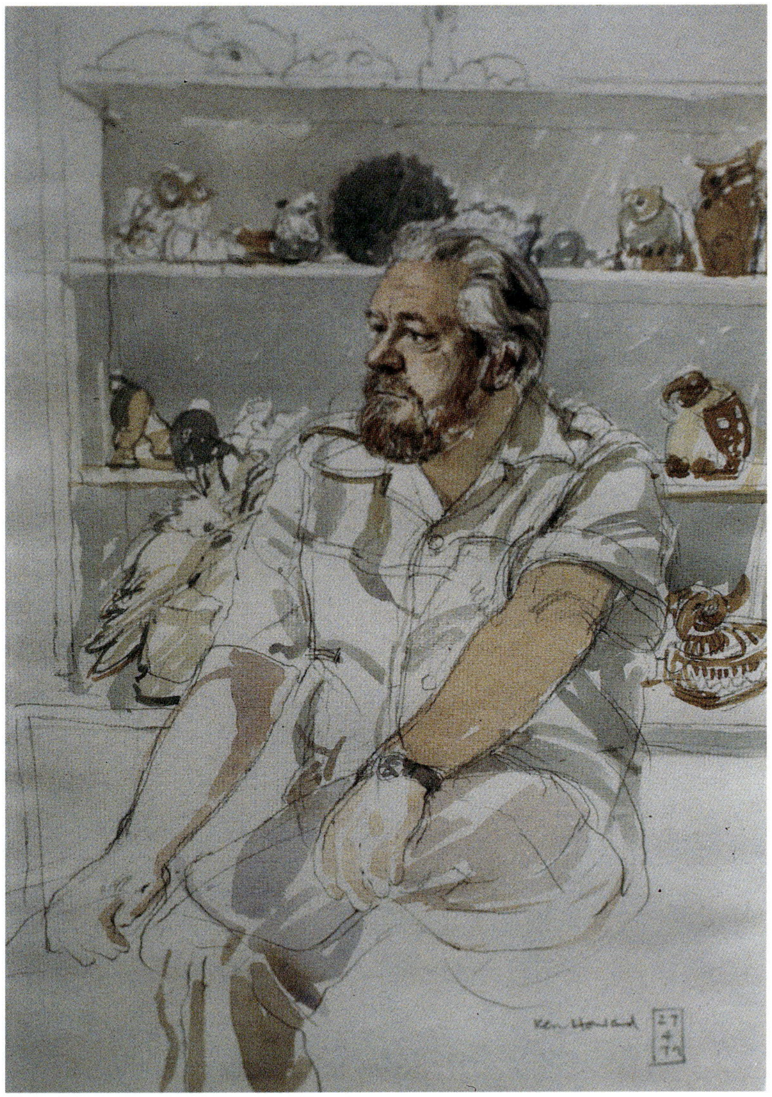

Gerald Durrell
Watercolour, 1979. 12 × 9ins.

He was a serious man in one way, and particularly about the plight of animals. But anyone who has read *My Family and Other Animals* sees another side – I don't think I've ever laughed so much.

'We went in for lunch and there were all these pottery animals brought back from his world-wide travels. I immediately said we must work in there, because those animals brought out the humorous side of him. I think in all I had two sittings for the oil and a sitting for the watercolour.'

Although the oil is a striking painting, Howard prefers the watercolour, which perhaps captures the man better. It also bears witness to the artist's marvellously economical use of elegant washes of watercolour – in this instance over a structural

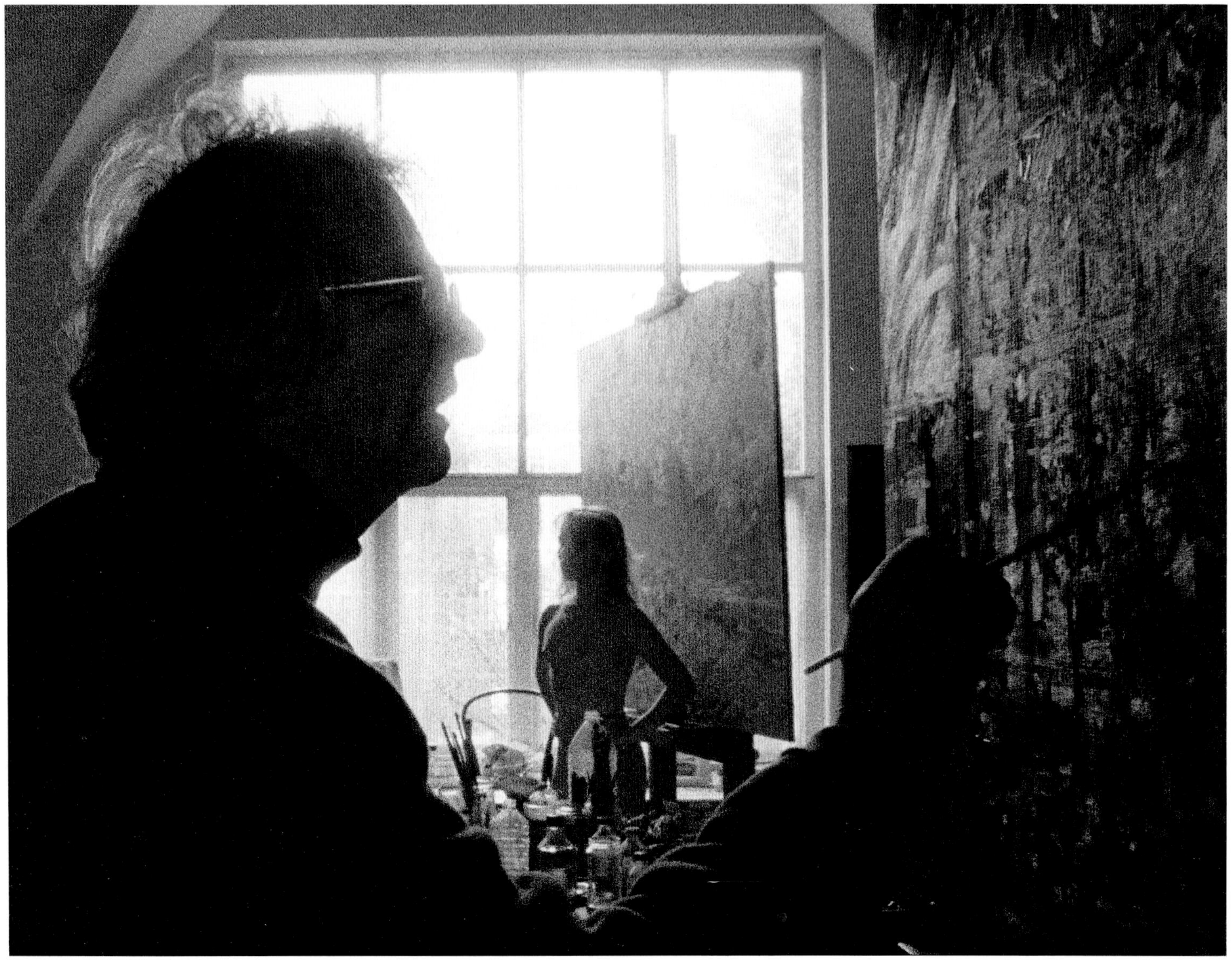

Ken Howard painting the model (Melanie) at South Bolton Gardens
Photograph, 1986.

pencil outline. This, and the other watercolours which intersperse the splendid series of oil paintings in this book, demonstrate the individual power that characterises his use of this medium.

We shall, indeed, see him questioning preconceived differences between watercolour and oil painting technique. Perhaps unusually, this does not mean that his watercolours have become more gouache-laden, but that the recent oils have been painted with fine glazes of thin colour. This manner is to be seen developing in *The Red Parasol*, illustrated on the dust jacket of this book. One of the richest and most gorgeous of his interiors with models, this painting reveals the unabashed eclectic in Howard, and in this case the influence of Whistler. Set in the living-room at St Clement's Hall, it features the same model in two poses:

'Being very interested in Whistler's orientalist work I became intrigued by his multiple-figure compositions, especially those set on a balcony. I was painting a series of kimono and parasol paintings and decided I would try to compose two figures. I started with Saskia and Valerie posing, to get the relationship between the two. Once the composition looked right I just got Valerie to switch poses as I worked.

'With the south-facing window, you get an extraordinary blaze of morning light reflecting off the sea. This picture really epitomises everything that I feel about light – the light source itself being in the picture, the light coming through the parasol and being brought far into the room, coming through the honesty plant and being reflected off the coffee tables in the foreground.'

In many ways *The Red Parasol* is one of the consummate examples of Howard's interiors of the 1980s. It has poise and balance, it is exotic and rich, it is freely and lusciously painted, and it catches the rising Cornish sun.

This book includes examples of Howard's work from each stage of his career. The artist is still in mid-career, and moving with conviction and at a pace into unexplored territory. Thus the principal intention here has been to draw breath and take a series of snapshots of this career to date. What is special about the text that follows is that these snapshots will be illuminated by the artist's own words. Ken Howard articulates with lucidity and openness the painter's priorities and concerns in the making of a work of art.

The reader will also have the opportunity of judging his present standing as a painter. To this end emphasis has been placed on gathering together a significant body of his work from the last decade or so, compiled under the subject headings which have most interested him in this period.

As has been observed, a consuming interest informs the majority of this work. The more his own fascination for the light source grew, the closer into it J.M.W. Turner seemed to stare. Ken Howard also gazes deep into the sun. We see this in the paintings, but it is a matter for speculation whether they carry conscious symbolism. This question can be considered as we leaf through the illustrations. Howard does, however, offer a clue:

'After I left National Service I became disillusioned with the conventional church and for a time attended Quaker meetings at Muswell Hill. Later, in Italy, I also looked at Catholicism, but I never found the same conviction I had at the beginning. Somewhat disaffected, I stopped looking for God in formal religion. For many years religious symbolism did come into my work, from the strong emphasis of the cross in some of my railway compositions to the *Ulster Crucifixion*. But now I get my strongest conviction that there is something beyond us, something mysterious, when confronted by nature and particularly by the magic of light.'

War Artist

For both practical and security reasons Howard was transported from assignment to assignment by armoured vehicle. In this instance he is seen in the care of his Alma Mater, the Royal Marines. Being so closely guarded was not always to his liking, however:

'On the whole I didn't like them to take me to where I was actually going to work in the Land Rover. They would take me to the approximate location and I would get out and wander into the area by myself, without any army cover. I never wanted to provoke any reaction from the local people and if I hopped out of the back of the Rover in somewhere like Leeson Street, there would immediately be antagonism. I reckoned I was more liable to get shot at if I went down a street with a couple of soldiers who would stand around watching over me while I drew, than if I just walked in and chatted to the locals before starting to work. I mainly tried to disassociate myself from the army.'

Roden Street Patrol (*Overleaf*)
Here the artist reveals some of the urban dereliction resulting from, or in some cases leading to, the troubles in Belfast's divided communities. Someone brought up in the London Blitz must have responded with empathy to such a physical scar on the city. As official artist – an appointment reviving memories of many of the outstanding recorders of World War II, but curious for being so close to home – Howard took on the task of providing a rounded account of the Northern Ireland scene and the soldiers' role therein. Although he made numerous commissions for the regiments, the work he produced for the Museum and exhibitions in London do seem to represent an objective view. In the cause of safety and security, his day was inevitably shaped by that of the army. Yet he clearly made use of the time available to him on his several tours, to talk to the local people and depict something of the reality of their surroundings:

'If, in fifty years' time, someone looks at my drawings in the Imperial War Museum and says "Is that how they lived during the troubles in Northern Ireland?" – that will satisfy me. I didn't want to make any judgement on whether the Catholics, or the Protestants, or the army were right.

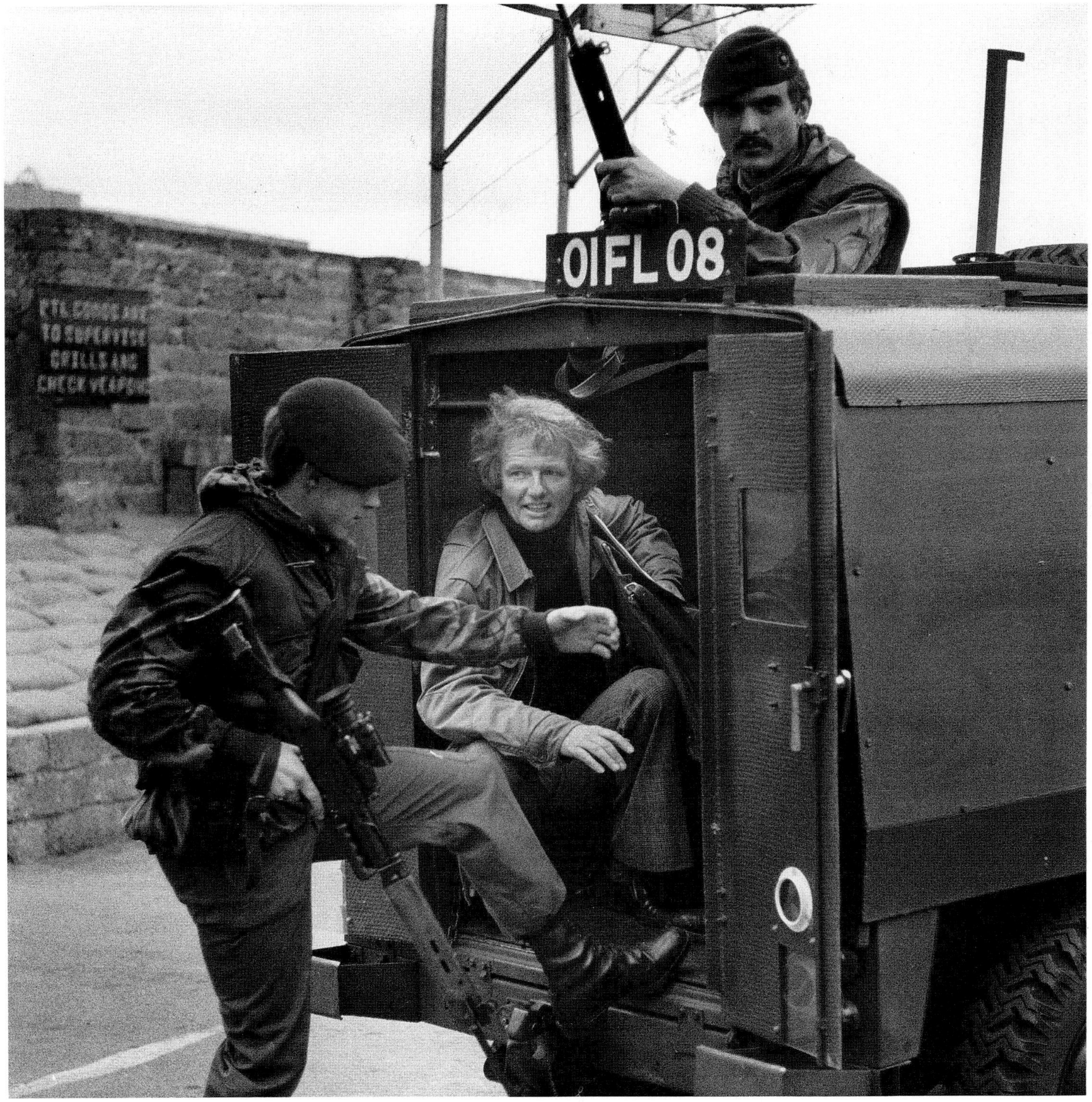

Ken Howard in an armoured Land Rover, Northern Ireland
Photograph, 1978.

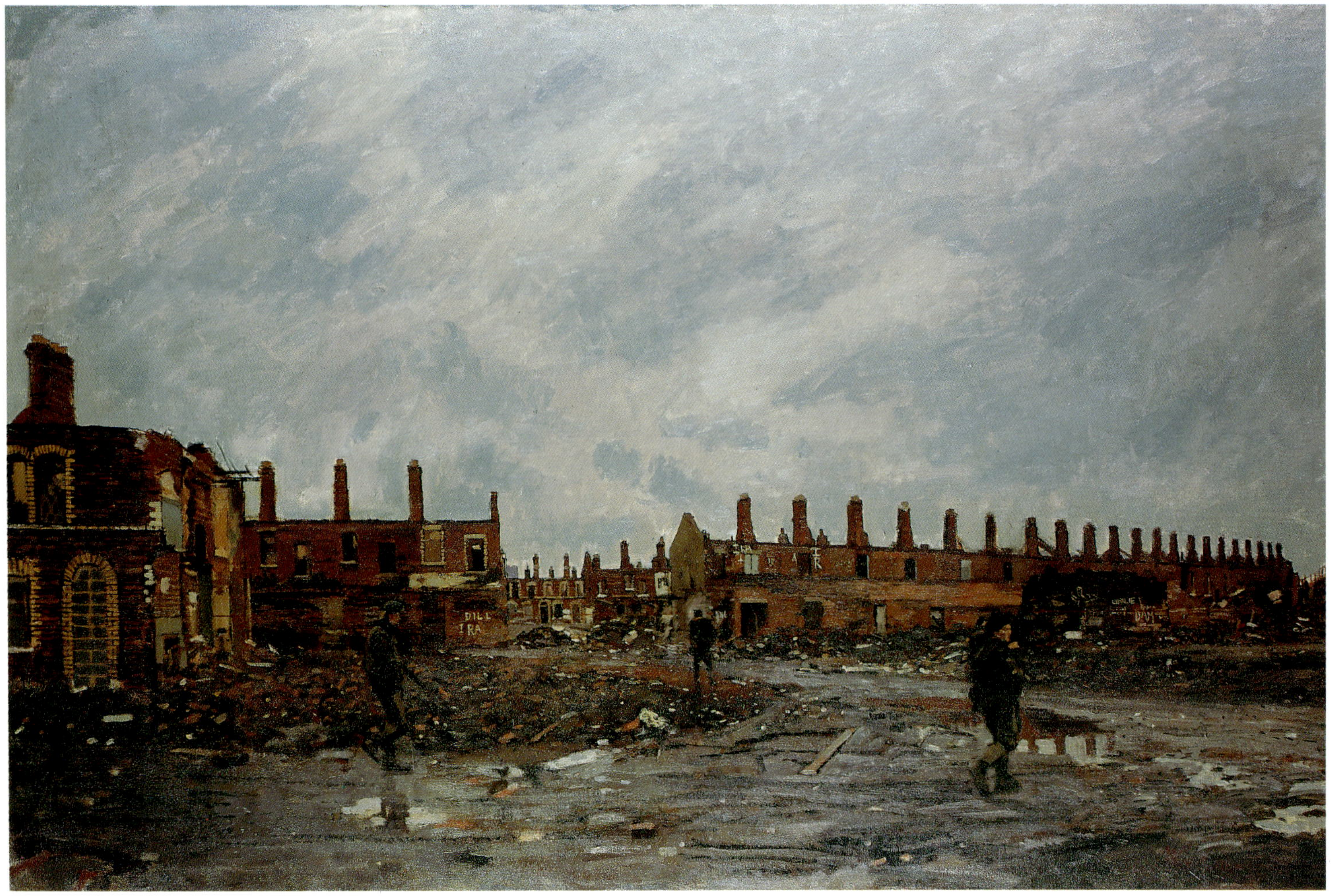

Roden Street Patrol
Oil on canvas, c 1979. 60 × 72ins.

'If I had got off the boat from Liverpool and gone to stay with a family of Protestants, I know I would have had sympathy with them, and if I had stayed with a Catholic family I know I would have sympathised with them. But I happened to get off the boat and go to live with the army, and I have a lot of sympathy with the job they have been trying to do. I'm not that thick-skinned – the place did affect me. On the other hand I had a job to do there, and that was principally to record the life of a soldier in Northern Ireland. The best way I could do that job was in a journalistic manner.

'All the houses shown in the *Roden Street Patrol* were derelict except three, where the old people insisted on staying. Therefore they had to have the normal services – for example, the postman used to come. It was ridiculous amongst all the bombs and derelict buildings. As soon as the families moved out to new flats the army blocked up the windows to stop the IRA using the houses as stores, and immediately the local lads came in and took the lead off the roof.

'It was a Catholic street – in Belfast you get a block of Protestant houses and a block of Catholic. I was sitting there drawing and the kids were playing around me and talking to me. All of a sudden a really big bomb went off nearby, and these kids didn't even stop, they carried on playing. I was really shaken – I'd jumped off my seat – and out of nerves I said to one of the kids "Good Lord, what was that?". A little girl said "It's nothing mister – it's just the f****** Prots blowing up the town again". Those children were tragic, with their vacant looks, growing up to be used to that sort of environment.'

The painting of Roden Street does not reveal such activity, typical though it was of the conditions under which the artist worked. Neither would we imagine anyone could be living in this wasteland, visibly populated only by the passing army patrol. The central vista of distant streets gives a poignant glimpse of the extent of the devastation. The starkly silhouetted chimneys, like rows of gravestones, provide a series of vertical elements in a composition whose otherwise uncompromising horizontal stress – reminiscent of the early railway yard pictures – serves to emphasise the monotonous extent of urban dereliction.

Ulster Crucifixion

Howard's concern for the predicament of the children of the conflict-points of Northern Ireland found its most significant expression in *Ulster Crucifixion*. This large triptych might be seen as an emblematic summary of the artist's early experience in the province. It is certainly the culmination of a series of paintings which emphasise and make symbolic use of the graffiti of strife, which he found adorning the walls of Belfast. It was a casual event that planted the central image in the artist's mind:

'I was drawing one day in front of this grotty wall in a wasteland – all the roofs were stripped – and I saw this little boy playing. He climbed up a lamp post and swung from it, and I suddenly saw that he looked as though he was being crucified. I asked him if he minded if I took a photograph and did a drawing of him in my sketchbook. He replied "No, mister", so I gave him a couple of bob and he shinned up the lamp post again. Eventually he said "Mister can I come down, it's painful". He suffered for me, and I did the drawing.

'So I had the idea of this boy crucified in my mind, but I couldn't see it in terms of a picture. Some time later I went into another area and found the wall you see in this painting. On it was all this graffiti – "UVF", "Army Out", "No Pope Here", even a football slogan – a complete hotchpotch. It struck me that these themes were essentially the same as those surrounding Christ's crucifixion – politics, the army and religion.

'I thought this wall and that boy would work together. For a long time I'd wanted to do something with the death figures, or skeletons that the locals in the Catholic areas paint on the walls. This one, Toshy, was someone who died of what they used to call lead poisoning – he was shot by the army, and he was a bit of a hero. The army used to paint these figures out, and then the locals used to paint them back in, and then the army painted them out. They became incredible visually.

'I decided I wanted to use two of these figures and make it like a triptych, with a predella of an army patrol. On the back I was going to have photographs of IRA members, because to the locals they are almost like saints, but eventually the graffiti spread all over the back.'

For Howard the triptych was clearly a major personal statement and he was upset that the Royal Academy's hanging committee placed it badly. It might have seemed a 'difficult' picture at the time, particularly for an official artist and potential Academician to be presenting. This difficulty, and his disappointment with its position at the Academy – where it failed to sell – might have led the artist to submit *Ulster Crucifixion* to the John Moores Exhibition in Liverpool. The celebrated biannual competition produced what was at the time one of the few prominent, regular avant-garde exhibitions in the country. Howard might not have considered the Moores his natural milieu, but his neighbour,

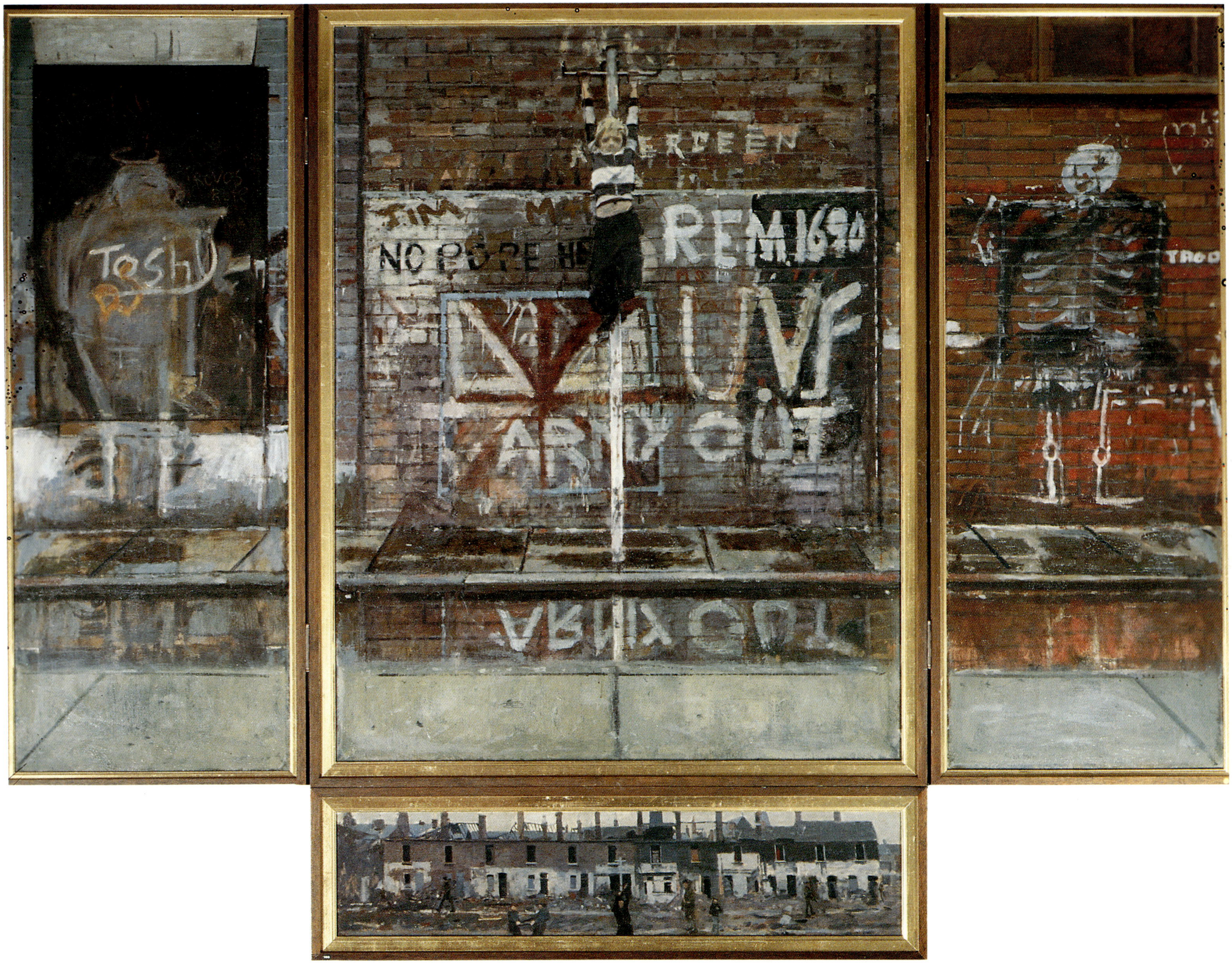

Ulster Crucifixion
Oil on canvas, 1978. 48 × 72ins main panels,
9 × 36ins predella (RA 1978, No 1009).

the widow of Jacques O'Hana of the O'Hana Gallery, had handed him the forms and the painting was available. It received one of the coveted awards – to the artist's surprise – and a mixed press.

It is possible to regard *Ulster Crucifixion* as a near masterpiece. The fact that Howard has yet to work again in such an uncompromising, harshly realist vein as the graffiti paintings might suggest that he was not entirely comfortable with the genre. These works do, however, sit convincingly at the end of a line that commenced in the railway yards and the Plymouth barracks. The rectilinear, abstract design this particular painting so clearly hinges upon also underlies much of the artist's later work. Nevertheless the morbid symbolism of the graffiti series, and particularly of this triptych, may have been felt to have a disquieting effect within the context of his *oeuvre*.

Ultimately any flaw in the triptych probably stems from the very painterliness of Howard's art. By the late 1970s he was capable of exploiting the seductive qualities of oil paint and of manipulating the medium to achieve astonishingly naturalistic effects. In *Ulster Crucifixion* the potent images of the boy and the graffiti are almost too blatantly real. What results is a most disturbing juxtaposition of painted and scrawled images.

In the faithful, near life-size representation of the graffiti ghosts of the two 'thieves', the artist is rekindling and participating in a folk art, whose origins in human culture pre-date the classical science of representational painting. It is this ancient imagery which, with iconographical correctness, forms the body of the triptych. Used before to portray City of London churches, the medieval triptych format's religious connotations are even more clearly alluded to here. The graffiti Calvary forms a painting within a painting, with the wall as its support. Indeed it might be seen to become the painting itself.

In the narrow picture space between the wall and the canvas hangs the boy's strained body. He almost seems to swing beyond the canvas into the observer's own, real space. He is painted with a classical realism far removed from cave art, and his startling presence represents ancient tragedy in 1970s Belfast.

Although it was painted for his own purposes, not for the Imperial War Museum, *Ulster Crucifixion* must stand as one of the most potent depictions of the troubles in Northern Ireland. Unfortunately it is now in North America, rather than on public display in the United Kingdom.

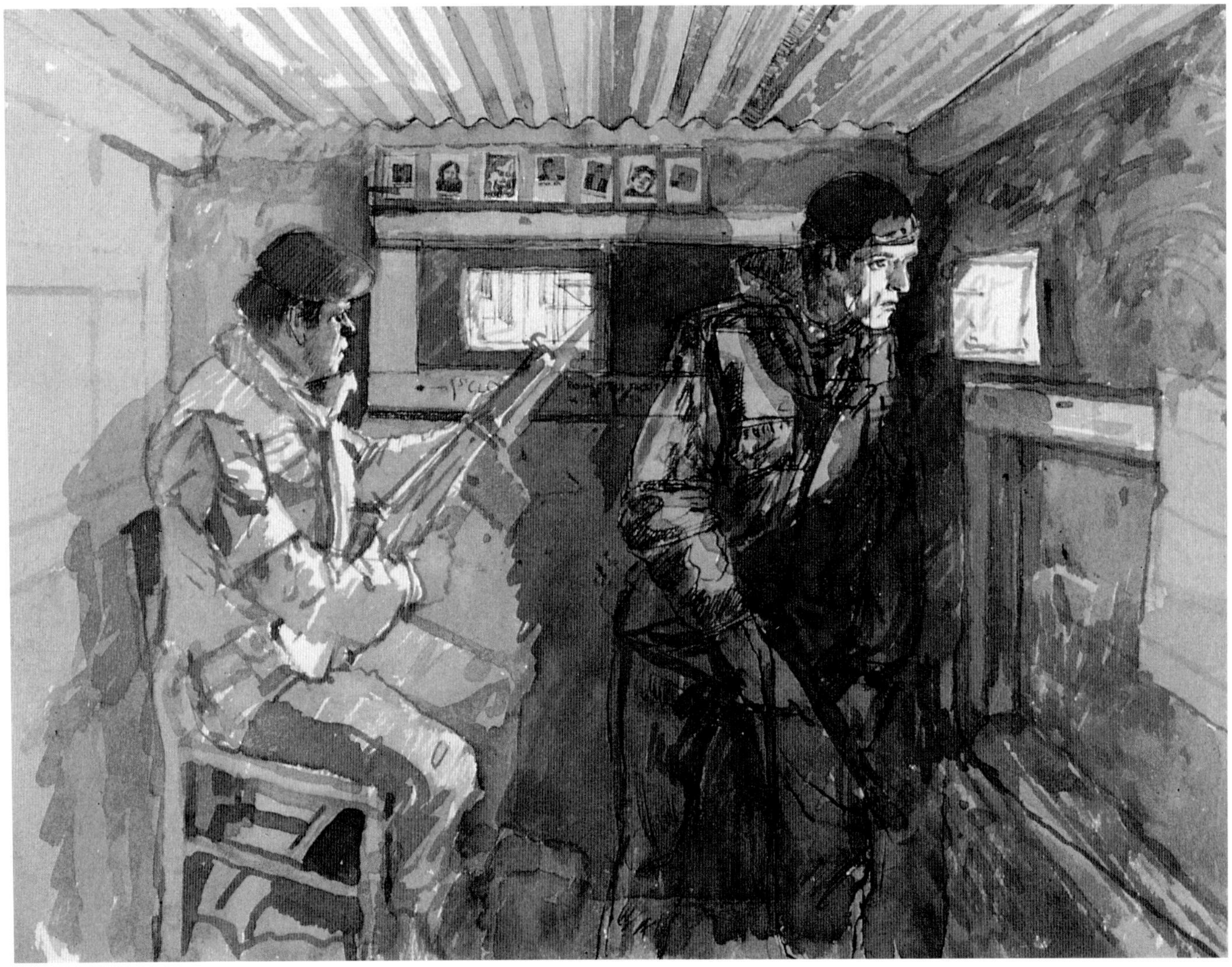

The Sanger
Pen and ink and wash, 1973. 15 × 22ins.

The Sanger

The two monochromatic studies on these pages, of soldiers on watch inside the sangers – concrete pill-boxes – which guard police stations and army barracks across Northern Ireland, are among the drawings specifically commissioned by the Museum. In shades of sepia, they are fine examples of war reportage and were produced in awkward conditions. Their vivid sense of reality and wonderful economy of brush-marks, notably in the Divis drawing, clearly flow from the artist's intense experience of his subject. Forced to work close up to soldiers in a heightened state of awareness, he must have shared in the tension.

These studies also serve to demonstrate how correct had been Carel Weight's judgement in recommending Ken Howard to the Imperial War Museum. The years of commissioned drawings, working up sketches for the telephone directories in hotel bedrooms and recording events in the casualty ward, had prepared him well for recording the inside of an army sanger. Nonetheless, the level of tension must have been a new experience:

'In Northern Ireland all parties relied very much on collecting information, and a lot of soldiers spent a lot of time sitting in sangers, just watching the crowd go by and making notes that so and so was in the area.

'This one that the soldiers could just about stand in was near the notorious Divis Flats and was nicknamed "The Coffin". While they were sitting there the local girls would come along to talk through the holes to the men. On one occasion a girl was chatting up a soldier and persuaded him to come out of the sanger to talk to her. As he came out he was shot and killed. As his friend came out to pull him back in, he too was shot and killed.

'This drawing I built up when neither figure was with the other figure. I went in there to draw and soon one fellow went off duty. I then only had an hour with the other one. They wouldn't bend the rules to let me have any longer with the soldiers.'

Resulting from these constraints the drawing retains a lack of finish, which if anything adds to the sense of immediacy that is a hallmark of good reportage. We are also given an insight into the artist's working-method. The more complete, standing figure was brushed in first and then an economical ink line applied to the basic structure that had been established. On top of this a further wash has established the tones from the dark shadow to the light touching his face. The other soldier left before Howard had finished with him and exists simply in his first wash stage, bathed in an even light, too bright for a sanger interior.

'One of the striking things about working in Northern Ireland was that I could never expect them to change their routines because of me. I always fitted in with their routines. Therefore I would be doing a drawing, knowing that the next minute my subject might disappear. So it made it all terribly urgent, and I think the drawings have an immediacy.

'Sometimes, when teaching in the life class, I've snapped my fingers and asked the students what they were thinking of at that moment. A lot of them would look guilty and obviously weren't thinking about drawing – they were miles away, thinking about what they were having for dinner that night, or whether they were going to the pictures. You know an art school model is going to be there for several hours, but these soldiers might be gone in two minutes. Something might happen and they might be called away. So there was always an urgency and I always concentrated on my drawing.'

OP in the Divis Flats
'I had to get used to working in very difficult circumstances. This observation post was on top of the Divis Flats and you had to go up about twelve floors in the lift. There had been cases when the lift doors had opened and the people had been sprayed with bullets, so going up there made me quite nervous. Because one was a sitting target on top of the flats, I had to crawl into the OP with the soldiers. Inside there was very little headroom and I would draw lying on my stomach. It was so cramped that I couldn't look at the night-sight near me on the left and see the man at the other end. I had to turn my head through 180 degrees, and that is where the old knowledge of perspective which we had to learn as students really came in useful. I established an eye level and keyed everything in, so that I knew there was a common denominator through the drawing, from which everything else could grow.'

This remarkably controlled study gains a dynamic composition from this extended perspective. Despite the panoramic effect, the cramped conditions are emphasised by the strong horizontals and the looming ceiling. The handling of the brush, particularly in passages describing the men, reveals the artist at his ravishing best. No mark is superfluous and each brush-stroke is made with that rare combination of vigour and precision that characterises the greatest brush drawings, from Rembrandt to Hokusai. Made some five years after the less complex drawing of *The Sanger*, this study shows what a master of his medium and his conditions Howard had become.

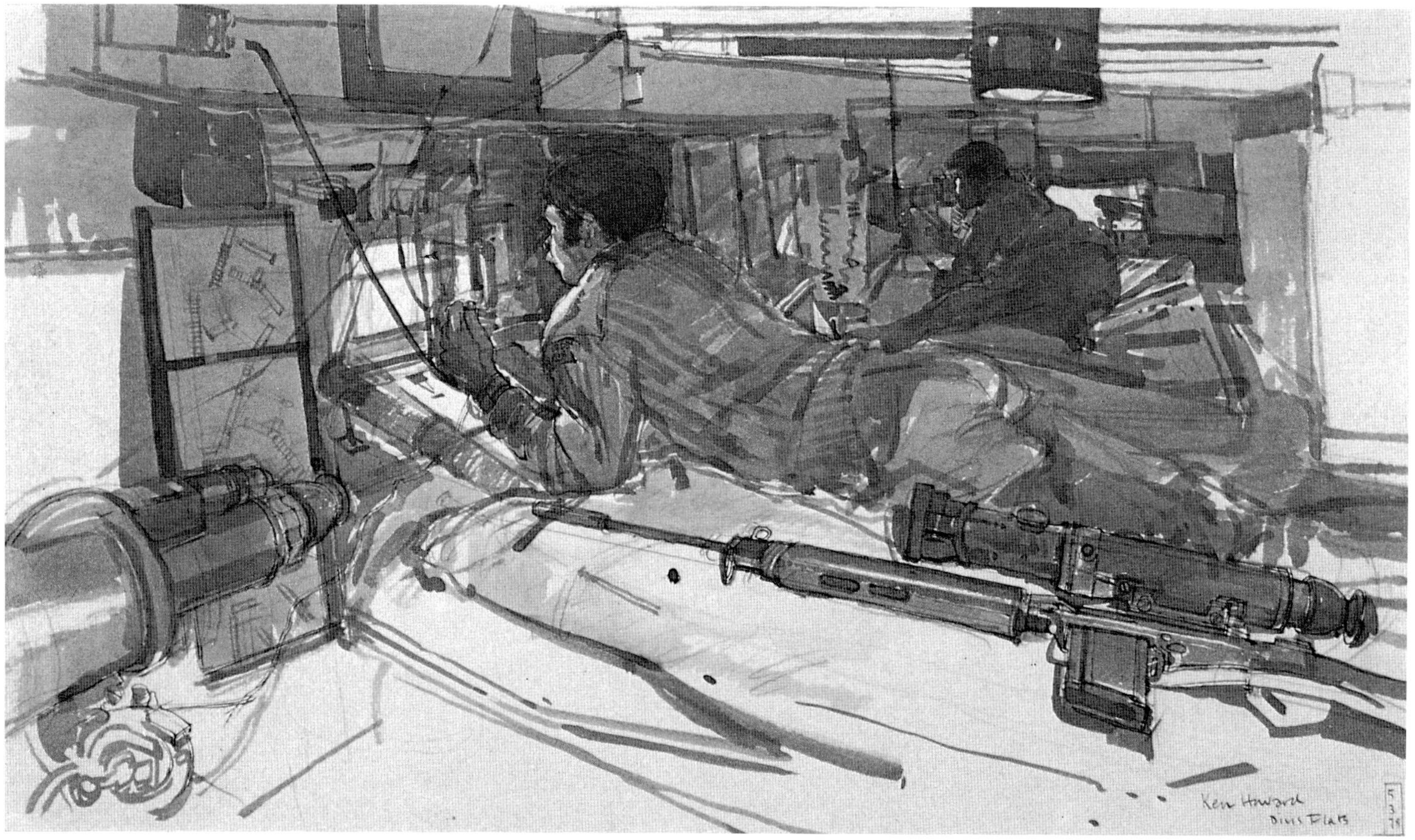

OP in the Divis Flats
Pen and ink and wash, 1978. 15 × 22ins.

The Barrack-Room at Fork Hill (*Overleaf*)
A more ambitious composition than either of the sanger studies, this drawing nevertheless retains their sense of truthful reporting. Once again the artist has apparently been forced to down tools before completion of the work. In fact the lack of 'finish' in some of the foreground areas is a device intended to add depth to the scene. These passages are peripheral to the angle of the observer's vision, which is concentrated on the figures in the middle-distance. These are by contrast densely detailed and are also thrown backwards in the composition by the plunging perspective.

Such techniques serve to convey the confined space of the barrack-room, where one's eyes can only focus on a relatively small area of the scene at any one time. It is the artist's chosen task to select and stress this area of interest. Guidance for the spectator's eye is a common enough device in the history of art; but not all art is made this way. At one extreme, the influence of John Ruskin on some of the Pre-Raphaelites and their followers led these painters to consider every detail of the scene before them with even-handed concentration and technique to match. Even in skilled hands such overall detail can become mechanical and art-less, although it has certainly resulted in many master-works over the ages. The consideration of these problems affects many artists at some point in their careers, including Howard:

'For a long time I went through a stage when I was worrying how one was seeing – whether one saw the end of a person's nose, and everything else in the face was blurred. I thought if you painted like that it would be much more like the way you see. But I also wondered whether we see more episodically, going from the eye to the ear or to the hair. Of course when we paint we have to do that to an extent, as we are charmed by so many different bits. But eventually I began to think one should fix the highlight on, say, the nose and work out from there.

'I suppose I was conscious of getting a focus in this drawing by developing one part of it. I was thinking in such terms in those days, and I did several of these drawings where there is one key figure and then the drawing fades away until it's simply indicated with the brush and no colour. Another thing that happened was that I started to mix my media in a fairly unconventional way.

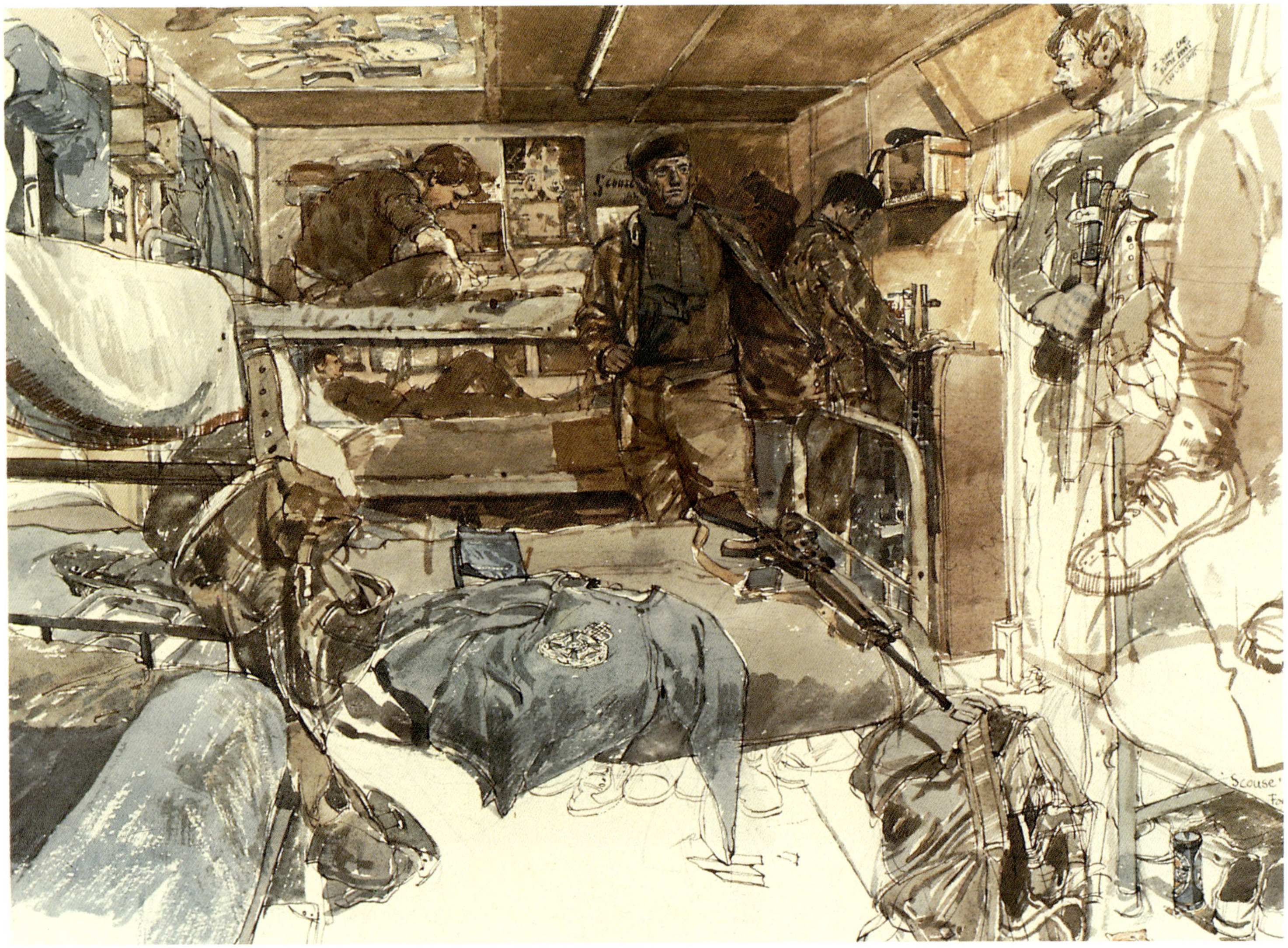

The Barrack-Room at Fork Hill
Pen and ink and watercolour, 1978. 15 × 22ins.

I did drawings with sepia ink and when they were established I used watercolour over the ink.

'With this subject having such a focal point I had to ask the man taking his jacket off to pose for me. That's why the barrack-room became a good place to draw, because out in the sangers you couldn't ask a soldier to pose. You just had to be there and try to follow the drawing through to a conclusion. In the barrack-room the soldiers were off duty and you could get then to pose, and they were flattered.'

These barrack-room drawings were much admired by the soldiers, especially those whose likenesses were destined for the Imperial War Museum. The habitually faithful portrayal of the soldiers and their surroundings must have inspired many of the regimental commissions Howard began to receive in Northern Ireland. As word went around the invitations mounted up. Howard embarked on a helter-skelter series of financially rewarding commissions, which was to take him to all those parts of the world where the British armed services were based. His understanding of service life meant he fitted in well with the troops and the drawings that resulted suggest they felt at ease as his models:

'I have got this funny knack of catching a likeness and when I drew soldiers in Northern Ireland – I couldn't help myself – it always looked like them, they weren't just any old soldier. In a way it complicated things a bit, because when the regiments started to commission me to do drawings they really wanted them to appeal to the whole regiment. Of course it would end up that Captain Jones and Sergeant Smith were clearly the two main figures in the drawing. But I couldn't do anything about that. I wasn't going to start worrying about making everything generalised, which would be entirely contrary to my philosophy of drawing.

'This philosophy is best summed up in a phrase of Ben Shahn, the American artist, which I think runs like this: "When I draw a pair of trousers I want people to know if they are a ten-dollar pair of trousers or a fifty-dollar pair of trousers". To take this example, this does not mean you should start off thinking you must draw Captain Jones. What it means is that you must try to get accurately the shape and form of what is in front of you. If you get that shape and form right – even if you don't put in one facial feature, even if you draw the back of the man's head – it will be like him.'

Boat People

Exhibited at the Academy two years after *Ulster Crucifixion*, this canvas is the culmination of the major imaginative paintings with which Howard concerned himself in the late 1960s and the 1970s. Its subject is clear, but the manner of its genesis complex. The finished work, in a restrained earth palette and simple, open composition, is one of the artist's most moving achievements.

'I was in Hong Kong doing a commission for the Gurkhas and spent some of the time drawing the view over the bay and the city skyline. During this time I knew that these refugees were out there on the freighters burning in the sun and being prevented from landing. So after the *Skyluck* finally ran aground I went out to see it – a very powerful image with its angled masts and the bay and islands beyond. Then I was shown a photograph of the people coming off the boat and climbing the hill. Immediately the image gelled in my mind. I had seen the boat people in the camps and felt I knew enough about them to include them in my painting of the grounded freighter.

'In those days some enterprising Vietnamese would hire a boat and sail to Hong Kong with his passengers, not knowing whether they would be accepted or not. At the time a lot did get in. With the terrible conditions in the camps, one can argue about the rights and wrongs of them being there, but that is all a matter of opinion and discussion. My concerns as an artist were somewhat different. When I saw the photographs of these burly Green Jackets helping babies and old men up the hill I knew I had to make a painting.

'I was asked on a number of occasions why I didn't make the people look more dirty, starving and miserable. To do that would have been to dramatise it. In Hong Kong there are squatter camps – cardboard cities – where the immigrant Chinese live. I remember one day passing a squatter camp resident going off to her job, and she was immaculate. The same was true of these people on the boats. They still did their laundry and kept themselves and their children clean. They didn't look as if they'd been suffering for weeks and weeks. So I painted the truth. What's true is usually far more interesting than what we think ought to be true.'

Boat People
Oil on canvas, 1979–80. 60 × 72ins (RA 1980, No 115).

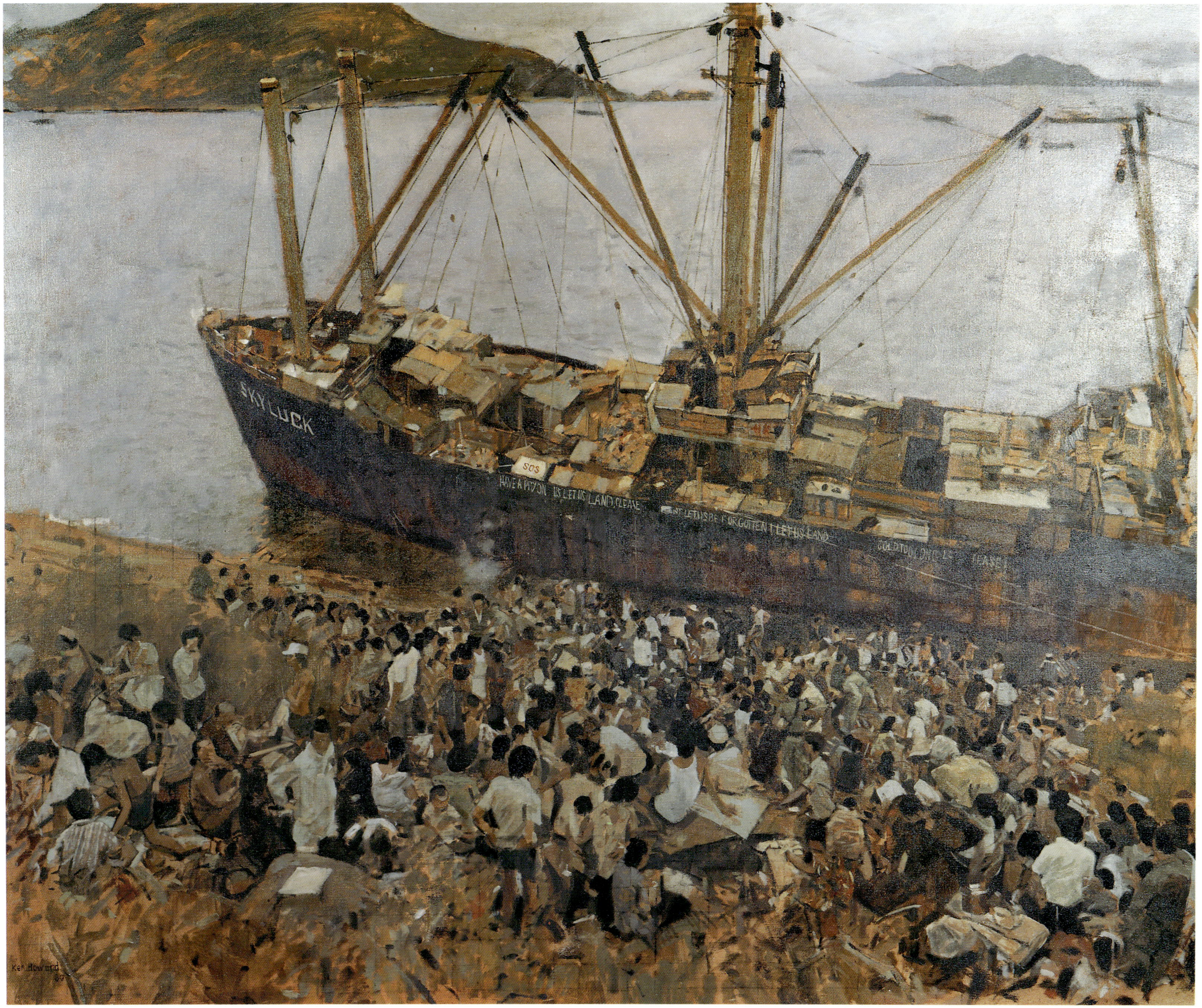
SKYLUCK
SOS
Ken Howard

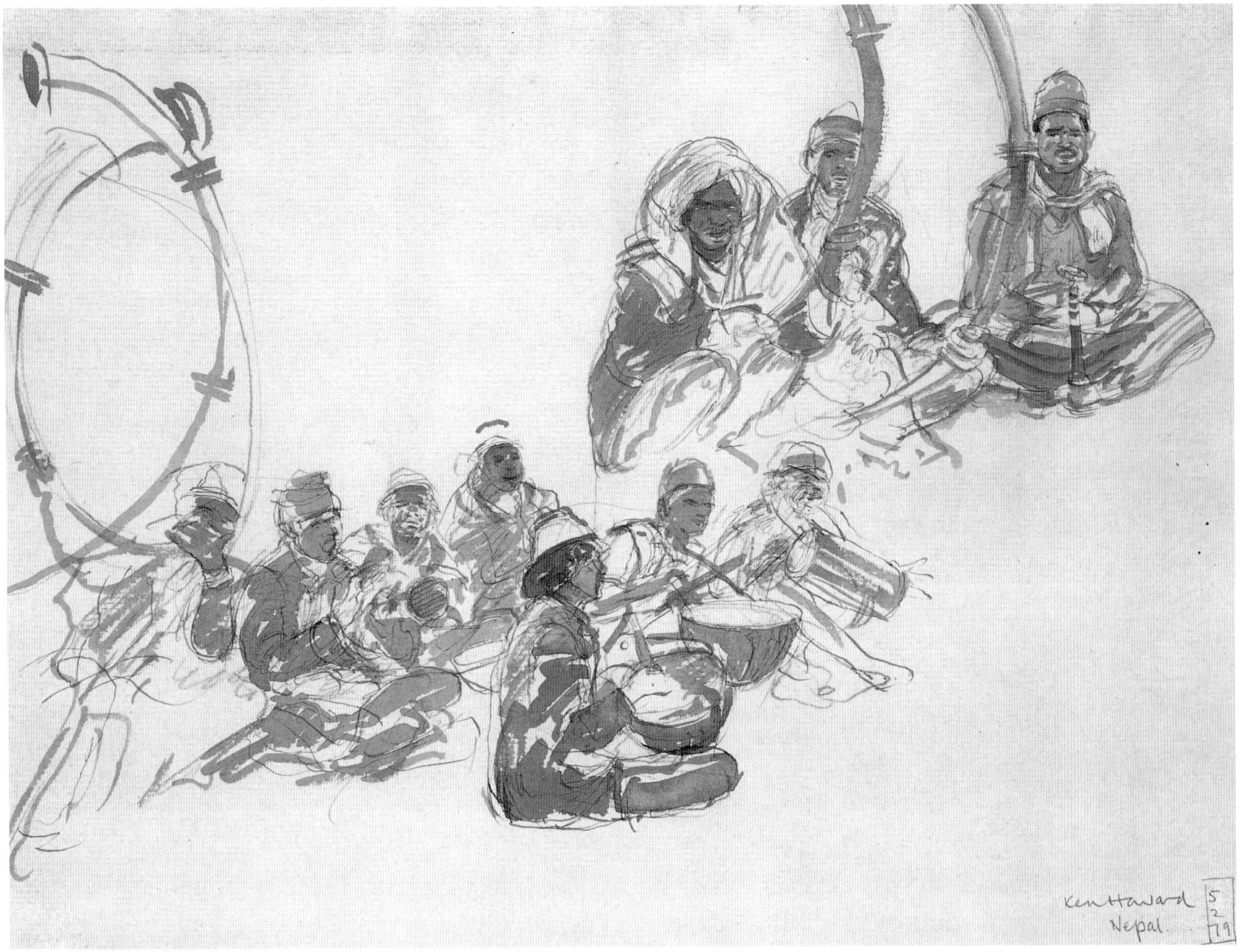

Damai Band
Pencil and wash, 1979. 10 × 13ins.

Damai Band

At what was a restless time in his life – between marriage to Annie and the time when Christa was finally to come to England – Howard was eager to take up opportunities to travel and work, whether in a military or a civilian context. Through his armed services commissions overseas, Howard made many excellent contacts. *Boat People* had originated while working for the Gurkhas and it was through his contacts with this regiment that he ended up in their native Nepal:

'I had been asked there by Colonel, now General, Peter Duffell, who at that time was commanding the 2nd KEO Gurkha Rifles and who was going off on a mountain trek. He was interested in writing a book about the home life of the Gurkha and asked me to do the illustrations.

'The Gurkha soldier typically retires from the army in his early thirties. He returns as a pensioner to the village where he grew up, to build a house with his savings and start a family. The Gurkhas are of necessity very self-sufficient and even the bricks for the house building are made on the edge of the village. There is no glass in the windows, no corrugated iron roofs, because these materials would have to be carried through the hills.

'We went on a trek through the villages in the area where Peter's regiment recruited. Part of his mission was to pay the "pensioners" their annual pension. It was never an enormous amount, but by Nepalese standards it wasn't bad. We arrived at a village and on its edge were met by all its inhabitants and the village band. The musicians and artists are usually from the Damai caste – the lowest caste. The band led us through the village and the children danced for us. They slaughtered an enormous goat for us in a field, and when we got to the field the Damai sat down and started to play – they were beating their drums and playing these enormous horns which made an incredibly deep noise. They were quite frenetic.

'Then Peter said to me he wanted a drawing of this scene for his book. I told him he was mad, but started to try to draw amid all the dancing children. While I was doing this they had a break, which is shown in the top right of the drawing. Then they carried on again, and so did I. In the end I lost my cool and gave up. But later, when I looked at the drawing again, I thought it worked almost because of the conditions. It couldn't have been posed like that and although it's a slight drawing, it is very accurate.'

Indeed, like the Northern Ireland sanger drawings, also made under adverse conditions, the *Damai Band* reveals the artist at his most urgent and telling. Slight in terms of the amount of marks on the paper it may be, but the imperative to record rapidly a fast-moving event has brought his instinctive draughtsmanship to the fore. As considerations of picture-making are cast to the winds, the raw quality of the marks on the paper is graphically and movingly obvious.

Village near Machhapuchare
'This drawing was made the morning after. I can survive on little sleep and I can work long hours – and we had sat up most of the night. Once they had fed us they bought some girls down from the hills to dance for us. Usually it's the boys who take the female dancing parts and they would never normally allow females to dance for a stranger. But Peter was like a god, being the officer who recruited in that area of Nepal.

'The night went on and on and I crawled into my tent at about four in the morning, only to get up at six-thirty. I went to sit on the edge of the wadi that ran round the village. Some locals came out with hard-boiled eggs for me, but I just had to draw this view, which I completed in about two hours.'

Such was the pressure to make drawings that Howard was consistently completing three daily. To keep up this rate he had on occasion to part company from the main party and go into the villages, where his subject matter lay. On one such expedition he slipped on some rocks while crossing a river and, instinctively saving his drawings from the water, badly hurt his left hand. When he eventually got medical attention he was able to carry on drawing with his all-important right hand. Despite this set-back, the output barely subsided and the artist found the constant demands of his subjects suited him well:

'After about two weeks I really began to feel my strength. I don't play cricket, but I think I could liken it to being a batsman who is beginning to see the ball grow larger and larger, to the extent that by the prime of his innings he can't miss it. I think one feels one's way into a drawing – tentative at first and doing a bit of measuring here and there. As the day goes on all such aids drop away and then one is really drawing. Surprises happen, like the head being absolutely right in relation to the body, which just couldn't have happened in the morning without making measurements. At its best it becomes complete command.'

This tonally subtle drawing demonstrates the artist's command of his technique. Although without quite the vitality of the *Damai Band* study, the pen and sepia wash are handled with an un-mannered directness. The hills rising up to the sharp peak of Machhapuchare are unfolded with a clarity born of experience. The eloquent marks belie the speed of working – a factor that becomes evident in much of Howard's later work.

Sadly the planned book was never written, but the whole series of Nepalese drawings is probably one of the most honest attempts at travel topography made by a contemporary artist. The evidence is that Howard managed to get to understand the landscape and people well enough for his purposes. This is confirmed by a characteristic anecdote that also helps illuminate his idea of the essence of drawing, already discussed in relation to *The Barrack-Room at Fork Hill*:

'Someone saw a sheet of heads I had done and was able to point out to me which one was from which caste. Of course I hadn't known this when I sat down to draw. To a Westerner they tend to look very similar and to me they were all Nepalese. But I had drawn their heads in such a way that they were unmistakable.

'When you sit down to draw, you don't say to yourself this man is going to look North Nepalese. You're more aware of drawing one shape against another, and if you draw intensively the truth of what is inside those shapes will emerge. The more you draw the surface the more you will show the real character of what's underneath. But you still have to remain removed from the subject and concern yourself with visual things.'

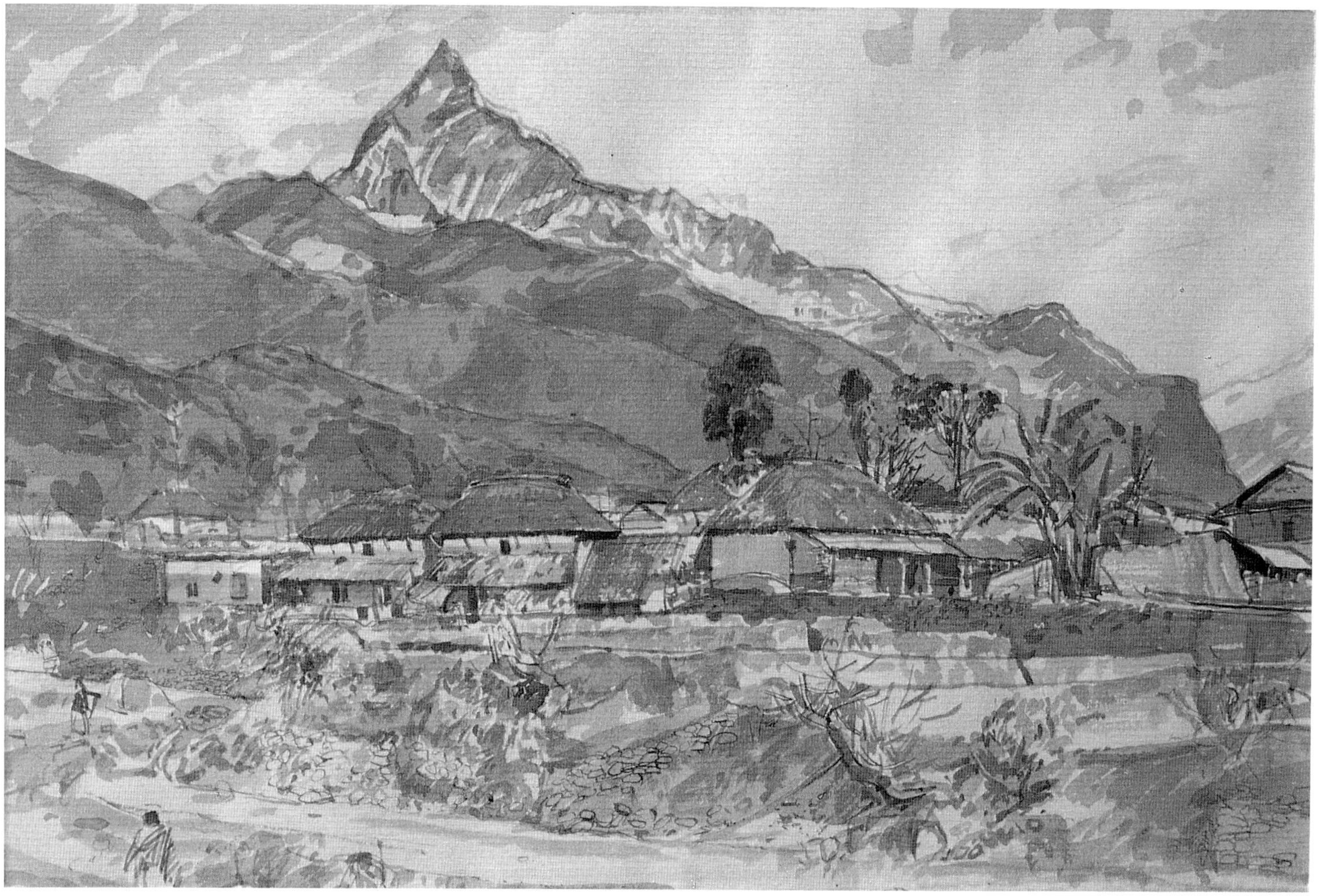

Village near Machhapuchare
Pen and wash, 1979. 10 × 13ins.

Travel and Landscape

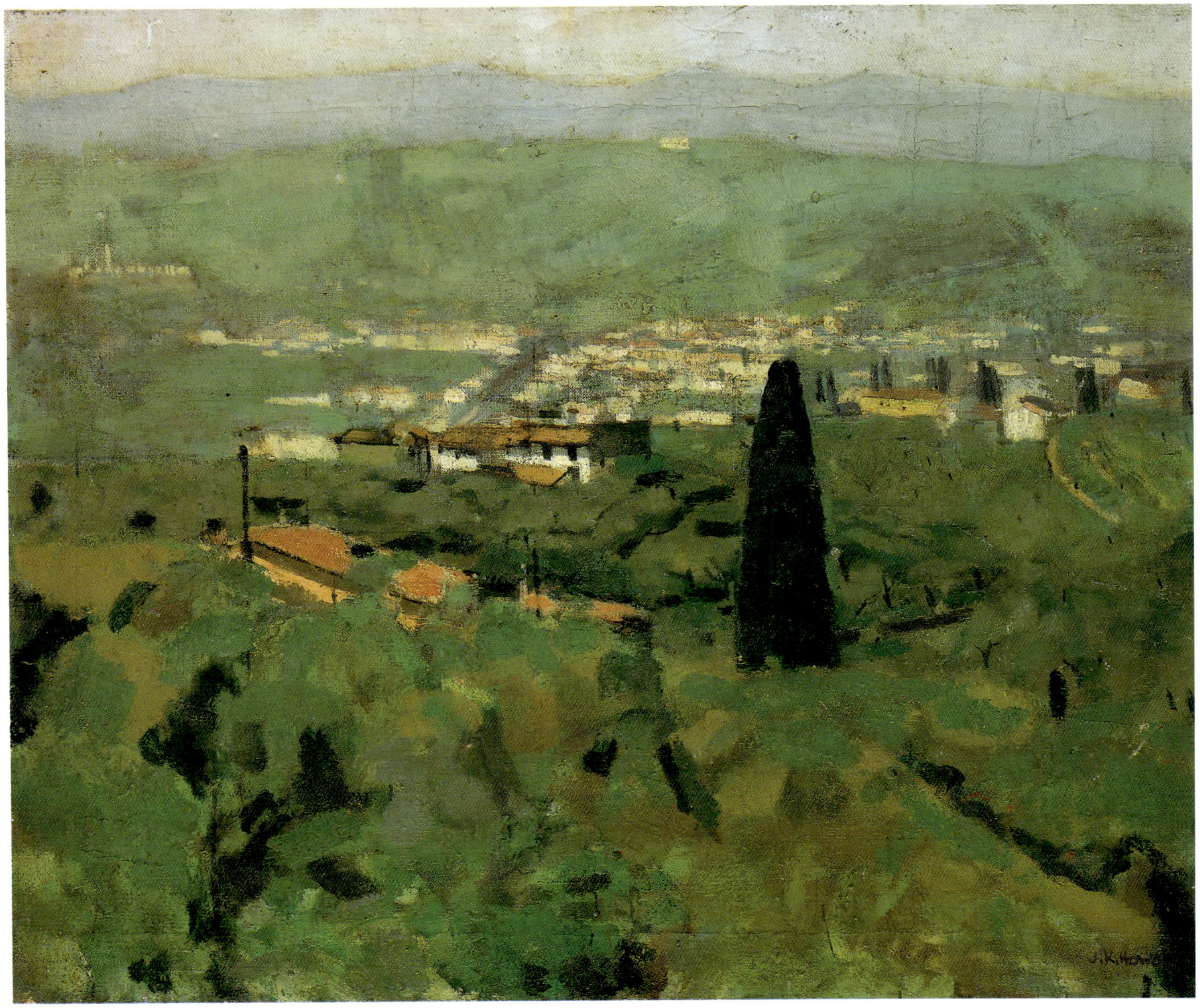

From the Viuzzo dei Monteripaldi
Oil on canvas, 1959. 20 × 24ins.

From the Viuzzo dei Monteripaldi
The paintings and drawings in the previous section, loosely gathered together under the theme of the 'war artist', were either made to commission or resulted from commissions. In essence they are records of people or events in their lives. The sequence of works in this section moves us closer to Howard the pure painter, and are the fruits of his personal response to landscape and urban scenes, often while travelling. In one or two cases his presence may have arisen from a commission, but he was nevertheless able to depart from a planned itinerary to find subjects that suited his aesthetic interests. These pictures conclude with the street scenes in Florence which, with the subsequent Venice series, have dominated his recent travels.

The journey starts on Howard's first visit to Italy in 1958, following his graduation from the Royal College of Art:

'I went off to Italy on my scooter. On my way I fell off three times and nearly wrote myself off once. The scooter was very unstable, being loaded with stuff for the year, and I used to get cut off the road by lorries. When I arrived in Florence I met an Italian medical student, who was looking for somewhere to live and wanted to learn English. We took a room in a house belonging to an American and I got straight down to painting in perfect weather from September to Christmas. I then met another American with a studio in the hills and moved in there.'

The Florentine hills are a place of refuge in summer months, when their green slopes provide relief from the searing heat of the dusty valley in which the city lies. In the winter the climate can be cold and damp, but importantly Howard's studio afforded fine views over the surrounding hills and distant mountains. For the first time he painted a series of landscapes. As the series developed he searched for a language to suit the Mediterranean shapes and colours.

This painting, taken from the studio, exhibits a lighter touch than the earlier railway sidings panels, which may not only be attributable to the luminosity of the scene:

'My work began to change. I arrived in the hills with the early Italian landscapes of Corot in my mind, but after some time working there I felt I was beginning to get an understanding for the Impressionists. My roots were architecture, factories, North London, and suddenly I was dealing with real landscape and looking for guidance. So the first pictures I took back to England and showed at Wildenstein's were more Impressionist-influenced than any of my earlier work. As this influence matured, my work became much more faceted – it began to be more broken in colour, more to do with marks. I became much more interested in the way one form comes up against another and the way colour changes right the way around something of supposedly consistent colour.'

The young man's evident joy in his lightened palette has produced light brush-strokes – almost playful if compared with his earlier work in England. The painting's pleasing texture is abstract rather than descriptive, although some of the sharper brush-marks suggest that he might have been impressed by Cézanne's paintings of the not-dissimilar Provençal hills. Ken Howard the painter, the picture-maker, was emerging.

Morning, Santa Magdalena del Pulpis
Following his first visit to Spain, during which he toured the museums to confirm his love for that country's artists – who were sparsely represented in England – Howard's second visit in 1955 was undertaken principally to paint the country and people. He went again in 1961 with Annie, to whom he was by this time engaged. She liked to spend the day by the sea and he would therefore make early-morning excursions in their first car to paint, before it got so hot that the beach beckoned. At about four in the afternoon he would return again to work until the sun went down.

He chose for his subject the village of Santa Magdalena del Pulpis, in the hills behind the Costa Dorada, to the south-west of Barcelona. He was to develop a warm affection for the quiet village and its inhabitants. During the next few years he returned to the village on a number of occasions, finally staying there in the local hairdresser's house – there being no hotel.

'I think the fact that it was rustic, unspoilt, drew me to the village. There were virtually no vehicles when I used to go there – maybe the odd car came off the main road to make the drive up into the hills. I got to know the people in the house very well, although my Spanish was terrible. By that time Spain was changing pretty radically – and when you were down on the coast you realised how beautiful places like this were.

'I first went to Spain because of my passion for her painters, but by this time I was getting more and more interested in light. The Spanish light is very extreme and I came to realise it was this which was pulling me back there. I think the quality of light always had been the motivating factor in my pictures, but I wasn't always conscious of it. My interest in it really came to the surface in Spain. I started to try to paint very particular light effects, and sometimes I had six or seven canvases on the go at the same time. I would work on one from six in the morning to seven-fifteen, one from seven-fifteen to eight-thirty, and so on. The next day I would work on the same canvases. In Spain I could do this, because every day I got up and the sun was in the same position. I could lock straight back into the picture I was working on the previous day. It's very different in England.'

If this was a method consciously derived from Monet's similar practice, Howard's technique and analysis of the stark sunlight of Mediterranean Spain were his own. Staring directly into the light, Howard did not see it diffusing into Impressionist haze, or even smothering the structure of things in Turnerian manner. Indeed, the painting illustrated here, taken characteristically *contre-jour*, is as reliant as the railway pictures on solidity of form and structure in the composition. The overhead wires, dark lines trailed through the bright sky, are the upside-down negative of the glistening railway lines cutting across the dark ground. The familiar interest in vertical and horizontal elements is as strong as ever. Each surface is given its own defined position within the pictorial space and each wall has a plasticity – a tactile presence – that recalls Utrillo's Montmartre.

Within the context of the selection of work in this book, *Santa Magdalena* may be seen as something of a milestone in Ken Howard's career. From his lucid portrayal of the effects of light, shadow and local colour, one might be forgiven for thinking he had lived in the Mediterranean all his life. Confronting the sun head on, he found he liked it bright and hot. This painting is a forerunner of so much, from the sparkle of Cornish beaches to the baking streets of modern Florence. It hints that he was beginning to find that a new aesthetic landscape lay between him and the sun, the source of light.

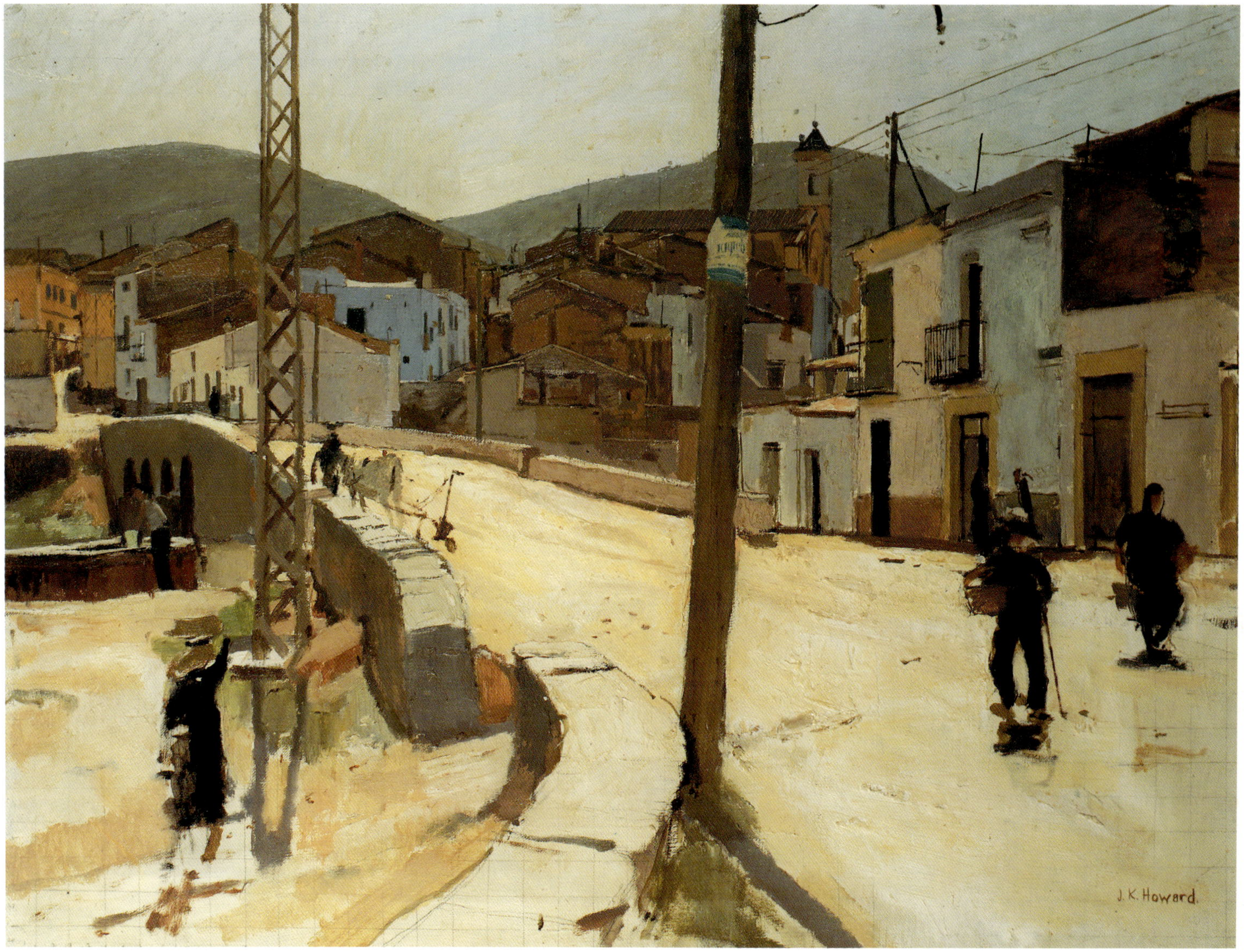

Morning, Santa Magdalena del Pulpis
Oil on canvas, 1961. 28 × 36ins.

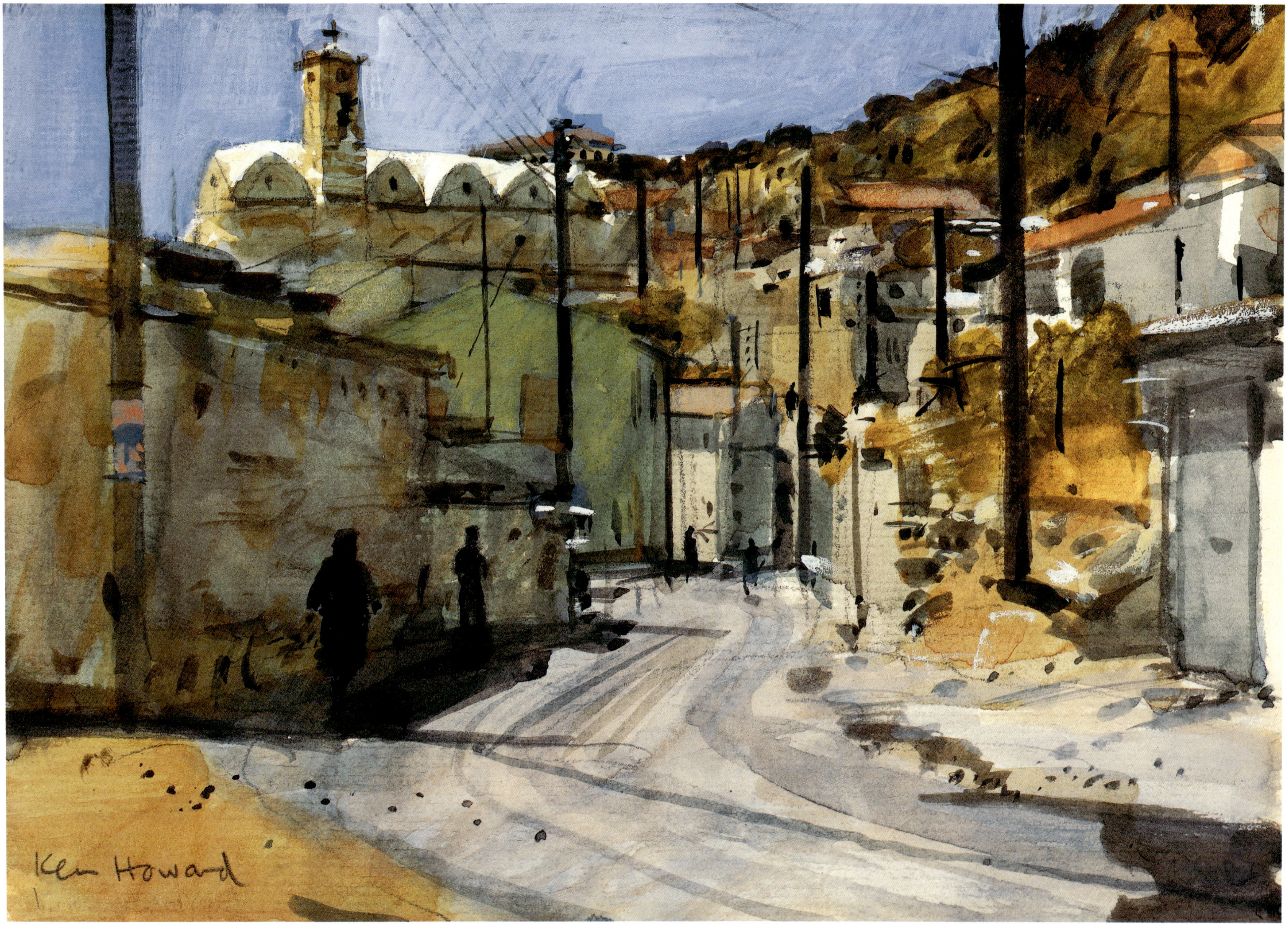

Pissouri Village, Afternoon
Watercolour, 1982. 7 × 9ins.

Pissouri Village, Afternoon

'I started going to Cyprus in about 1975, not long after the Turkish-Greek war. There were two sovereign bases – at Episkopi and at Dekalia – and I used to work between the two. After a hectic series of commissions in England, a doctor told me I was suffering from nervous exhaustion and that I should lay off work for a couple of weeks. I wrote to the Devon and Dorsets to tell them I couldn't go to Cyprus as planned. They replied that I should come and live with them, and paint the commission if I felt like it. So I did, and I went up into the hills and found Pissouri. After that I went to Pissouri whenever I was in Cyprus, which was a lot.'

The doctor's advice reaped rewards for Howard, although it is unlikely that he would have obeyed such orders for long. Over a decade after the Spanish paintings he again reacted strongly to the brilliant Mediterranean sun. The artist's consistency is evident when we compare *Pissouri, Afternoon*, painted on one of his later visits to the island, with *Santa Magdalena*. Compositional mirror images, they both employ the effects of *contre-jour*, using the sharp silhouettes of telegraph posts and wires to divide up the shapes of the subject. In the later work this division is made much less dramatically or self-consciously. Over the course of the intervening years the artist had apparently learnt to express his painter's gifts through a less formally obvious, though still extant, compositional structure. In the next decade this structure was to become less obvious to the observer, but it was always to underlie his art.

Another development of note is that Howard is to be seen using bright, liberal washes of watercolour. The pencil outline is scant and the paint is worked with verve and confidence. His fluency with the brush is described by Howard with the fervour of a significant experience:

'While I was painting at Pissouri that time, I did what I think is probably the best set of watercolours of my life. I hit one of those patches, where I really felt completely at one with the medium. Using watercolour is like playing the violin or another single instrument. Suddenly you can be at one with it and there is no gap between the image that you're seeing and what's going onto the piece of paper – it all flows together. That never happens using oil paint, which is like trying to conduct an orchestra, trying to pull all these disparate bits together to make the whole.

'I was painting the set for an exhibition in Nicosia and was working under pressure to complete the watercolours. In my haste I became liberated. I could look at my subject and intuitively see if something should be transparent, or whether it was opaque and needed a bit of gouache. My technique was completely free. It was fantastic. I have never found it quite the same ever again. I may get back to it one day, but I can't force it. I think the reason it came to me at that time was because I'd been working a long time on commissioned watercolours and was ready for it all to come together.'

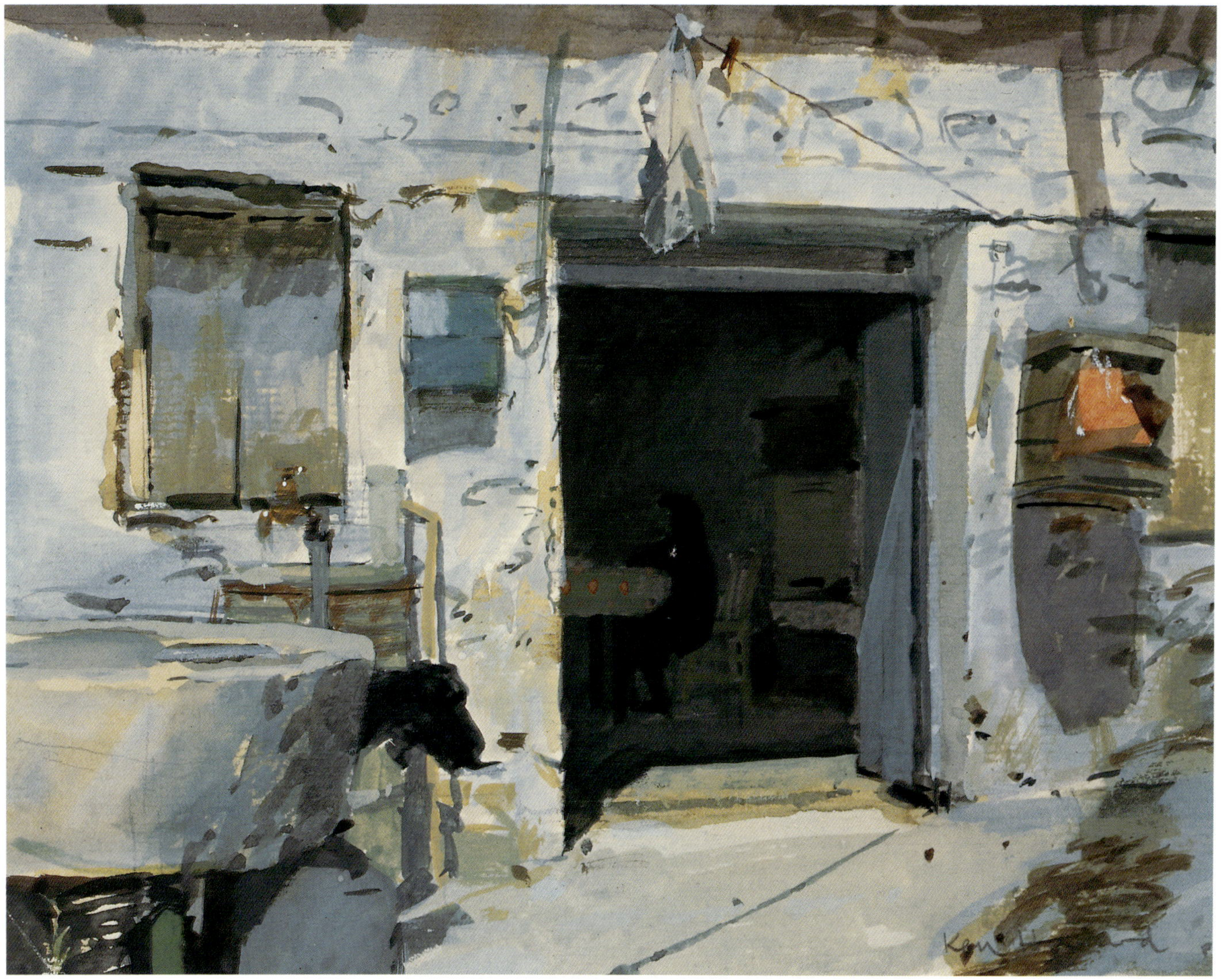

Midday Light, Cyprus

In the dazzling midday sun, when most sensible people are retiring inside, the artist is to be found outside, looking into a house in a hill village near Pissouri. A very different conception to the previous work, this watercolour is successful for a simple eloquence that equally well demonstrates Howard's mastery of his medium. Apparently contrary to his own belief, it is a mastery which is also evident in many later watercolours, painted in Venice and Cornwall. Unlike those later works, however, this is painted with large areas of bodycolour, which he used extensively and with great freedom in Cyprus.

Nonetheless, this particular image was not achieved with ease. Even sitting in shade, as he presumably was, the reflected midday light bouncing onto his paper sheet would make it hard to read the tonal relationships he was laying down:

Midday Light, Cyprus
Watercolour, 1982. 7 × 9ins.

'I lost my cool completely with this. I thought I just couldn't get it down. I thought it was getting bogged down and losing its transparency, so eventually I got a large brush and rubbed some water over the paint. When it dried it seemed to work. I tried to do it again the next day and couldn't – one of those happy accidents.

'When I was a young man I was rather precious, and thought that painting was an entirely conscious act that you must have total control over. Now I realise that sometimes there is a need to recognise the fortuitous accident and preserve it. It's more as though the act of painting is flowing through you. The older you get, the less you are consciously putting things together and the more instinctive, less self-conscious you become.'

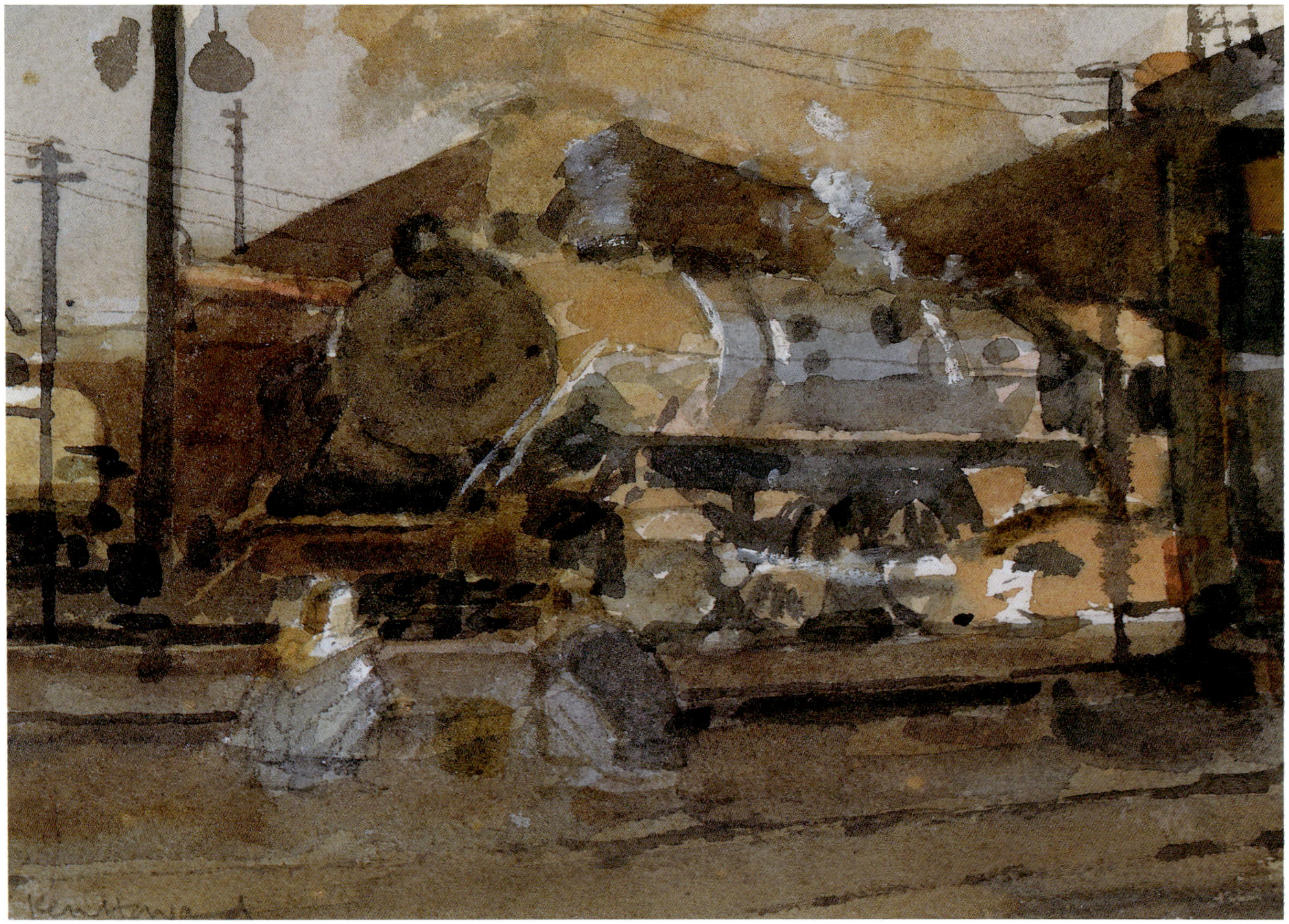

Jhansi Loco
Watercolour, 1984. 5 × 7ins.

Jhansi Loco
With the Hunting Group Award presented to him in 1982, Howard received £5,000. He decided to take Christa to India, where they stayed for a time with Brigadier John Cornell, the British Military Attaché in Delhi, and his wife Caroline. The artist was aware that he might be able to renew his acquaintance with steam railways, but it was not long after his arrival that he found himself taking on commissions to paint the Asian Games horse-riding champion and after that General Vaidya, Chief of the Indian Army Staff. The General, whom the artist remembers with warmth, was later to be assassinated, shortly after he commanded the operation to regain the Golden Temple of Amritsar.

With the proceeds from commissioned work, Howard ended up spending none of the Hunting prize. A successful exhibition also helped and he was to return with fewer drawings or paintings than he had originally hoped. Of these he was most satisfied with a series of watercolours of the railways, notably a set made at Jhansi:

'One advantage about working on the locos was that I could for a time get away from the hundreds of people who would gather round whenever I sat down to draw elsewhere. The problem was that they would stand in front of me, as well as to the back and sides, making it quite impossible to work. I had to get special permission to work there as the railways are the main means of military communication in India, although this didn't prevent me from being arrested and thoroughly interrogated on one occasion.

'The railway sidings were absolutely marvellous. Once again one felt that the scene could change at any time. I think it's crucial to my work to have a sense of excitement, and I loved the urgency which the uncertainty created. In the railway yards women used to pick through the coal dumped from the train's boilers, in search of unburnt pieces. They wore beautiful saris, which got covered with coal dust – sad but absolutely stunning visually. And the big old Indian trains were splendid. Although I love trains I couldn't tell you anything about them. To me they are like enormous animals as they heave into motion. Queuing up to go into the shed they were like a line of heaving bison or bulls.'

In examining the series of watercolours, mostly made on the spot, one is aware of the excitement felt by the artist. Although the locomotives are generally dominant, this is not railway portraiture of the nostalgic variety practised in Britain. Any identifying detail on the shining, heroic beast we see passing behind coal-gatherers – in the first illustrated watercolour – is largely ignored. The brush is wielded at speed over a small sheet of paper and the vigorous handling serves to emphasise the latent energy of the locomotive. Howard may not be able to explain the technicalities of the steam engine but he understands its characteristics.

Even if it is not an example of engineering nostalgia, the *Jhansi Loco* is painted with greater affection for its heroic qualities than the engines which steam up Monet's series of paintings of the Gare Saint-Lazare. Howard would admit to the inspiration of Monet's superbly objective series, in which the locomotives are but the working part of a scene chosen primarily for its atmospheric effects. For Monet, however, Saint-Lazare was everyday, modern life. In the age of diesel and electric, it is hardly a surprise that Howard should approach the subject as an enthusiast.

Steam and Smoke, Jhansi
When compared with the rapid, freely-washed spontaneity of the previous study, this larger watercolour bears the hallmarks of an exhibition piece. It is more conventionally composed. This having been said, it still captures the energy and movement of the locomotives, is wonderfully atmospheric and truly redolent of India.

The handling of the brush is quite delectable. Retaining suitable opacity in the highlights of steam and reflections of sun on steel, the watercolour is otherwise exceptionally translucent, giving both depth to the shadows and an unmistakable naturalism to the smoky, hazy blue sky.

Ken Howard meeting the President of India, accompanied by General Vaidya
Photograph, 1984.

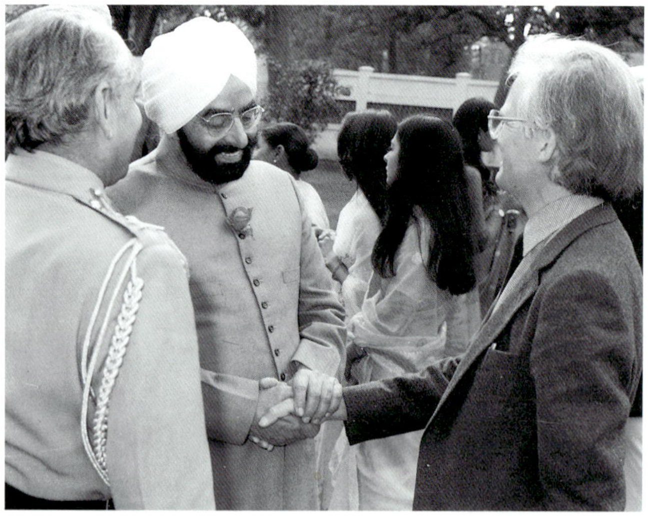

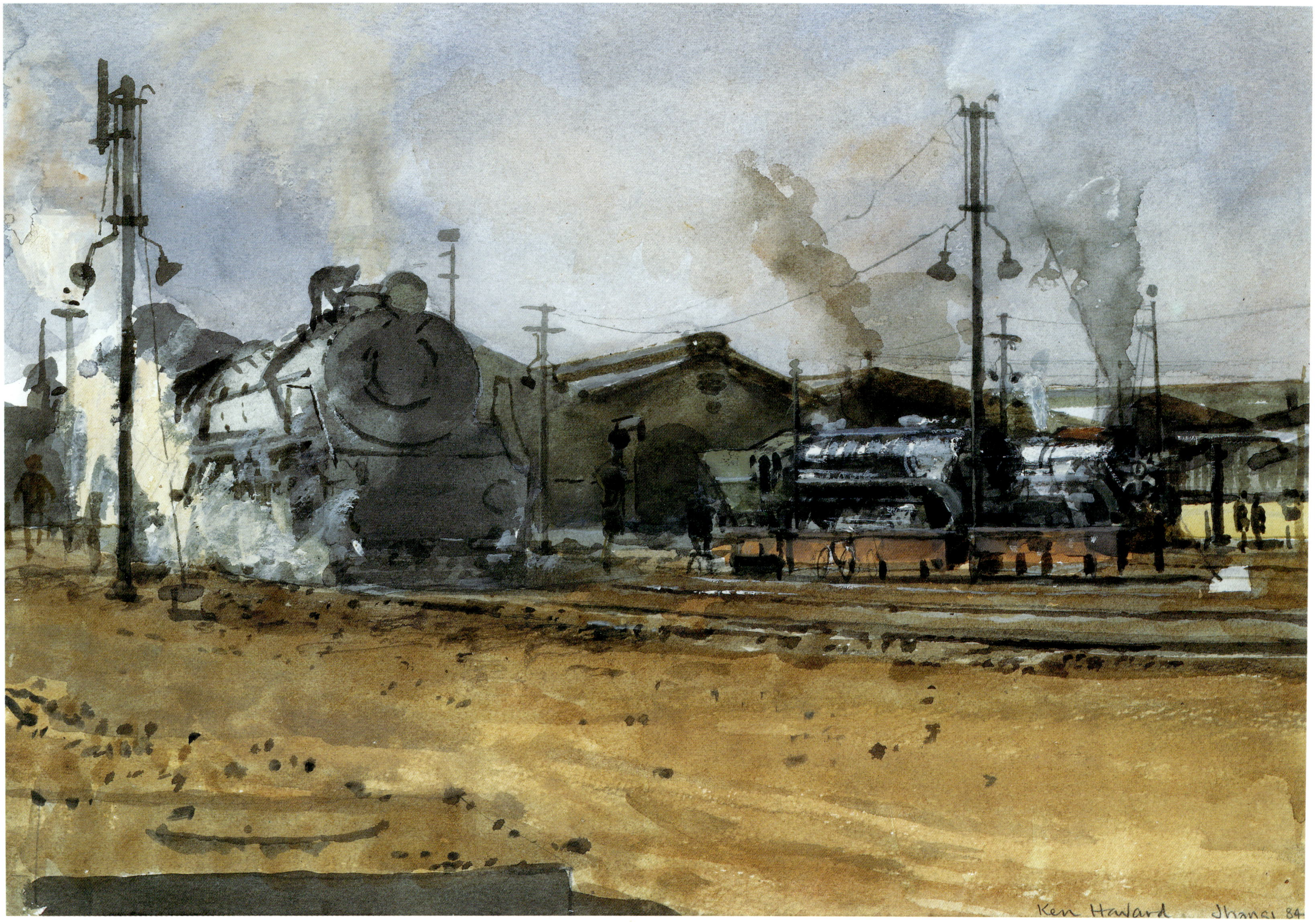

Steam and Smoke, Jhansi
Watercolour, 1984. 15 × 22ins.

With typical honesty to his subject, Howard made not only a faithful record of the Indian railway yards, but also, as he relates, a literal transcription of the atmosphere itself:

'After I had finished these watercolours I took my portfolio to show to the Minister of Railways. He wanted to have one in particular and, on being asked why that one, said it was because he could see the train had just been in for its three-monthly service. I asked him how he knew that. Apparently, when they come out after this overhaul, there is a particular colour of steam that comes out of the funnel that only happens when the boilers are refilling, or the water is new, or whatever it was. To me it was just another bit of steam but I hadn't been able to help myself recording that particular colour. It wasn't that obviously different. But I suppose the changes were about as marked as those from one tribe of Gurkha to the next.'

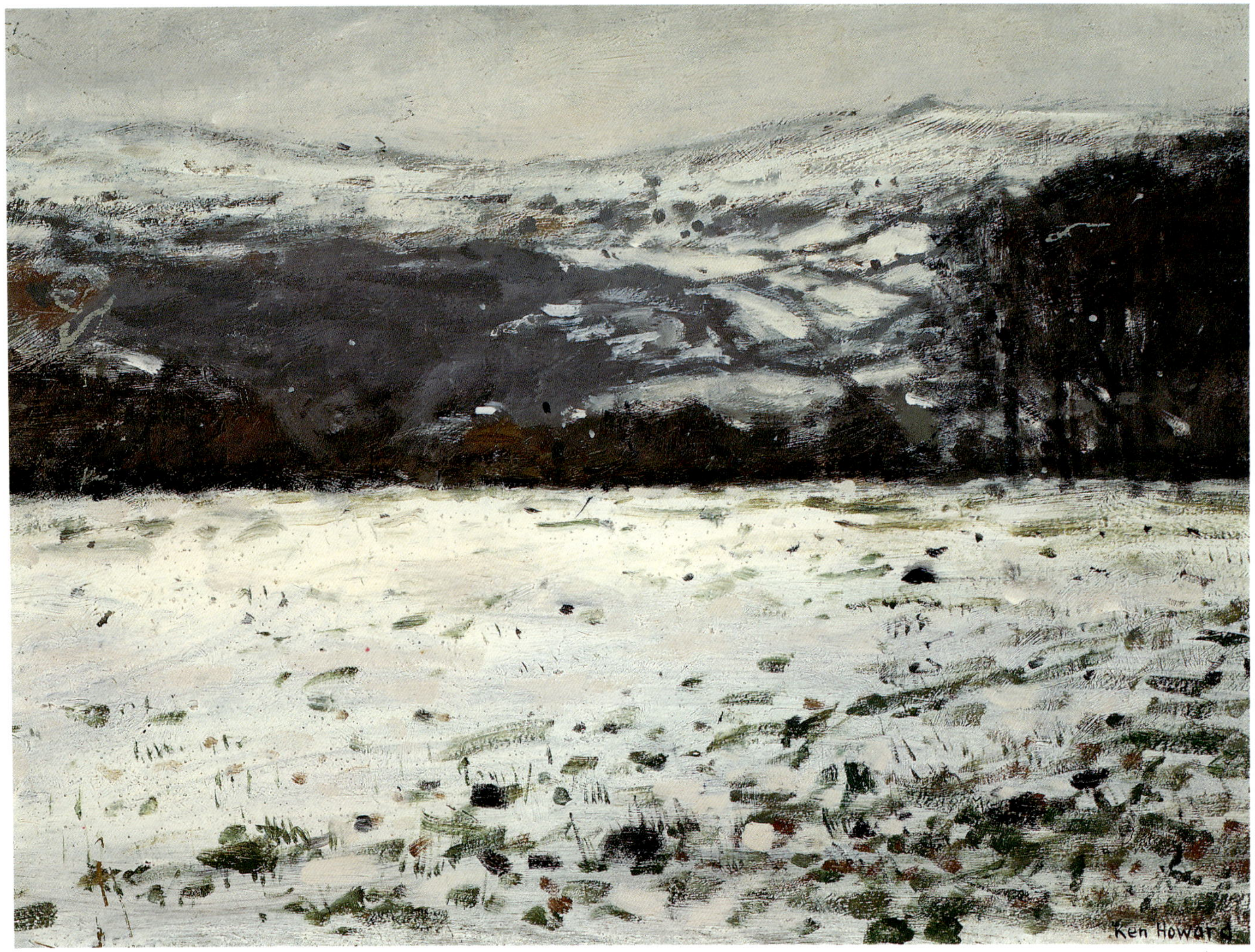

Snow at Sampford Spiney
Oil on panel, 1978. 12×16ins.

I worked until I was too cold to go on and would rush in to warm up by the fire, and then straight back out again. If you've got an image that really excites you it doesn't matter what the conditions are.'

As demonstrated by the painting illustrated, Howard was conscious enough of the cold to paint it. This is a real snowbound landscape, not a romanticised memory painted in a warm studio. The greys and silvers, aesthetically pleasing as they are, convey English gloom and cold as surely as Santa Magdalena is hot. Painted in one brief session and as simple in composition as snowy moorland demands, the reality of the scene is beyond question. When asked if he is ever tempted to enhance nature – to bring in a tree to enliven the composition, or even alter the colour of the steam emanating from a Jhansi loco – Howard responds:

'It wouldn't really be a question of just changing the steam, because when you look at nature you see that all the colours around that steam adjust themselves to its colour. As soon as the steam comes out you see those surrounding colours differently.

'In the same way there is a story of an artist and his son. The son believed you could do whatever you liked to a painting, and the father – like myself – believed that everything in nature is harmonious and fits together; that if you change one thing you change everything. The father was painting a view from a window and the son came and said "That is a fine painting, but the tree is completely wrong where it is – it doesn't work in the composition". The father replied "Well, it's there, and I'm going to paint it". The next day the son came in and had another go at his father. On the third day he came in and looked at the canvas, and said "Good Lord, you've taken the tree out – how marvellous". And the father said "Yes, look out of the window". He had chopped the tree down.

'I would have to do the same, because then I would see the landscape in the new terms without the tree. Immediately the tree goes the rhythms change, and immediately the steam changes colour, the rhythms of other colours change. Nature is constantly pulling things into a whole. On Dartmoor, when I felt like moving that tree on a hill over because it seemed to balance that farm over there, I was terribly conscious that the tree grew in that position because of the other trees around it and that it looked as it did because of the wind in that particular spot. You plant that tree over the other side of the field and it will grow as a completely different tree and will harmonise with its relative surroundings.'

For someone who declares himself not to be a landscape painter, this view exhibits a profound appreciation of nature and commitment to naturalism. There are

Snow at Sampford Spiney
The evidence of Ken Howard's travels within Britain is sporadic in his painting; certainly when compared with the journeys overseas. There have been a number of times, however, when he has settled down to paint in the vicinity of his home or studio. The group of river views, painted a few miles along the Thames from his house at Hampton, has already been noted. However, the only recent production of a significant body of straightforward landscape paintings was during his occupancy of a converted school on Dartmoor.

Howard had bought The Old School House at Sampford Spiney in 1969. He was to go on spending time there for some fifteen years until selling up shortly after returning from India, when he and Christa settled into St Clement's Hall, Mousehole. Howard had always wanted a second base from which to work, but Annie had not warmed to the idea of building a house on land in Santa Magdalena, offered to him by his landlady there. It was decided to search for somewhere in England and the silvery light and moorland landscape of Dartmoor appealed to Howard.

When he saw the school house while walking with friends, it was dilapidated. After much effort, permission was granted to convert it into a dwelling and studio. At this stage the London studio at South Bolton Gardens was shared, and not always an ideal working environment. As his marriage to Annie broke down and the travel commissions increased, so Sampford Spiney became an ever more useful retreat:

'Not for the first time, I almost became a landscape painter up on the moor. The principal reason I kept the studio after the first few years was to paint there in the winter, when I was really hoping for snow. I find that if I am a landscape painter at all, I am a winter landscape painter. I like it when you can see the bones of the trees – they're not fat with leaves – and you can see the structure of the landscape.

'I did get snowed in there a couple of times. In one case I worked there for about a week and produced an exhibition in one week's splurge of painting. Luckily I had plenty of paint, panels and canvases, and when the snow came I just went out and worked all the hours of light that God created. The imagery was so strong – it was so inspiring – that it was no effort, despite the cold.

painters and theorists who would argue that all the harmonising, let alone any enhancing, is done by the eye – and by the eye of the painter in particular. Howard would no doubt agree that he does to an extent play such a role. But, as he also states, this faithfulness to what is before him should mean that he avoids the repetition that the formulaic approach of the late work of Corot exemplifies: 'Like Constable, I would like to think I am looking at each new subject as if I am looking at nature for the first time.'

Ice Light, Bergun

In *Ice Light, Bergun*, the ice reflects the dazzling sun of the mountains and a brighter mood than the Dartmoor snow. In the late 1980s it became Howard's habit to spend Christmas and the New Year in Christa's native Germany, before travelling down to Switzerland with her daughters for a skiing holiday. Painted on one such occasion, this sparkling painting shows how at ease the artist is with the winter light:

'I haven't worked in many snowy places, but I've always had this love affair with snow. I don't know why I haven't travelled more to find it, because in England its presence is usually so ephemeral. Whenever it does snow here I wonder why I don't get on a plane to Norway, or wherever, to carry on with the subject. These skiing trips provided the ideal opportunity.

'This particular winter Switzerland suffered a lack of snow and the only winter sports were down in the village. So I painted by the ice rink. Rather like the railway tracks making a linear pattern in the foreground of the shunting yards, you would get the skate marks glistening in the sun, which was always relatively low. Of course I couldn't ask anyone to pose for me, as they were flying around the ice, and these figures are an amalgamation.'

This approximation of the skaters, painted in summary and energetic fashion, creates a great sense of their speed of movement. The sure brushwork and precise colour sense of the artist's maturity are strikingly evident in what is a fairly unusual subject. We become accustomed to the virtuosity of his handling of oil paint in the studio and beach paintings, but to see it so vividly here is like looking at nature anew.

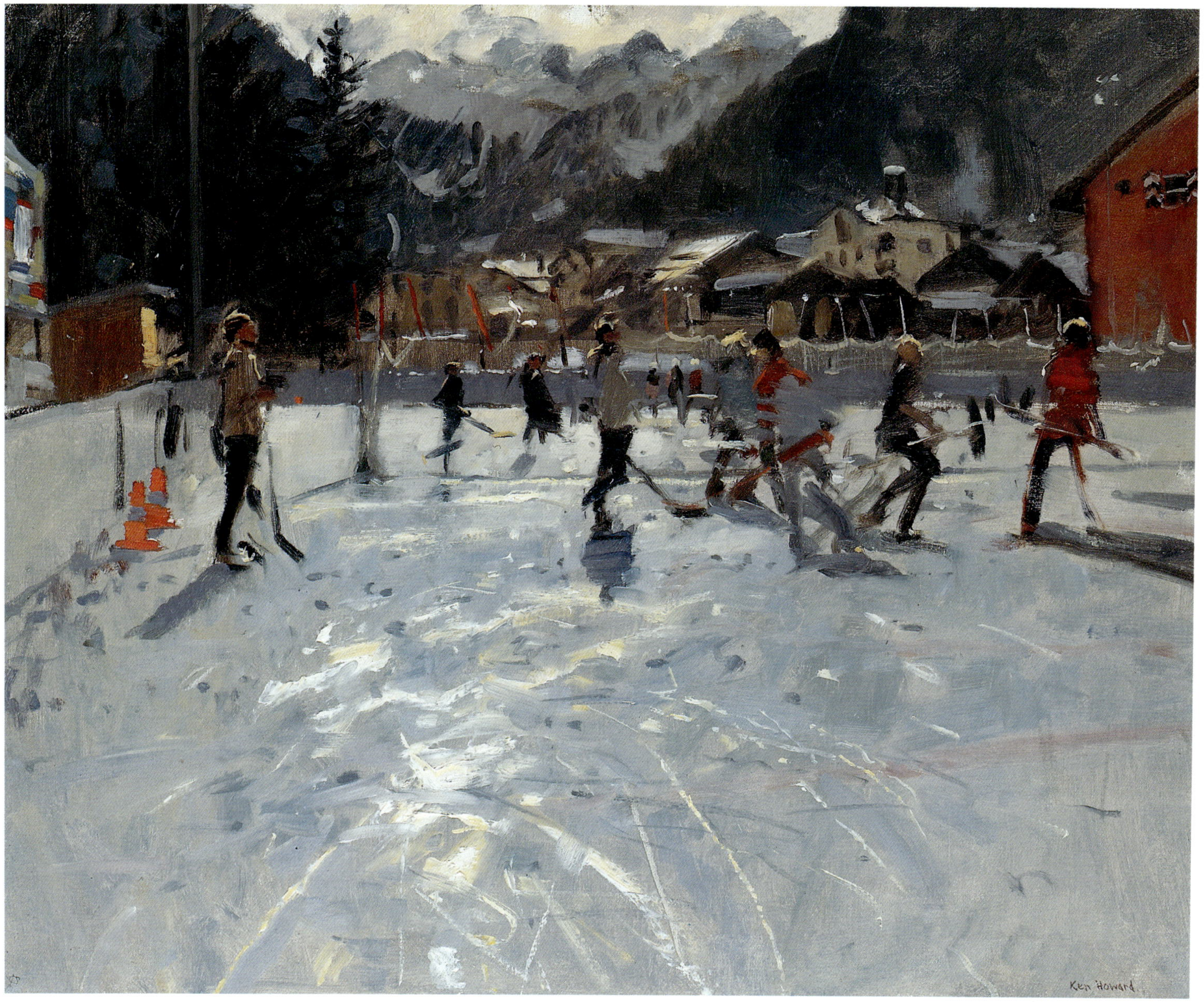

Ice Light, Bergun
Oil on canvas, 1988. 20 × 24ins.

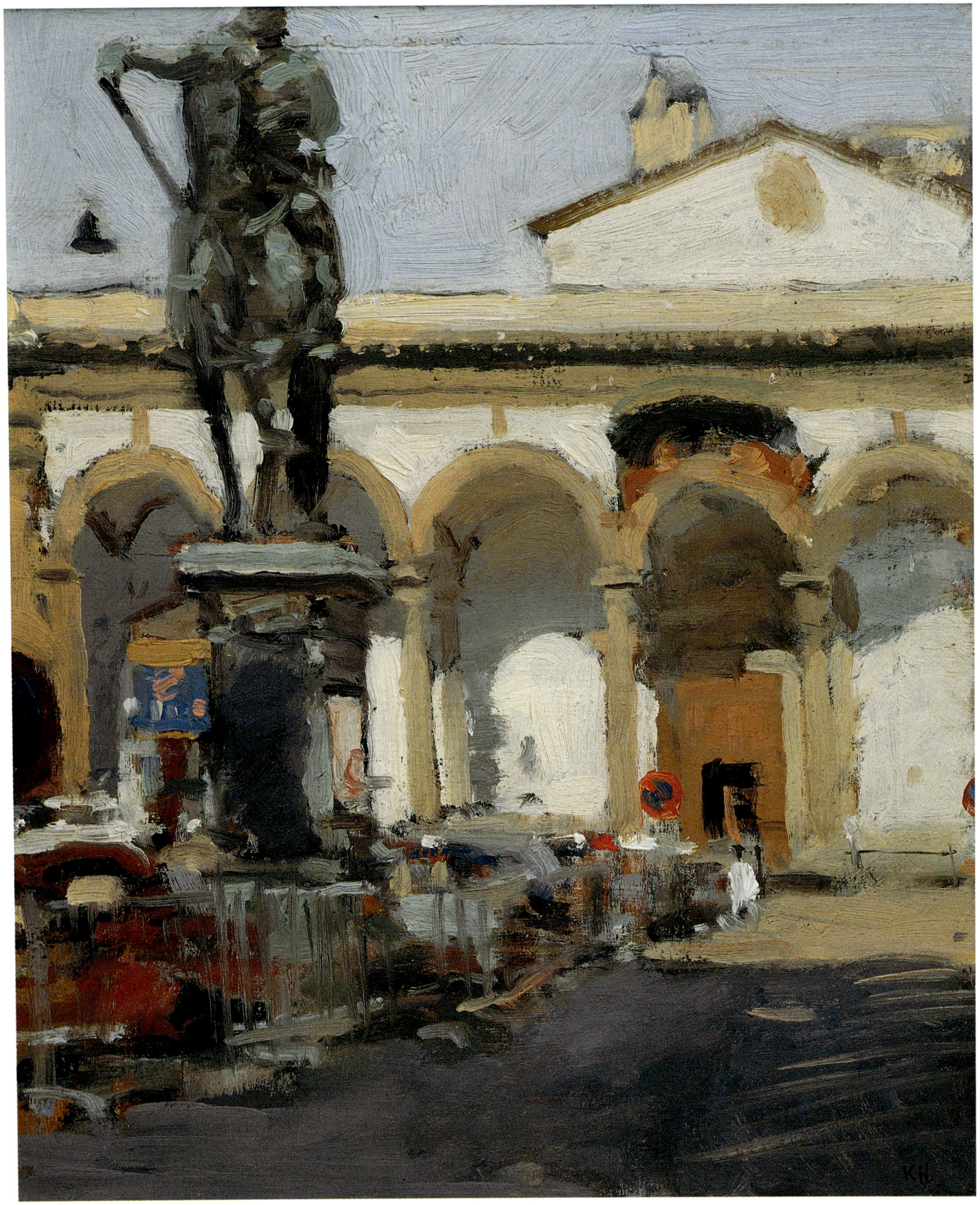

Piazza della SS Annunziata, Florence
Florence has drawn Howard back many times since he and Christa first revisited the city in 1978, nearly twenty years after they had met there. He recalls that initial meeting thus:

'Chrissie came to a party with her boyfriend, Tista. They had shared a bottle of Chianti and were quite tiddly and full of fun when they arrived. They had decided they would pretend Tista was Chrissie's uncle, so I was introduced to Chrissie and her uncle. I thought if that is her uncle I can ask her for a dance. We had only known each other for a few weeks when she went back to Germany, and by the time I saw her again she had been convinced that it was just a holiday romance. We were out of touch for fifteen years.

'We met again by accident in 1974. Over dinner with an old friend from Italy, whose best man I had been and who had long since emigrated to Australia, I asked after Chrissie. It turned out he was having dinner with her the following night in Cologne. I passed on my regards and hopes that life had been good. A couple of weeks later she rang to ask if I could help arrange an exchange for her children and that was how we met again.'

The return to Florence was something of a sentimental journey, and perhaps for this reason Howard was at first disappointed to find that the city had become engulfed in traffic. Unlike Venice, where, with some judicious editing, it is possible for a painter to pretend the place has not altered since Turner last visited, Florence has been indelibly altered by modern life. It is now a city of the motor car and the motor bike.

Perhaps surprisingly, many of Howard's paintings of Florence have seemed to revel in the street life. Realist that he is – and almost despite his love of the ancient – his paintings seem to accept and make subjects of the vivid colours and clamorous noise of vehicles and people, that are so characteristic of Italian cities. In this artist's Florence, the frenzied jumble of cars, railings and traffic signals co-exist with, and set in relief, the stately presence of Renaissance churches and palaces.

This picture shows just such a conglomeration in a famous Florentine square, surrounded by important early Renaissance buildings. At the centre of the square is an equestrian statue of Ferdinand I de' Medici by the *cinquecento* sculptor, Giambologna. Made on that first return journey, this painting demonstrates that by this stage of his career the artist had achieved a rare command of the depiction of textures through the effects of light. The plasticity of the sunlit, whitewashed wall of the church is as strong as that of the walls at Santa Magdalena and Pissouri. Yet here it is as if we can also feel the rough surface of the plaster in the broad, dragged brush-strokes.

Piazza della SS Annunziata, Florence
Oil on board, 1978. 10 × 8ins.

Now one of Howard's favourite pictures of Florence, this painting caused him some birth pains:

'As I was painting it I was almost crying, and a German came up to me to say how much he liked it. I told him how awful I thought it was and that I just couldn't achieve what I wanted. His reaction was to tell me to leave it alone and he would buy it. I refused to sell the painting, but the upshot was that I didn't work on it any further. Later, Chrissie looked at it and said it was the best picture I had done on that trip. It took me some time to see that. She can always stand back and see my work in this way – something I often find hard. Being a very fine painter in her own right must help.'

Morning Light, Via Cavour

Around a decade later, this painting finds Howard concerned with largely similar aspects of the Florentine scene. This is one of a number of paintings made along the broad Via Cavour, which runs north-east from the Piazza del Duomo towards the Convent of San Marco. Any misgivings he might have had about the bustling street life seem to have vanished, for here he is to be seen making good use of the visual cacophony. He appears to enjoy the foreground hurly-burly of cars, motor-bikes and scooters, punctured by the verticals of wind-shields, traffic lights and signs. In the middle distance this visual activity diminishes to a blur, out of which rise the four-storey façades of the Via Cavour, receding dramatically to a distant vanishing point.

Although this ground-level arrangement of shapes and lines has the realist's sense of the random, it forms a most satisfying composition. Clearly the artist has chosen his position with care. Having exercised that privilege, even if he then only painted what was before him, the ever-changing bustle of humans and machines – creating as it does that uncertainty the artist so likes – must have allowed him further possibilities of choice before finally committing brush to canvas.

It might be said here that such a man-made arrangement of lines and shapes cannot be subject to Howard's laws of natural conditioning, which change the nature of the tree on the hill, depending on where it is planted. After all, a traffic light will look the same, wherever it is sited. Howard's companion law of course counteracts this, for each element of the scene affects, and is affected by, its surroundings. This does not just happen from the scientific point of view of colour theory, but, more importantly for this artist, because it creates new shapes and affects other colours within the painting itself.

Such thoughts were probably far from his mind as he contended with the immediate problems of picture-making and controlling his representation of a fairly brief moment of light. The strong mid-morning sun on the façades is splendidly captured. In the next picture, painted under different light conditions, we shall view the gabled buildings on the left, from a position beneath the flag on the sunlit terrace.

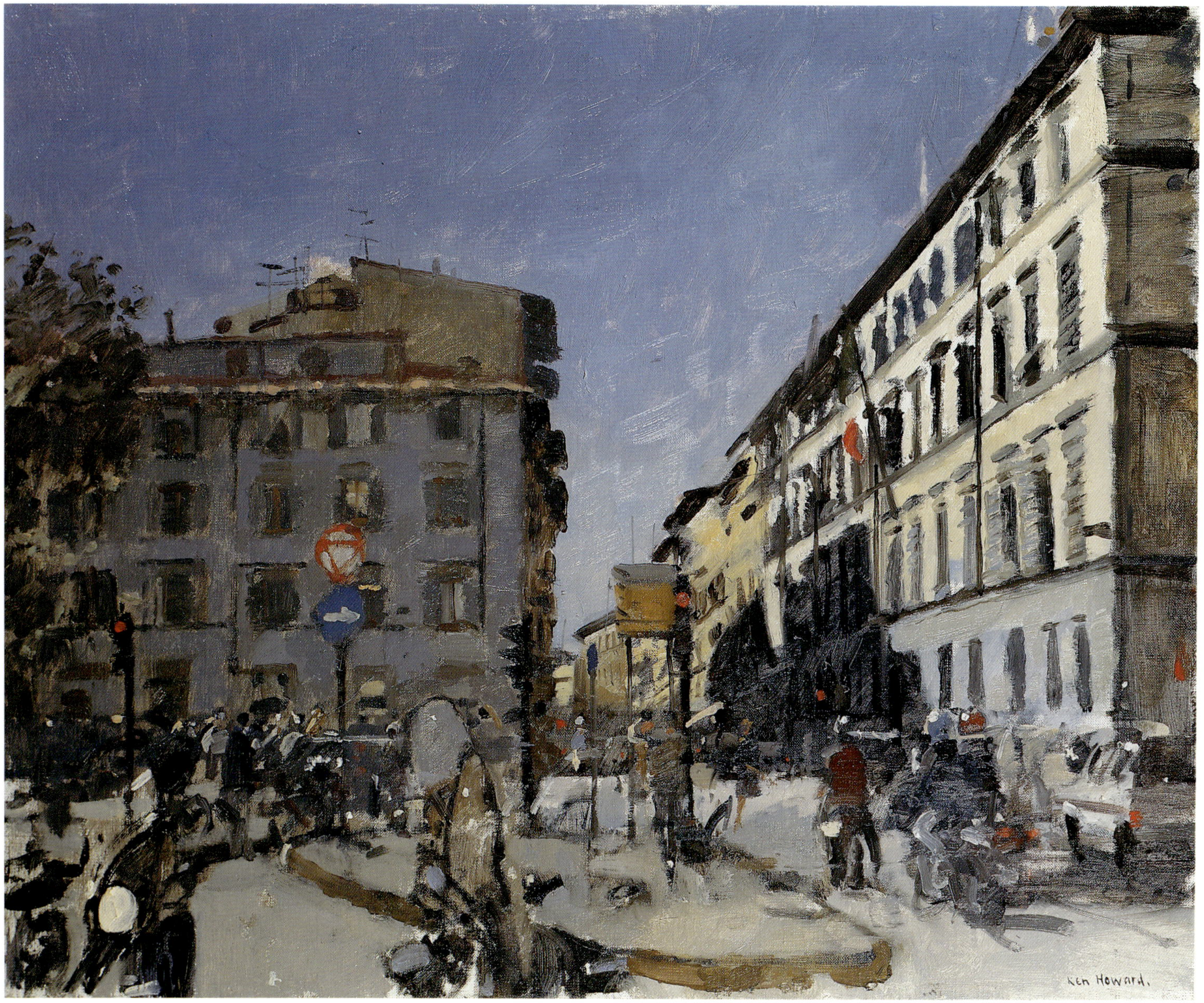

Morning Light, Via Cavour
Oil on canvas, 1990. 20 × 24ins.

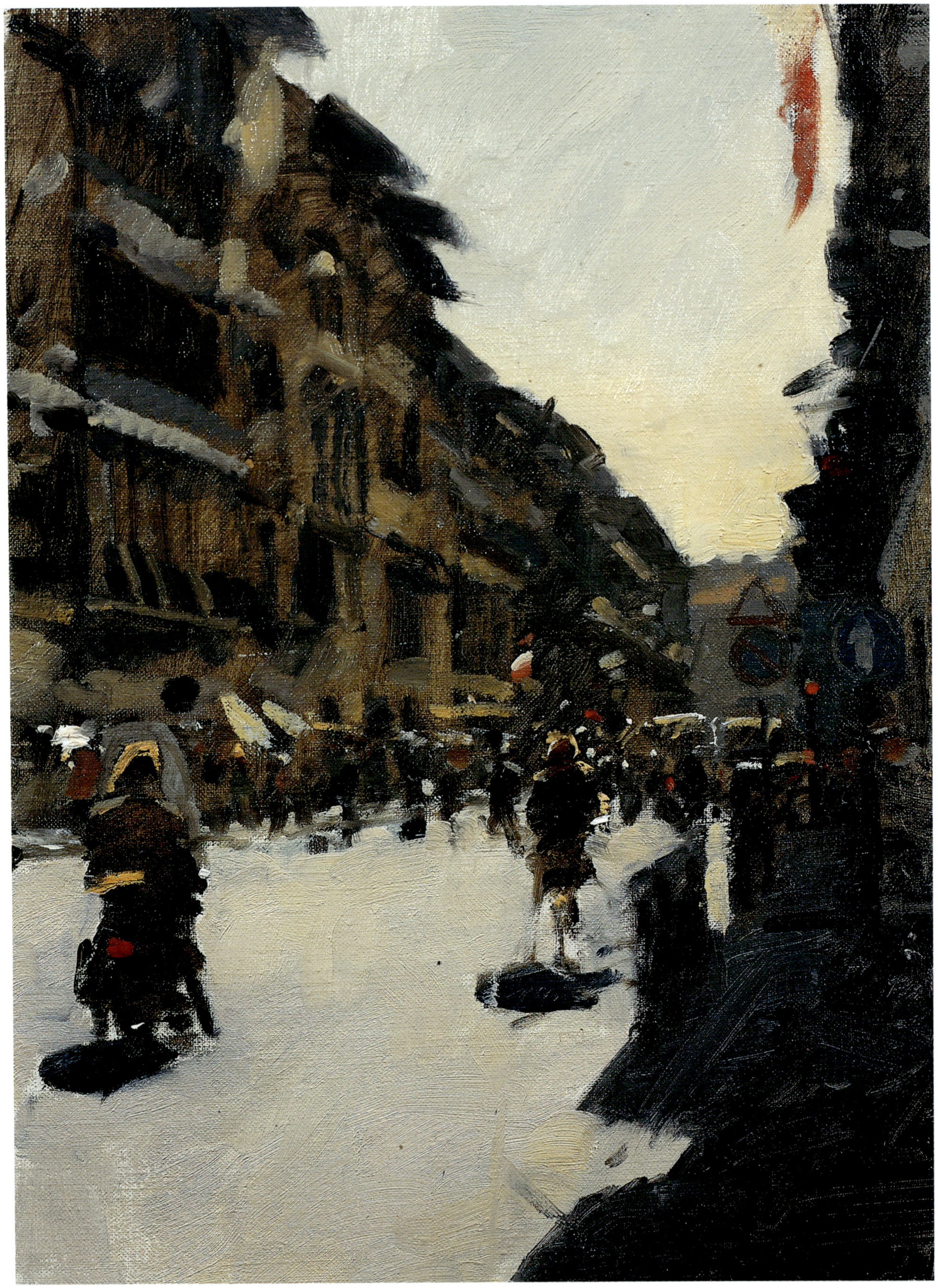

September Light, Afternoon, Via Cavour, Florence
This small, vigorous oil shows the previously shaded side of the Via Cavour as, a few hours later, it begins to be caught by the sun's rays. The light hits the street remorselessly, obliterating any road-markings the eye would take in at a duller time. Looking towards the lowering sun, the spectator almost has to squint to take in the scene. The powerfully contrasting *contre-jour* effect is brilliantly summarised with free and purposeful strokes of the brush. This is an example of the hand and eye working in absolute unison.

'This was the last painting I did on the trip that October. When I go on a trip like that I gradually become familiar with the subject and end up painting it very differently from the first tentative attempts. The danger is that towards the end I can fly too much and then the whole thing becomes too loose. Although this one is free, it did seem to hold together. I was pleased with both the strong contrasts and the very slight tonal change between the sky and the road, which I think gives the feeling of the sun starting to go down just out of the picture. About half an hour later the whole of the left-hand side of the picture was illuminated. I also like to give a sense of movement in a picture. I hope this is conveyed by the woman on the bicycle and by the man on the scooter, who is about to start off when the lights change.

'I realise more and more that, if you are going to be concerned with light and you are going to work on the spot, firstly you can't work too large, and secondly you must not allow yourself to work too long. Monet, of course, worked out how to do it. I do sometimes have two pictures on the go at one time, one for when the sun comes out and the other for when it goes in, or the light alters. An additional benefit of this is that when you change to another canvas, it is like standing back from the previous one. When you return to it you can see it freshly. With this painting I simply worked fast to finish in one session – about forty minutes – and if I had gone on any longer the effect on the buildings would have been lost.

'I don't always get the tonal range right, and have to struggle to attain it throughout the picture, unlike an artist like Fred Cuming, who has perfect tonal pitch. This one just came together. But by that time I had been painting in Italy for about ten hours a day, almost every day, for a month. One should be on form.'

September Light, Afternoon, Via Cavour, Florence
Oil on canvas, 1990. 14 × 10ins.

Venice

San Marco, Morning
Arriving in Venice on a Sunday morning, late in September, we gaze on the city's most venerable building. Within a carefully controlled composition on a fairly small sheet of paper, this work is painted with all the freedom and luminosity that watercolour has to offer. As we saw the subtle effect of the sun beginning to catch one side of the Via Cavour, we can now admire the skill with which the reflected light of the Piazza illuminates the portals of the Basilica.

Howard first visited Venice while on his scholarship in 1958–9. He studied Venetian art, but did not paint in the city on that occasion. Much later, as the numbers of British painters working there began to rival late nineteenth-century levels, he was encouraged by Bernard Dunstan and Diana Armfield to make a serious attempt at painting Venice. This is a daunting task for any painter, and many are unable to see beyond the vision of Turner, Bonington or Whistler. For Howard the encounter was an unusual one, and undoubtedly to his advantage.

He found he was able to relate the classic Venetian scene of light on the water, and the complexity of the city's reflected light, to his experiences on the beaches of Cornwall:

'When you get down to Land's End or the Lizard on a really bright summer's day, with the sea on either side of the peninsula, there is just the same feeling of the light being bounced off the water. It is as if the light fuses in the veils of atmosphere.'

The west front of the basilica is about as far from water as one can get in Venice, yet still that bounced light, which seems to be the Holy Grail for painters of the city, seems to flood the façade. The transparency of pure watercolour would appear essential to this particular achievement:

'On my first painting visit there I worked in oils, which was pretty disastrous. I couldn't get the effect I wanted and that nearly killed Venice for me. So the next time I decided consciously to do something different and just painted the alleys – no canals. Some of those were quite interesting, but somehow I still wasn't getting in close to Venice. So the next time I just took watercolours and decided simply to paint whatever touched me, even if it had been painted a hundred times before. As soon as I did that, I felt Venice begin to reveal herself to me. As soon as I wasn't any longer looking hard for a different

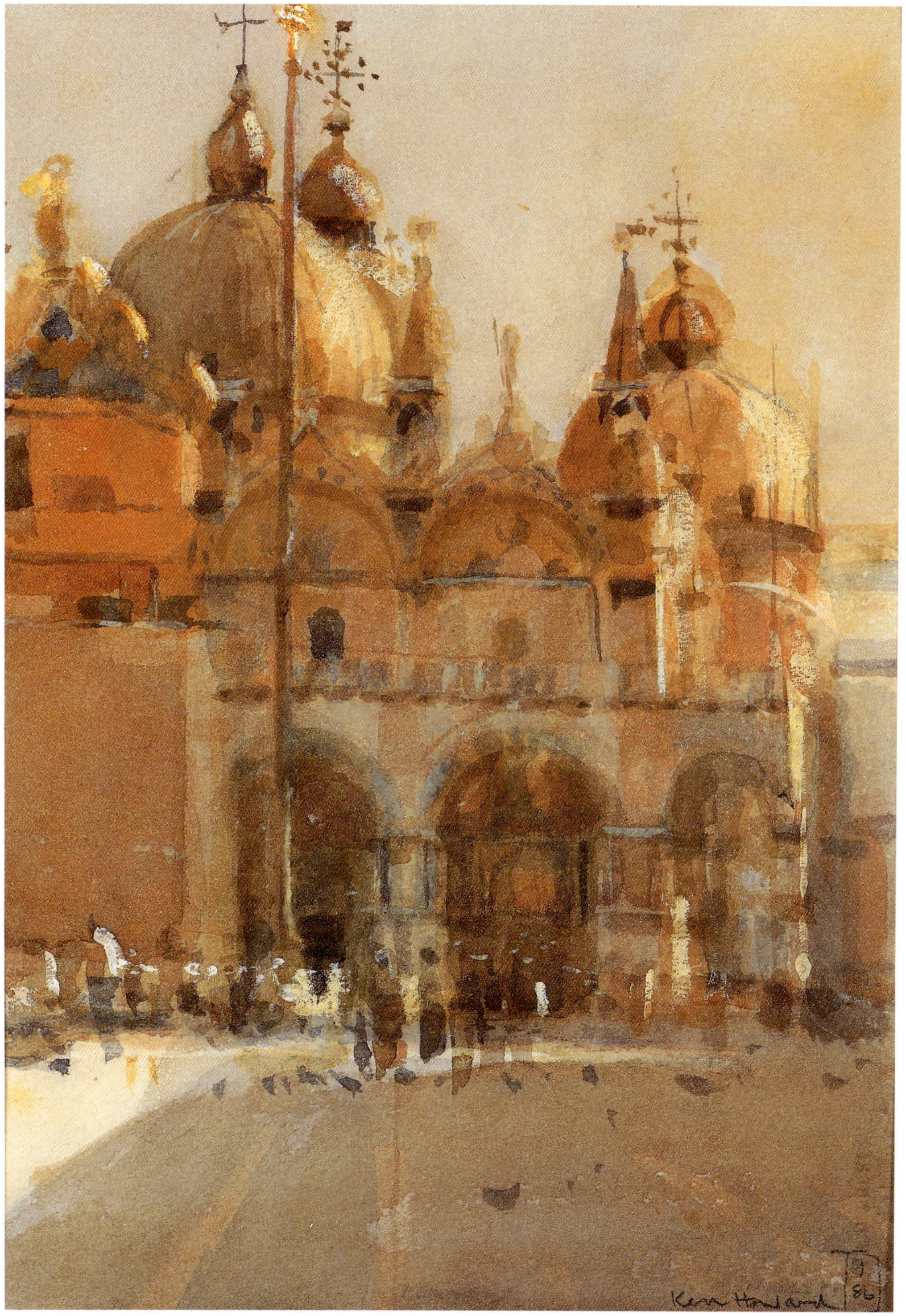

San Marco, Morning
Watercolour, 1986.
11 × 9ins.

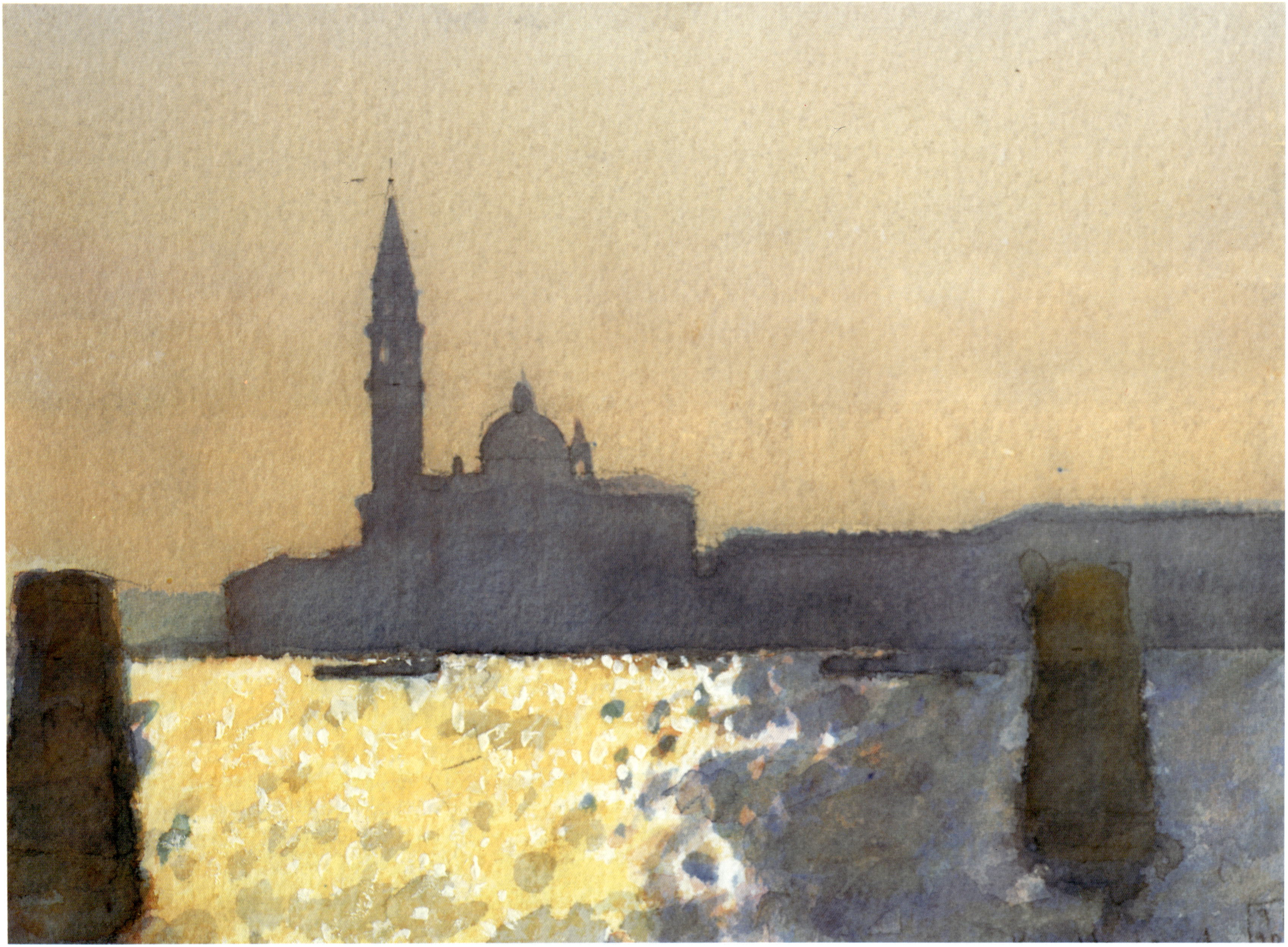

San Giorgio Maggiore, Venice, Brilliant Light
Watercolour, 1990. 7 × 9ins.

aspect of Venice, I began to find aspects that I think are mine.

'Venice is now for me a watercolour experience. Technically, what I do is to paint into the form and then, while it's still damp, I will bring a wash over the whole thing. This fuses the forms together much more. Then as it gets to a certain state of dryness I will sometimes drop another wash onto it. I will usually have two watercolours going at once, so that I can work on the one while the other is starting to dry – and of course if the light is changeable. For years I wasn't a very wet watercolourist – drawing and then heightening with watercolour – but now I'm getting more and more wet. I doubt whether I did any preliminary drawing on this one. I allowed myself to use a bit of Chinese white. When I am working just in pure watercolour, I can sometimes become a bit self-conscious about preserving the lights. Mostly, though, it is pure watercolour.'

Ken Howard does of course follow in a great tradition of British watercolourists in Venice. Naturally, in a city where the primary mode of transport is the leg, the mobility the medium affords should not be underestimated. Like one of the painters of Venice he especially admires, Walter Sickert, Howard has painted significant oils in the city, and one of these is reproduced in the pages that follow. It is, however, the series of small watercolours made over recent years that have established for him a special niche somewhere in *La Serenissima*.

San Giorgio Maggiore, Venice, Brilliant Light
Out over the Bacino di San Marco, the sun dances on the choppy water and the artist uses his characteristic rough paper to help his dragged washes to echo this sparkling movement. The sight of San Giorgio across the Bacino is often the first the visitor has when stepping off the *vaporetto* at San Marco. On a bright day, walking along the Riva degli Schiavoni, the view past the monastery island and over towards the Lido – with fast boats scudding and slow boats plying this way and that across the incandescent water – is surely one of the most inspiring in the world. Turning back into the narrow streets beyond the Piazza is, by comparison, claustrophobic.

In this watercolour, as in much of his Venetian work on rough paper, Howard seems to refine the subject to its absolutely bare essentials. He masses strong, solid shapes into an elemental pattern of limited tonal range. This is juxtaposed with the burst of light on the water and the softer, broad sky, which defines the characteristic silhouette. This simple, lucid image captures a common memory of the city as she first greets us:

'I never cease to get a thrill when I get there – the first moment, when you get off the *vaporetto* or water taxi – that first contact. And I think you always have to leave Venice wanting to come back to her. You can't, mustn't use Venice up in the one trip. When I go to the plane I always know I have to come back. There is still a lot for me to do there. Venice is still a bit beyond me on a large scale – I haven't got fully into it enough to have wanted to paint more than three or four large studio oils up to this point. At the moment I prefer to continue exploring the images I have discovered with small watercolours, like this.

'When I was much younger I believed that after you had painted something once you had to go and paint something else. Now I realise that the subject is never the same twice anyway. If I was told that from now on I could only paint this view, or that from the vaporetto stop opposite the Salute, I don't think I should be too unhappy. With 365 days a year to watch one image, each day that image would be different.'

Contre-Jour, Santa Maria Formosa
The scene is the Campo di Santa Maria Formosa, a fine square in the Castello district, to the north of the Piazza San Marco. This jewel-like watercolour presents a softer effect of *contre-jour* than the *Via Cavour* oil. The cause may in part be the reflected Venetian light, which bounces around buildings and squares and reaches deep into areas of shade. Howard's ability to make the watercolour contain the radiant light so particular to the city is quite breathtaking.

In the hands of such a gifted artist, it is indeed given to watercolour not only to describe these light effects, but to do so in close imitation of the real play of light. Although Howard has used Chinese white bodycolour to pick out some of the highlights in this work, he has principally relied on transparent colour. Thus, as the observer studies the watercolour, light is reflecting off the white paper surface and passing through the thin layer of colour back to the eye. Set amid the dark tones of the surrounding shadows, the result is striking and convincing, and the halos of the two girls concentrate the viewer's attention at the centre of the composition. Although it too is effective, the bodycolour addition of the street-light, the sun cutting right through the lamp, is comparatively less 'light':

'In the studio I love painting the model with the light coming through her hair or just catching down the body, and in Venice you get that constantly with people moving through alleys and across piazzas. As they go *contre-jour* the whole of their hair lights up like a halo, against a building behind, and that's a theme I might develop in the next few years.'

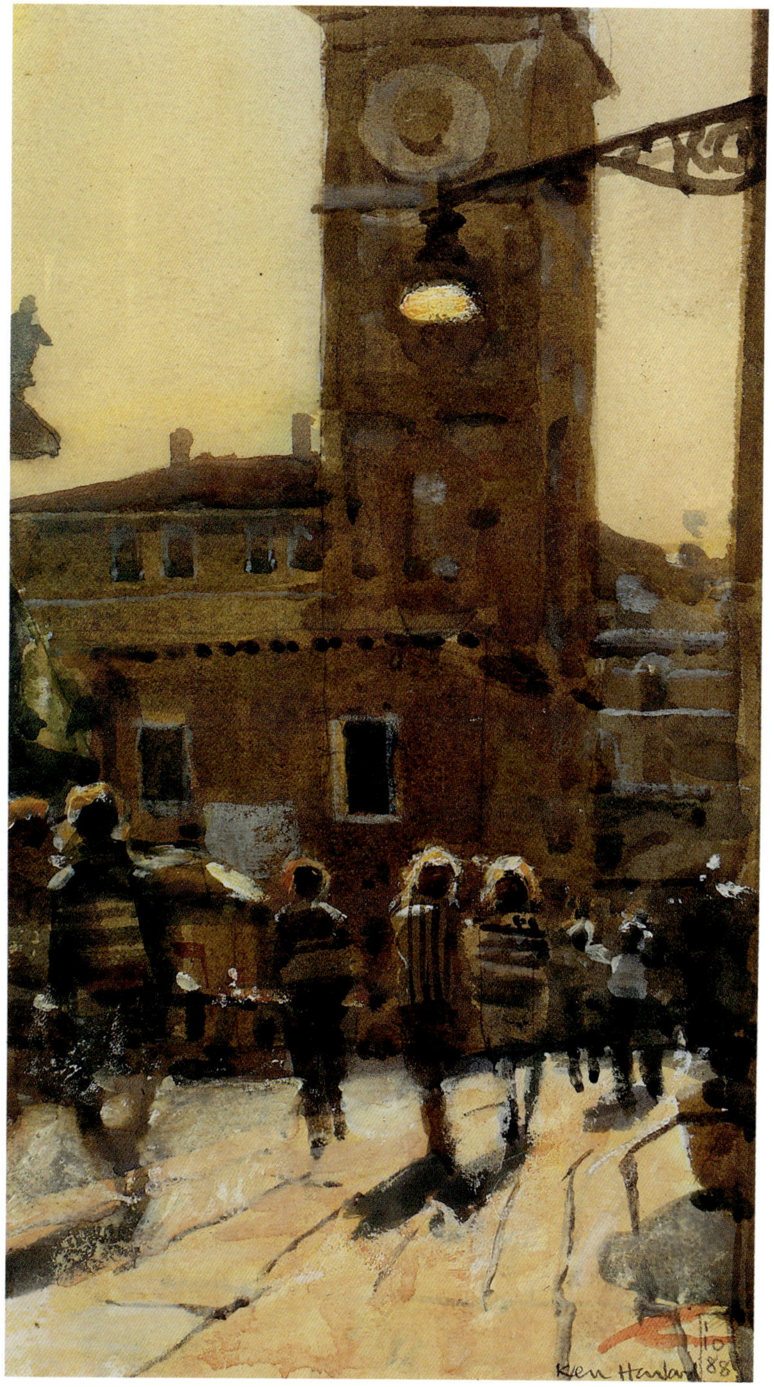

Contre-Jour, Santa Maria Formosa
Watercolour, 1988. 10 × 5ins.

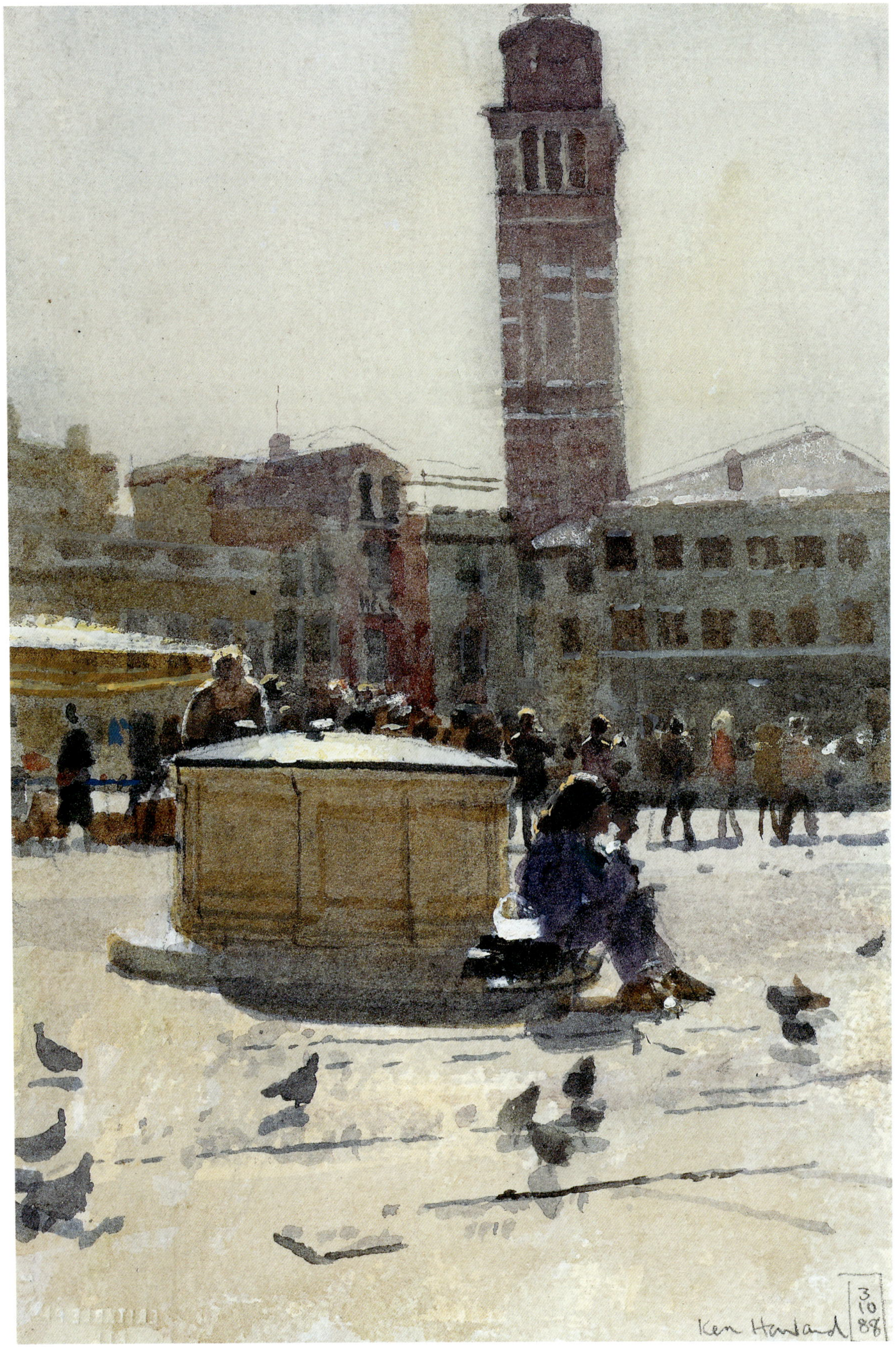

Lunch in Campo San Angelo
Campo San Angelo is one of the most open of Venetian squares, and one of the principal crossroads of the San Marco district. On a bright day the square is bathed in sunlight, which only periodically intrudes into the narrow surrounding streets. Two wells provide suitable resting-places to eat a snack and take in the sunshine. Seen *contre-jour*, with the sun high in the sky, the bright, white light has a depth suggesting a sense of space rare in Venice.

There is even room for a hint of aerial perspective – a thickening of the atmosphere between the foreground scene and the distant buildings. In the absence of any obvious lines of perspective, such as a street or building diminishing to a vanishing point, the artist uses aerial perspective to establish for the spectator the spatial dimensions of the scene. The group of figures in the middle-ground helps further to register the recession through this perspective.

Again the artist has washed the watercolour thinly, notably in the areas of shadow, to bring out both their visual depth and the reflected light. In this case the dominant light source for the shaded buildings would probably be the sun bouncing off the flagstones. The brightest place he has concentrated upon is the shield-like shape of the well cover, which acts as a horizontal foil to the vertical axis formed by the leaning *campanile* and the figure in mauve.

'In Venice I like to find themes to work on. Often the central interest or anchor of a theme is a particular light effect. The first thing that drew me to these marvellous wells that you get in the squares was this incredible reflection on the top of them. When the sun is in a certain position there is a sort of blaze. I started painting these well covers. Near this one was a place where people get their sandwiches, so the figurative thing began to creep in more and more. For some time in Venice I was really only interested in the water, light and reflection, and didn't use figures. Now the figurative element is often quite prominent and it was working in this square which started that off.'

Howard described earlier how he first painted Venice as a series of narrow streets. His present vision of the city is, by contrast, one of light, of space, of people relaxed. This is not the city of forgotten, silent, early morning courtyards; or of getting lost in dark alleys that turn into dead ends; or of recalling the films and books of *Don't Look Now* and *The Comfort of Strangers* – 'I don't find Venice at all sinister. I find Venice quite a magical and uplifting place – I think it is probably the single most magical place I've ever been to.'

Lunch in Campo San Angelo
Watercolour, 1988. 11 × 9ins.

The Grand Canal, Sunset
Some of the artist's favoured spots from which to work are the *vaporetto* and *traghetto* stops – jetties that service the motorised river-bus service and the two-man ferry gondolas that transfer pedestrians across the Grand Canal. On some stretches these jetties afford the only good view of the Grand Canal. Because they project out over the water, they can provide the artist with a panoramic vista and many potential subjects.

Howard has painted several views from the San Marco stop, situated at the mouth of the Grand Canal, opposite and to the east of Santa Maria della Salute. This is one example. From his position Howard watches the sun sinking towards the water, silhouetting the great dome of the Salute and the shapes of gondolas tied to posts outside neighbouring palaces:

'This is my favourite time of the early evening, when the sun is beginning to get down and the sky starts to take on that incredible glow that you get. And then the light begins to dance off the water. I'd been to Venice several times before I saw the light on the water as an image. Now it is one of my main preoccupations when working there.

'For many years I've been fascinated by working *contre-jour*, which somehow binds together the image and gives a feeling of wholeness. And of course in Venice you also get the sparkle on the water, which, because it is so light, reveals colour in other parts of the picture. For example, if you were to look at the sky without the light on the water, you would probably see it as much higher in tone and less colourful. Put in that sparkle and in this case the sky becomes a deep orange-green.'

As the September sun gets lower over the Canal its iridescent reflection grows in relative intensity and richness, and becomes more sharply defined against the darkening water round about. While this is happening the surrounding buildings undergo the most extraordinary sequence of transformations, providing unlimited fuel for an artist with Howard's interests and rapid technique.

Here he has captured all these effects with vigorous washes and strokes of the brush, making spontaneous patterns of dense, rich watercolour. Again rough paper has been employed to emphasise the jangling quality of the water, where the paper has been left white to give the highlights, and add further texture to the sky.

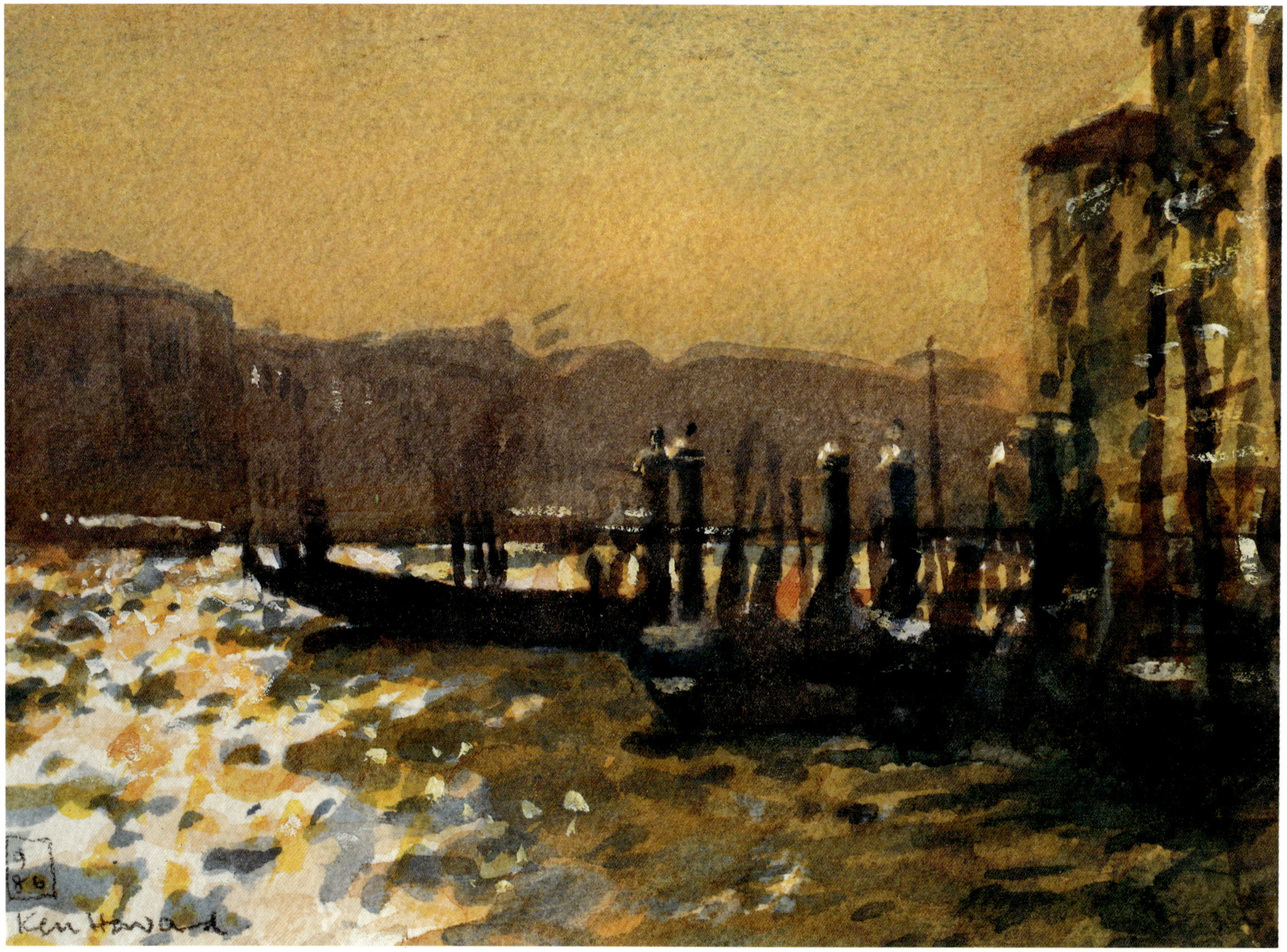

The Grand Canal, Sunset
Watercolour, 1986. 5 × 7ins.

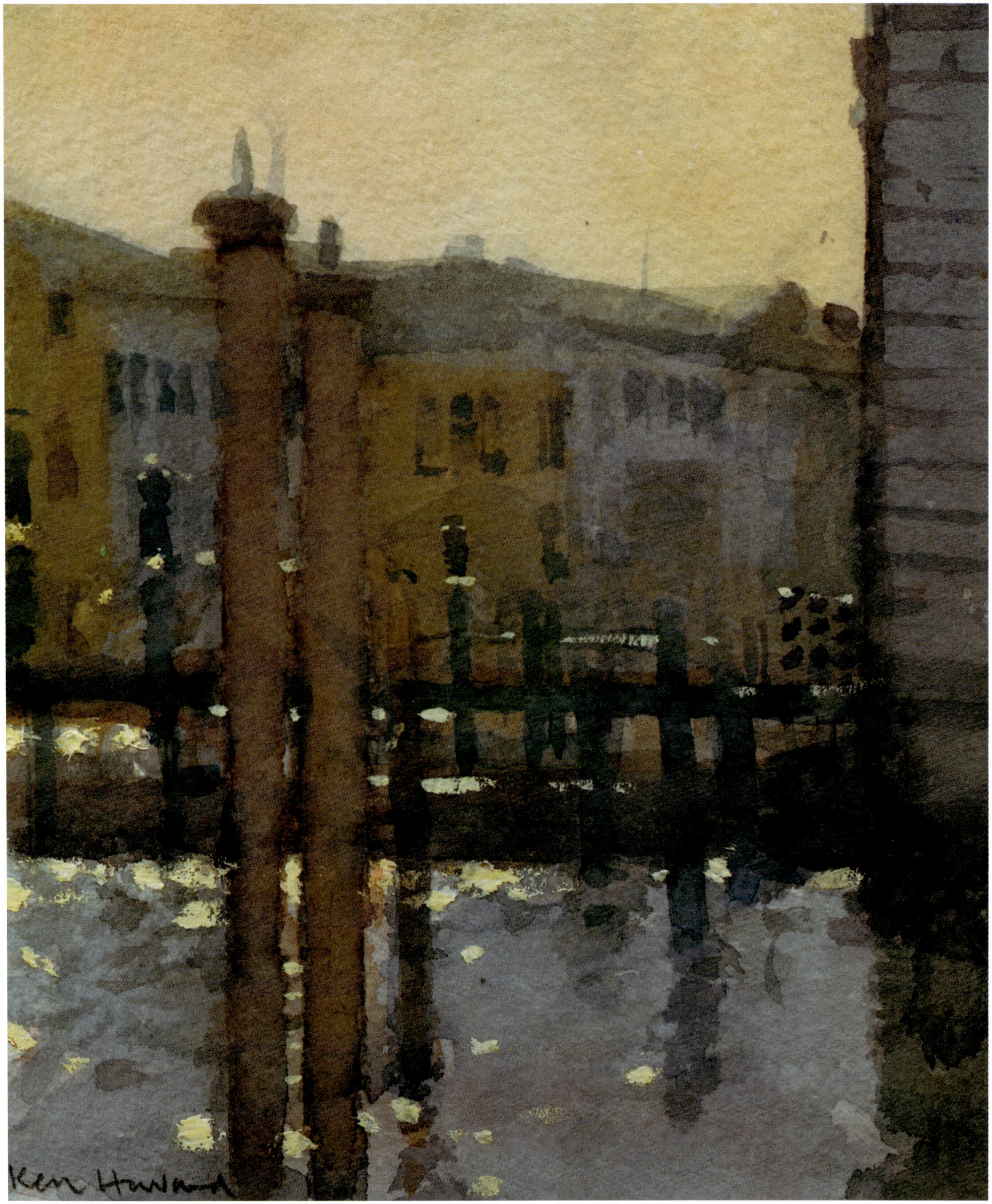

Venice, Green and Grey
Taken from Santa Maria del Giglio, the next *vaporetto* stop along to the west of San Marco, this watercolour looks westward past the Palazzo Barbarigo to the palaces on the southern side of the Canal. Although without an extensive area of sunlit water in view, it presents a more subtle and varied density of colouring than the previous work. As has been observed in discussing earlier watercolours of other subjects, areas of shade are described with thin, deliberate washes of transparent paint. The depth thus created is offset by the brilliant dashes of bodycolour, added for the highlights.

More than is perhaps usual in the artist's Venetian work, the picture is fundamentally an arrangement of strong horizontal and vertical forms. Across what is a relatively flat picture-plane, this grid-like arrangement is emphasised by the consistent tonality and repeating colour patterns.

'I suppose my interest in such angular shapes is one reason I am more attracted towards the townscape than pure landscape. I was pleased to find this subject as I got off the *vaporetto* recently, and there was a marvellous place to work from beside the stop.

'If it had not been for the foreground and middle-distance posts and landing stages, which obscured much of the reflected light, I would have been far more dazzled. It is quite easy to overstate the effect of light on the water and here the subject prevented me from doing so. Therefore you get this slightly understated light.'

Almost meditative in effect, this is one of the most beautiful and sensitive of the artist's more personal images of Venice.

Venice, Green and Grey
Watercolour, 1990. 7 × 5ins.

Pax Tibi Marce Evangelista Meus II

Among the small number of substantial oil paintings that have resulted from Ken Howard's Venetian trips, the west front of the Basilica San Marco is the dominant subject. In this he owes a conscious debt to Sickert, one of the most productive of major British artists in Venice at the beginning of this century. Some of Sickert's most important Venetian work centres on the Basilica. It includes a series of oil paintings of this view, all painted in London. These were all based on a single large, squared-up drawing that was made on the spot and is now in Manchester City Art Gallery. The several versions feature the façade in differing lights and colour harmonies, thus suggesting the influence both of Monet's cathedral series and Whistler's Nocturnes.

Howard's picture is likewise one of a few differing versions. The monumental composition shown here has a weight and poise reminiscent of his early architectural paintings, for example the *Westminster Abbey* illustrated in this book. Viewed from a point near the centre of the Piazza, the Byzantine forms of the west front take on a flat, icon-like clarity. With the three flagstaffs in a precisely central position, the image is uncompromising in its massive symmetry.

Across the plane of the façade the artist has woven a simple and subtle pattern of colour harmonies. As the sun rises behind the domes, the tints of the Venetian shadows touch and colour every element of the building. Beneath this is a dynamic treatment of the scene in the Piazza. The distant figures develop from the static on the left of the composition to the active and blurred on the right, uncoiling a strong sense of movement across the canvas that further emphasises the stature of the Basilica.

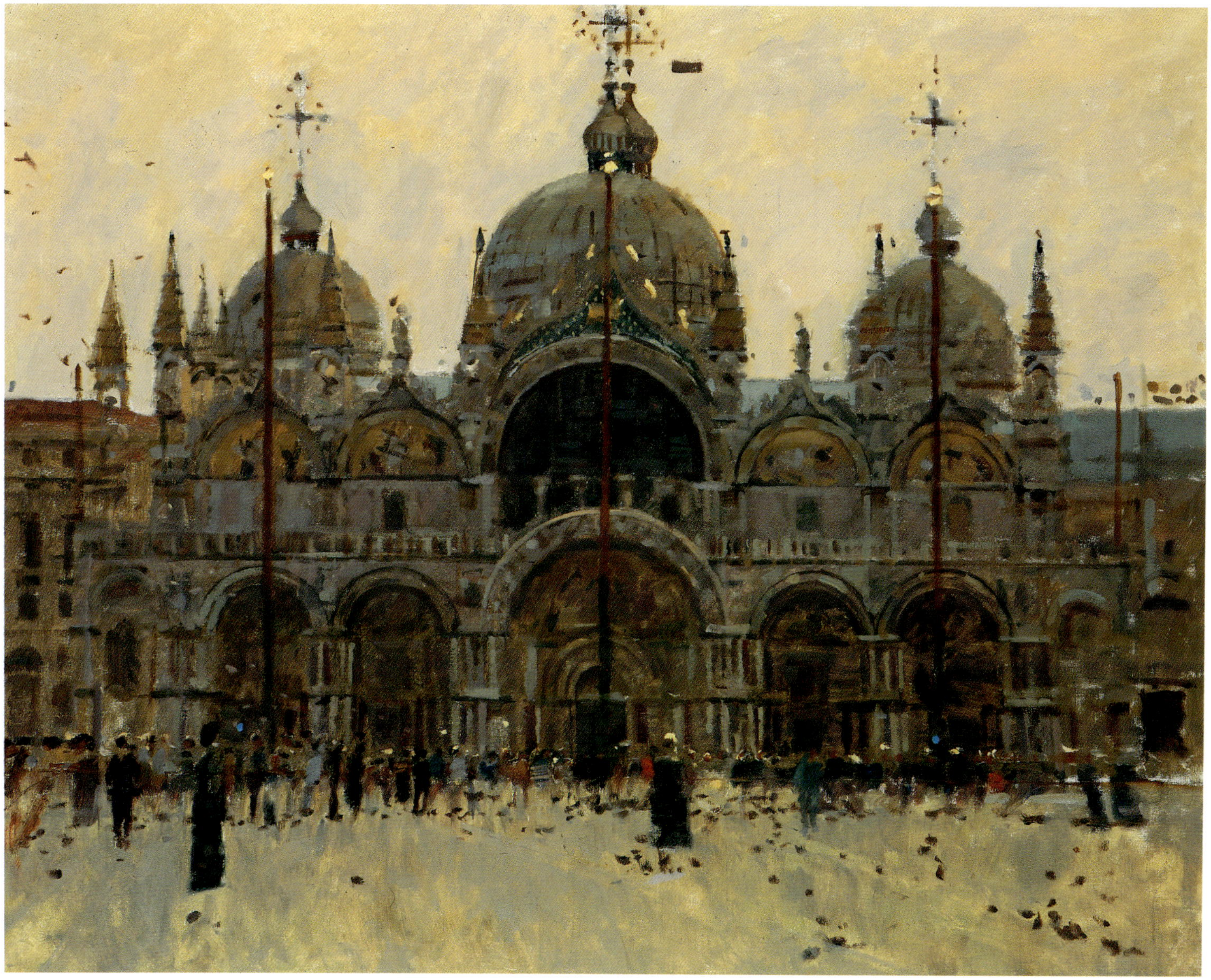

Pax Tibi Marce Evangelista Meus II
Oil on canvas, 1990. 40 × 48ins.

'One of my great loves has always been Sickert. I suppose I borrowed the composition as well as the title from him. But there is a difference. His Basilica sits right at the base of the painting – is seen close up, in other words. But I like to use the foreground to take the eye in. In that sense I don't feel I was stealing the image, for although I have admired Sickert since I was a student, I don't really work like him. I think the reason I find his work so powerful is that I am moved by the same images he was moved by – for instance, seeing things *contre-jour*, low in tone, limited in colour, with a very strong light effect.

'Another difference in the way I work is that I very rarely do so just from drawings and I don't really like the practice. In this case I did have one fairly precise drawing for reference, because, as for Sickert, it was only practical for me to paint the picture back in the studio. I also had lots of watercolours and oil sketches.

'The day preceding the painting of the picture, just before I went off for the plane, I stood in front of the Basilica and made notes and memorised as much as I could. There are stories of Whistler walking along the Embankment saying to himself "The sky is tone one, the river is tone two and the bridge is tone four", etcetera. When I work in this way I write these notes down – even laying out my palette – but I have to paint the subject very soon afterwards. The subject has to remain in my mind's eye. In a way I think the best way to work from drawings is to let the painting become a thing in itself, and not try to imitate the actual effect of what you saw. I believe that if you want to do that you should really be seeing the subject as you paint. Because I'm one of those painters who loves the sensation and truth of the thing I'm looking at, the only way I can get anything out of these large paintings made away from the subject is by doing them immediately on my return.

'On a few occasions, such as *Boat People* and *Ulster Crucifixion*, I have used photographic reference as well. This has always been black and white. I can't use colour, because it takes over, and I lose the image I had in my mind of how the subject was. One of my main arguments against the use of photography is that I believe drawing is a way of seeing. If I pick up a sketch-book and begin to draw someone's head, within five minutes I'll know more visually about that head than from years of just meeting and talking to the person.

'Photographs have their uses, but if you work the way I work, they can be very dangerous. They are superficially too similar to the kind of paintings I and thousands of others are trying to do, and they can deceive us about what we have seen, because photographs are not truthful. Of course Sickert was almost undone by photography in his later years.'

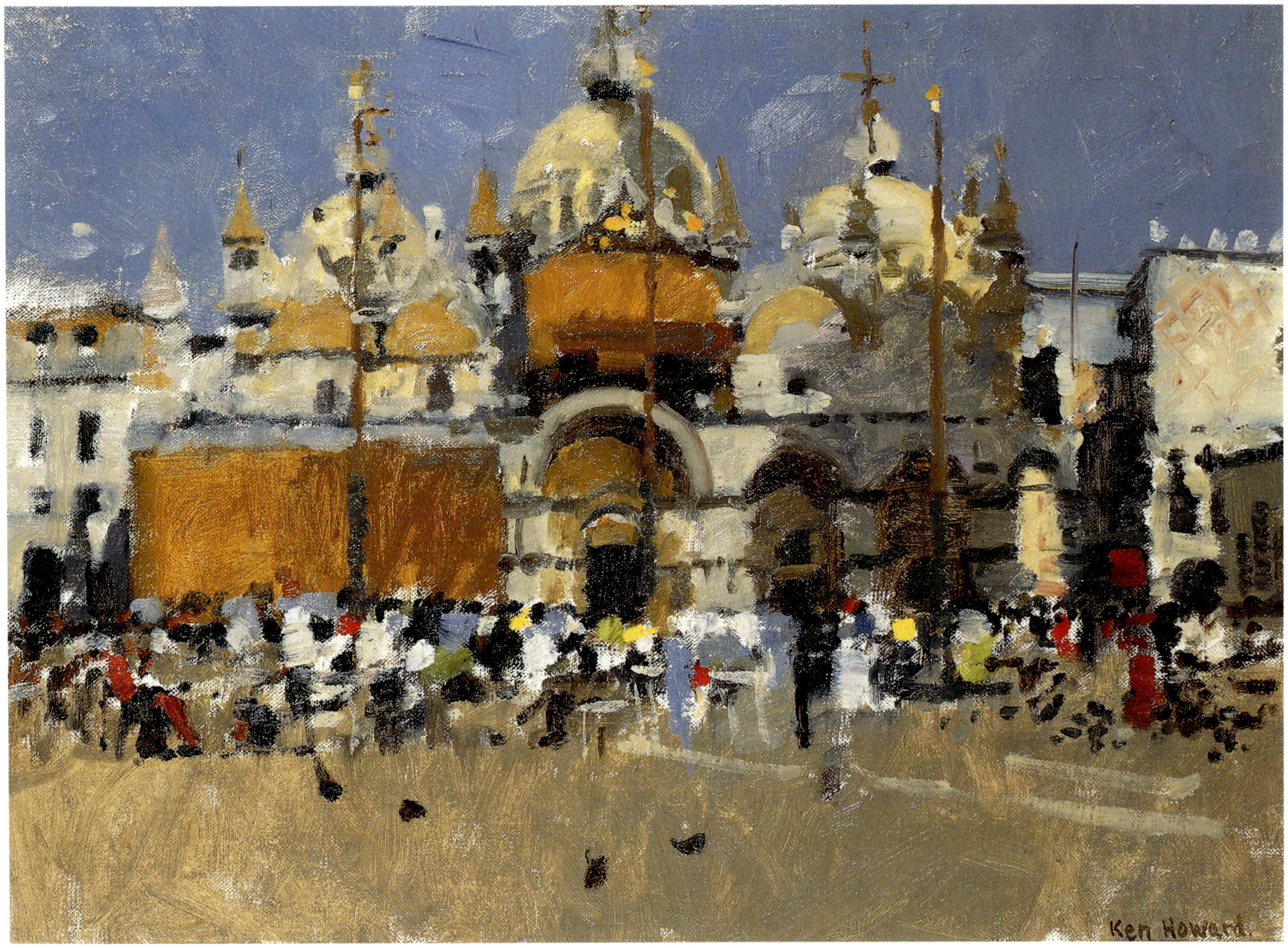

Basilica San Marco, Venice, September Light
Oil on canvas, 1990. 12 × 16ins.

Basilica San Marco, Venice, September Light
Taken in bright early afternoon sunlight, with the shadow of the Campanile San Marco passing over the portals of the west front, this small oil does not relate specifically to the previous work. It is, however, one of the several studies that were made preparatory to the *Pax Tibi* series, building up the artist's concept of the image until the final idea was crystallised.

If it lacks the perfect symmetry of *Pax Tibi II*, this composition is at least similar. In the studio painting the boarding that has covered restoration work in recent years is removed in order not to diminish the balanced majesty of the façade. The on-the-spot painting carries no such considerations and represents what was there on that day.

For a change we are here looking with the light, and the painter's palette is correspondingly bright and varied. Consequently, the sense of unity, the simplified tones and contrasting shapes of the *contre-jour* watercolours are replaced by a busy patchwork of free brushwork. The comparative lack of shade is perhaps one reason why Howard has chosen oils for this subject, bearing out his belief in the opacity of sun on stone.

One can almost hear the chatter of the crowd before San Marco. Placing himself in such an exposed spot, on so many occasions, one wonders whether Howard ever encountered the problems with curious passers-by that hampered him in India:

'It is completely different. I have always said I could never do a demonstration, but if I'm sitting on the beach and there's a hundred people behind me, it doesn't bother me in the least. I just love having people around. In the Piazza there are usually three or four people standing watching, but as long as they don't talk to me I am quite happy. The Italian has a certain respect for what you are doing, but the Indian culture does not accommodate this sort of activity. I shouldn't think that in their eyes my drawing even looked like what was in front of us.'

Riva degli Schiavoni
Here we are looking from the wide Riva, somewhere opposite San Giorgio, westward back towards the Salute and the mouth of the Grand Canal. For the artist this is a recently-found Venetian subject, for which he has hopes for the future:

'It has to be painted late in the evening, when the sun has got low enough for the light on the water to have become a block. I like the way it comes through to the side of a vaporetto stop and cuts across the surface of the Riva, reflecting off the stone. This picture is about light first of all, but also about the figures walking across the scene. This figurative element that I tend to introduce may be something of a weakness in me. I can't see an empty studio as having any potential as a subject.'

For a man who loves crowds and company, such an interest is simply one way in which he expresses himself in paint. Even the most disciplined realist must choose his image. The exercising of this choice has to be subjective and ultimately the painter can only convey onto the canvas what is inside him – how he reacts to the world.

The inclusion of figures in townscape and landscape also has distinguished precedents; in the work of Turner, for example. Previously unloved, Turner's figures are now considered by many to breathe real life and humanity into much of his work. We naturally relate to the scale and presence of such figures, who have been used by many painters as though to introduce the observer to the subject.

This small, confidently-handled oil is on a narrow panel, reminiscent of the railway-yard paintings. These small panels, now much favoured by the artist, are covered with muslin and gesso, giving enough of a tooth to hold the paint, but not accepting repainting very well. Thus Howard, intentionally or not, puts himself under pressure to finish each painting in one vigorous session.

Here the spontaneity of the technique is, as usual, extremely pleasing. The late afternoon light of an early autumn day is splendidly preserved in the economical brush-marks. The wonderful feeling of delight – like a deep breath – that the sight of this bright, fresh expanse of water and air inspires, is conveyed to perfection.

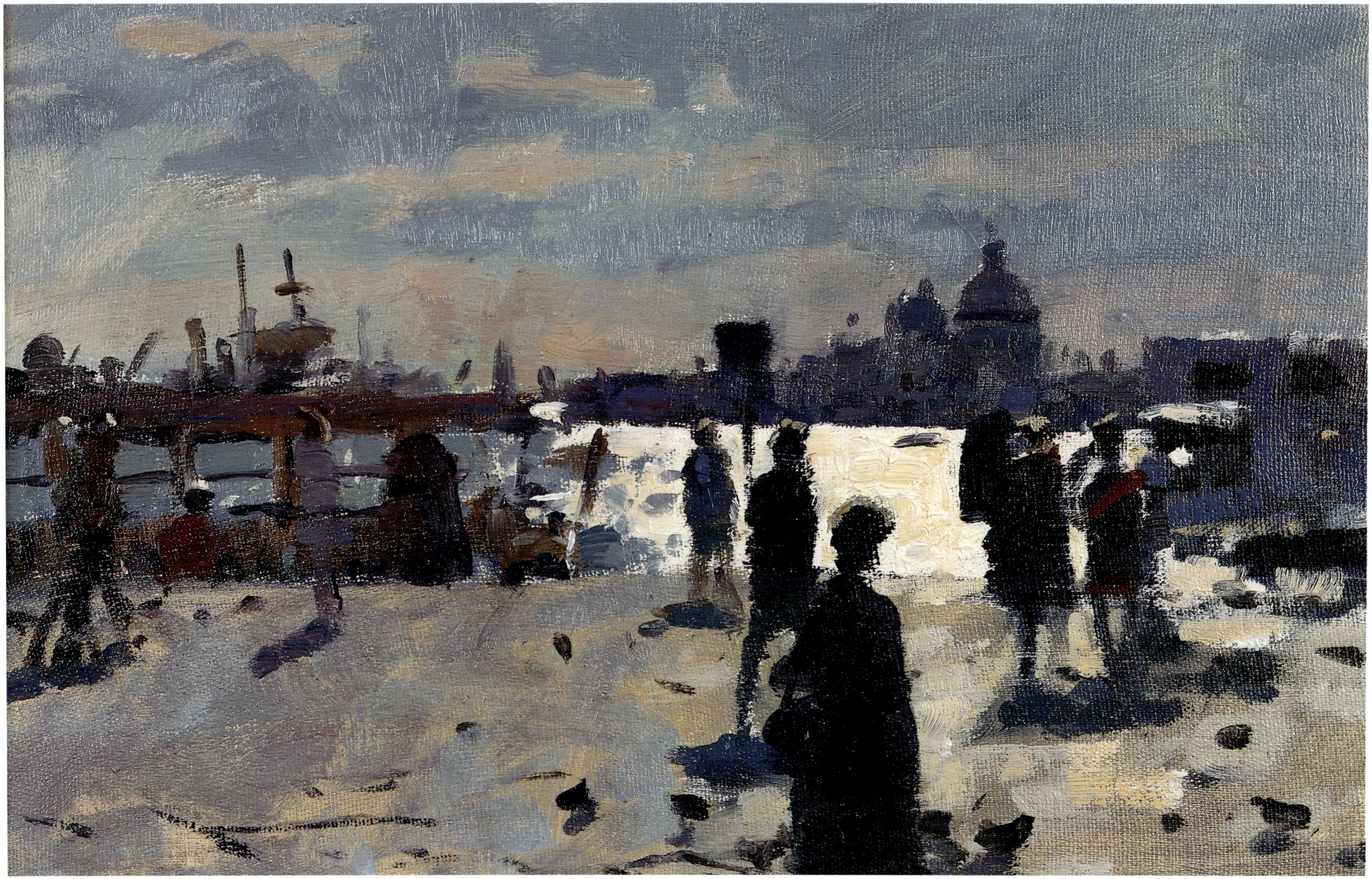

Riva degli Schiavoni
Oil on panel, 1989. 8 × 12ins.

The Cornish Coast

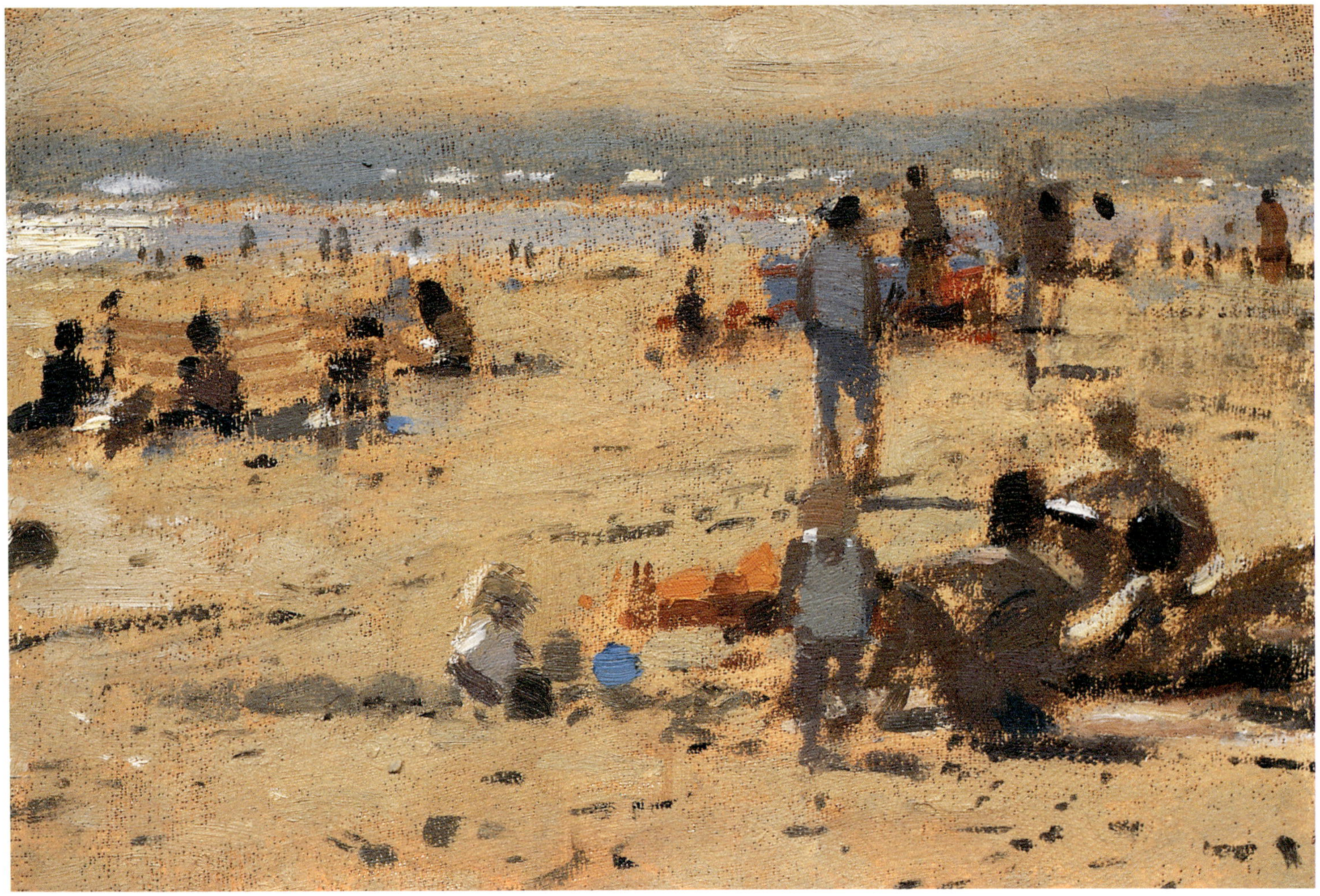

Marazion, Evening
Oil on panel, c 1988. 8 × 10ins.

Marazion, Evening
As the painting of the open view from the Riva faithfully caught a particular Venetian light, so does this superb study capture a very different effect. Here we are able to recognise the sultry atmosphere of the early evening following a hot summer's day on the beach. The dragged, dry brushwork perfectly describes the languid, hazy brightness, as the wetter, sharper strokes of the previous picture suited the clearer air and light.

The very natural groupings of figures are handled with great brevity and conviction. Some figures are most acutely observed. The description of the demeanour and actions of the woman and two children in the foreground, for example, are remarkably complete, considering their lack of literal detail.

The setting is a popular beach opposite St Michael's Mount, on the south side of the West Penwith peninsula:

'At this time in the evening, as the shadows begin to lengthen, the beach starts to reflect the warmth of the sky, which is no longer blue and turns to greens and yellows. Compared with, say, Sennen, on the north side of the peninsula, Marazion is quite a warmly-coloured sandy beach. Each of the Cornish beaches I paint has its own characteristics, which I hope come through in the pictures. I think it is important that one should be conscious of the particular, more than the general.'

A rare quality of the beach paintings that follow is their sense of particularity. Of all popular subjects for painting, beach scenes are among those that are most commonly generalised, however delightfully. So often sun, fun, sea and sand dominate the scene, and the painter could be on any beach. Howard sees beaches as populated landscapes, invariably full of colour and flooded with sunlight. Realist and likeness-maker that he remains, he respects and likes to convey the individuality of each location and each moment, as he would in any landscape painting. This beautiful and lucid oil sketch is a prime example. It seems to be utterly true to life, light and time.

'By the end of a day's painting, a little panel like this can be finished quite quickly – about forty-five minutes to an hour. That wouldn't be possible first thing in the morning, but by this time – after six or seven hours' practice - I should really be seeing, and have control of my materials and palette. By this stage there should be no fumbling. I want to paint as one speaks – naturally and directly, without fumbling and chewing it over – just speaking. I once read that Monet said he wished to paint as a bird sings. Monet's ambition was much higher than mine. To paint as a bird sings is a very high thing to aim for.'

St Michael's Mount from Marazion

Ken Howard has produced an extensive range of images of the West Penwith beaches, in oils and watercolour. The oils vary considerably in scale and ambition. Larger paintings, like the present canvas, are often extremely complex pieces of picture-making, involving the arrangement of upwards of twenty individual figures. The scene here is once again Marazion, somewhat earlier in the day. The artist has turned to the right to look straight out to St Michael's Mount, a few hundred yards over the sea.

'A couple of years ago I went to Marazion, principally to see the dinghies, and realised then that much of the day one could work *contre-jour*, with the light on the water. Also, the images on that beach are very good. At high tide the sea comes up a long way and the people are gathered at the top. But when the sea goes out, you get an enormous expanse of beach, almost as far out as St Michael's Mount itself.

'What particularly attracted me to this subject were the red sails of the dinghies near the sea – with the light coming through them – and the staccato notes of all the figures in the foreground. The light also cuts through the windbreaks, against which the shadows of figures are thrown – a very exciting image. I painted the picture in the studio, from a number of studies.

'I would very much like to be able to work on this scale on the beach. The trouble is that I need to build up to it. I would need to paint throughout a run of two or three weeks of constant sun before I felt confident enough to take a big canvas onto the beach. English weather isn't that reliable. It has always been my ambition to be able to paint a 40 by 48 inch canvas outdoors, with the same breadth and brushwork as the smaller panels.'

It is in the later paintings of studio interiors – when the artist's subject is before him and inconsistent weather can be ignored – that this breadth has happily translated to the larger canvas. With the complicated transcription onto the large beach canvases of figure groups from various studies, it is perhaps inevitable that Howard finds his painterly freedom inhibited. Ever since the advent of *plein air* painting in the nineteenth century, the unstudied spontaneity and freshness of this direct approach to nature has been highly prized by many. Howard is probably right in saying that, away from the subject, his brush-marks become more uniform, less animated. To all but the most perceptive of observers, however, some of his less formal, studio-bound paintings can be taken for works made on the spot – a tribute to his acute visual memory.

This composition of *St Michael's Mount from Marazion* is carefully managed, and the overall handling even. The symmetrical composition and fairly flat lighting from a high sun impart a certain sense of stillness. Yet the brushwork is vivid and broad, sufficient to convey the artist's keen understanding and memory of his subject with absolute conviction.

The Mount, set in the sparkling sea off Marazion beach, is sharply visible and clearly delineated through a hint of aerial perspective. In its central position it accentuates the flatness of the picture-plane by hemming in our seaward gaze. As ever, this picture is utterly faithful to its subject, as any visitor to the scene will recognise.

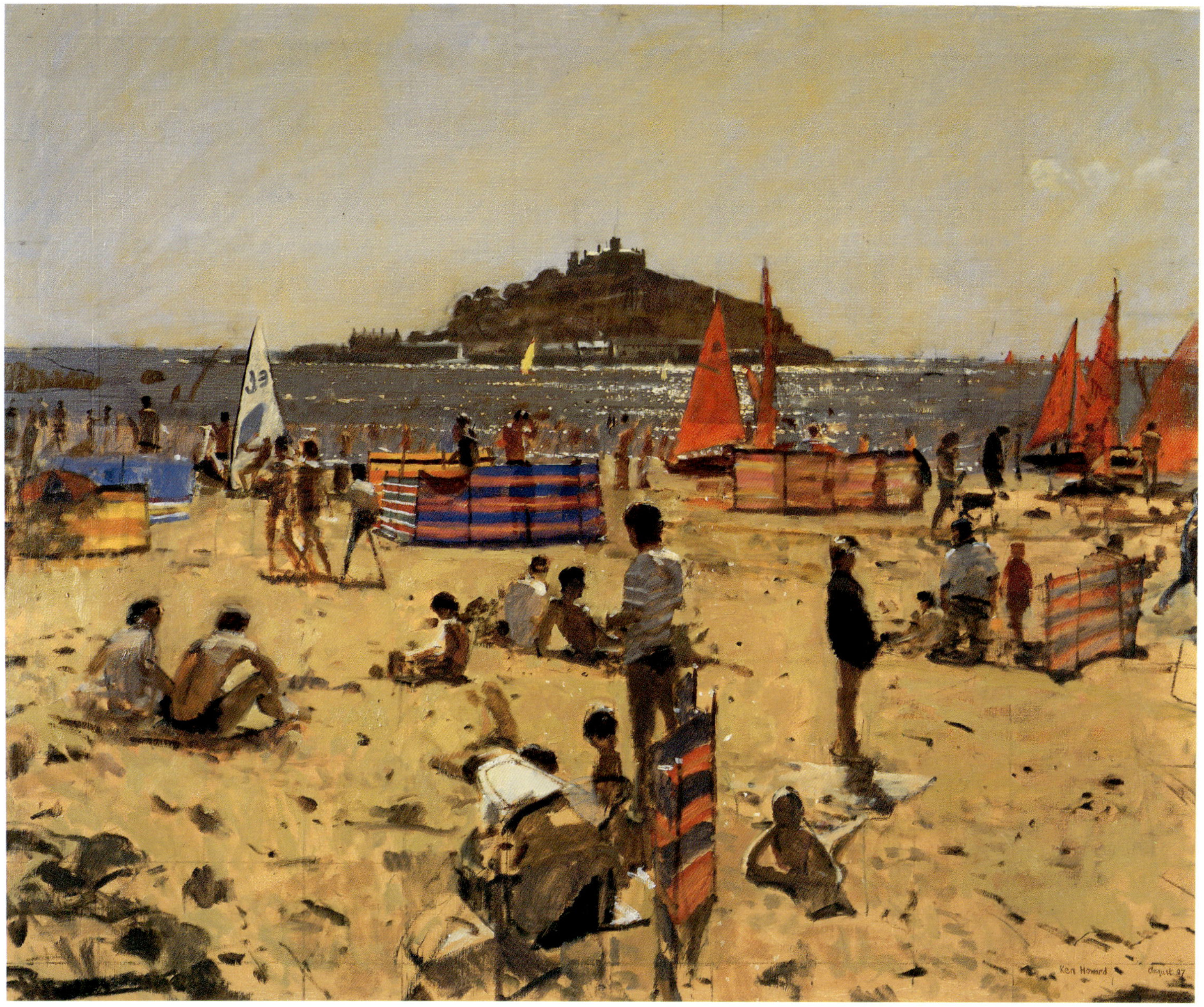

St Michael's Mount from Marazion
Oil on canvas, 1987. 40 × 48ins.

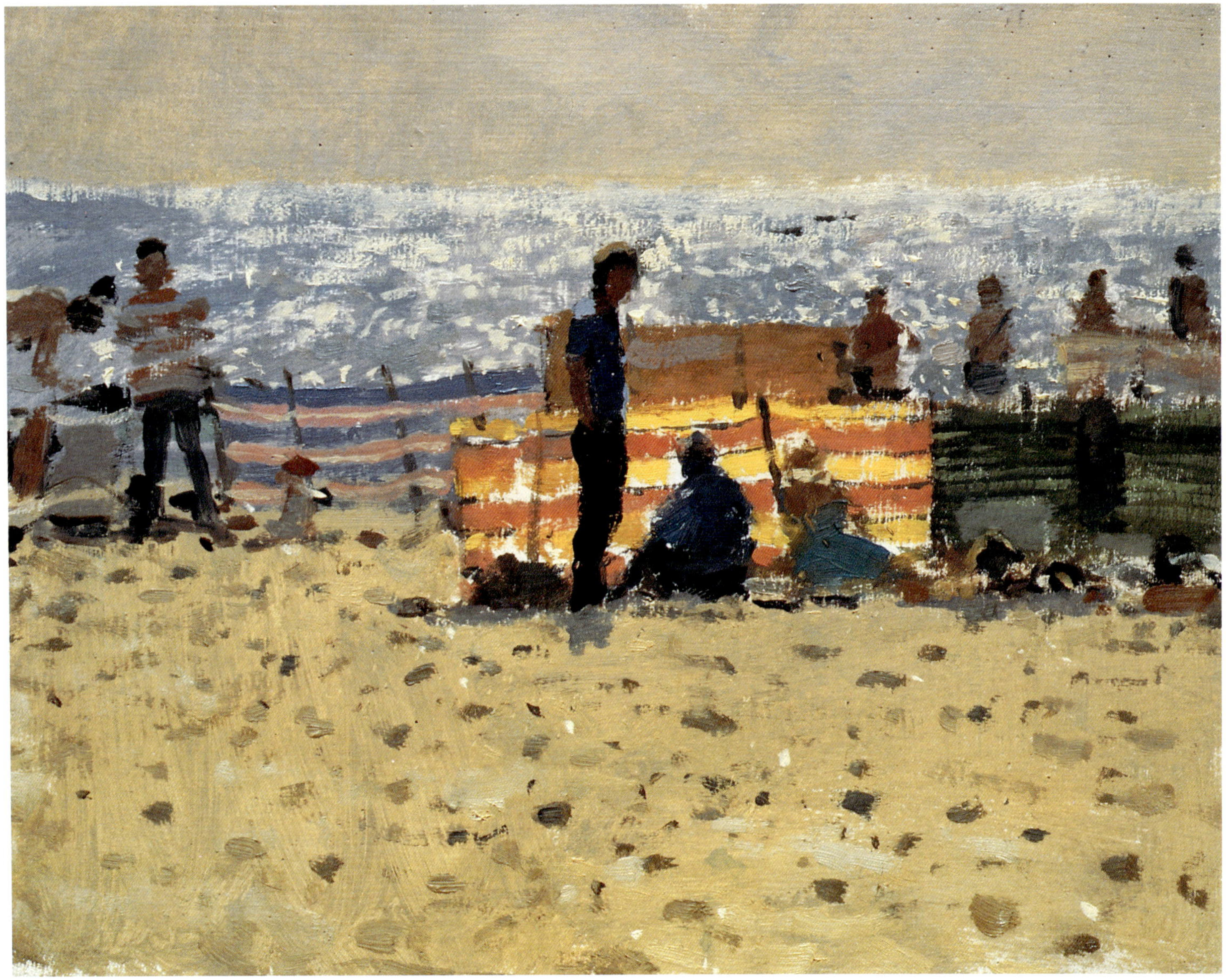

Red and Yellow Lightbreaks
Oil on panel, 1988. 8 × 10ins.

Red and Yellow Lightbreaks
We are here looking straight out over a shining sea at Porthcurno beach, south of Land's End. Like *Marazion, Evening*, this is one of the vivid small oils, painted directly and with speed before an ever-changing subject, that are in many ways the quintessential beach paintings. These brief notes of a precise moment and a precise light effect bring the artist closer to his subject, further refining and elaborating what he knows about the beach, the sea, the light:

'As with all these small panels done outdoors, I paint the picture in one "wet". I can't allow the panel to dry in between sessions, because the gesso ground takes some of the oil out of the paint, which therefore tends to sink. If I do it in one wet, the whole painting goes in together as it were. It finishes up with a very beautiful mat consistency and all the tonal values stay in their right relationship to one another during the drying process. This is very important to me, with my interest in tone.'

Here we may note both the artist's control of the tonal scale of the painting and also his fascination for the way the sunbathers' windbreaks catch and hold the sunshine, into which he stares. Howard makes simple but effective use of the varying tones of the silhouetted figures to emphasise the *contre-jour* effect and to give some sense of space and distance between the closely planted 'lightbreaks'. The straightforward, centralised composition means the observer's attention is not distracted from the middle-distance scene. The free brushwork is so handled as to encourage us to read into this area considerable beach activity.

The artist has only recently become a regular visitor to this beach:

'Porthcurno didn't mean very much to me for some time. It's a very narrow beach facing directly south. You're in the sea before you know where you are and all the lightbreaks line up along the water's edge. It has always been very much two-dimensional – you never get much sense of depth. One day I began to see it as a subject because of all this, and then it became more and more exciting for me. I love this brilliant sparkle of light that you get off the water and I love the strongly silhouetted shapes of the figures against the lightbreaks and against the water, particularly in the morning. That's why I like to get to the beach quite early.'

Lightbreaks, Sennen
Taking the lightbreak theme one stage further, this rather larger and more carefully composed picture retains much of the free brushwork and vigour, if not the spontaneity of the more immediate previous example. The elaborate arrangement of lightbreaks establishes a high-key middle-distance, capturing the sunlight striking down over the shaded wall at the back. The sparkle of light is carried on into the foreground across a diagonal arrangement of figures and sailboard, while the stark shadows in the sand reinforce the harshness of the light and contrast with the colour of the windbreaks.

The sharp tonal contrasts demonstrate once again that Howard possesses a natural tonal pitch. The seemingly random array of tones over the surface of the canvas are in fact taken carefully up the scale from the darkest to the lightest. If the artist pitches his darkest tone too dark or too light, the natural order of that harmonious scale makes it inevitable that he will end up with the lightest correspondingly dull or bright. The same rule naturally operates in the other direction, depending on one's working methods. Try to embrace tones that are too far apart, in order to bridge a gap, and the harmony breaks down and the scale snaps. Too close together and the tones will become confused and muddied – most inappropriate, in this case, to the subject. Sennen beach presents an altogether different challenge from Porthcurno, as the artist explains:

'This is typical of the things that I do at Sennen in the summer, when I want to paint looking into the light. Because it's a north-facing beach, whenever you're looking out to sea you're looking with the light. I discovered that the best thing was to go down towards the sea and look back up the beach. So a lot of my Sennen pictures have no sea in them at all. I often include the long dark wall that lies below the car park, which, being extremely dark, is a marvellous foil against the lightbreaks. Once the sun has got up a bit – by ten-thirty to eleven in the morning – it's cutting right down into the people on the beach and into their windbreaks.

'Of course it is a bit embarrassing that one has to

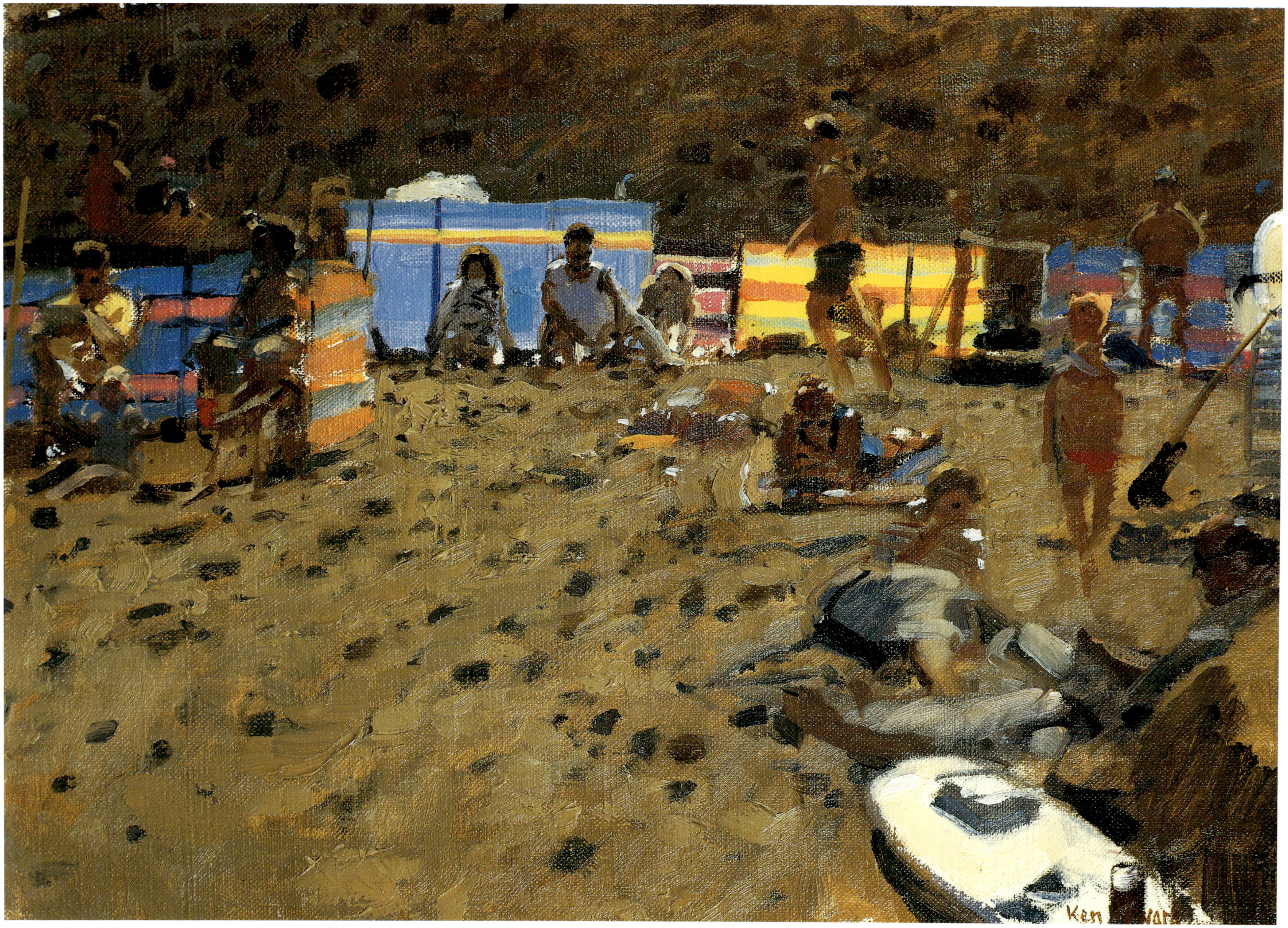

stand out in front of all these people, who are themselves looking out to sea. There's this strange fellow standing there painting, looking back at them from the sea. They are, as it were, on a stage – or I am on a stage, depending on which way you look at it. Still, I can't afford to allow myself to be bothered by things like that. If I have decided I am going to paint the image, I've got to go ahead and do it.'

Lightbreaks, Sennen
Oil on canvas, c 1987. 18 × 26ins.

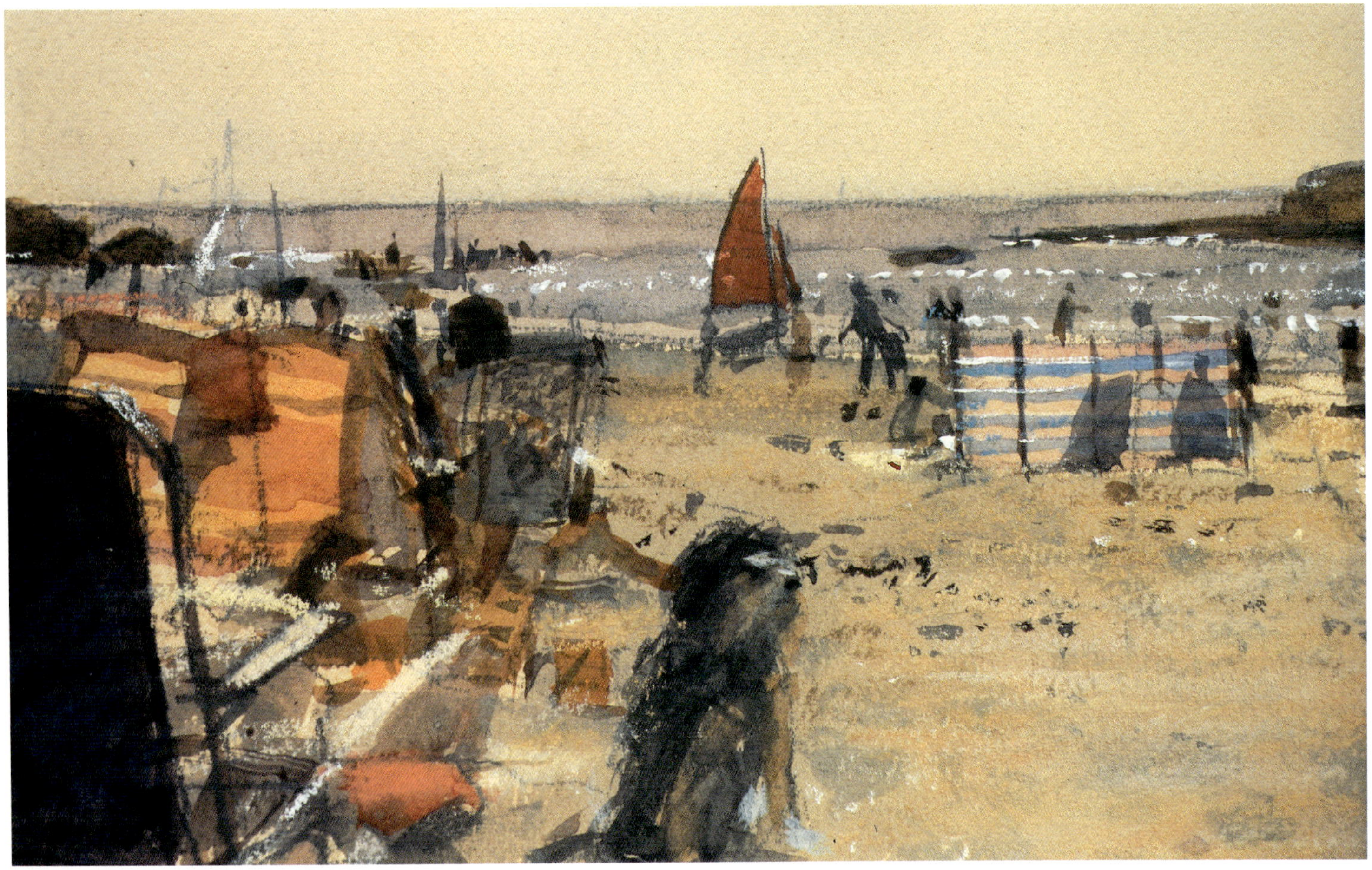

Beach Dog
Watercolour, with bodycolour and pastel over pencil, 1988. 5 × 7ins.

Beach Dog
Ken Howard's watercolours of the Cornish beaches tend to be similar in intent and manner to the small oils on panel. *Beach Dog* is one of the finest of them. Over a small sheet of paper is spread a great amount of visual and textural interest. Like the Cyprus series it has been assembled with assurance and technical freedom, using whatever medium was necessary to achieve the desired effect. It also introduces, in the form of the relaxed but possibly distracted canine, a rare touch of humour to Howard's work. The result is a true visual transcription of the excitement and enjoyment he found in the subject.

The setting is again the golden sands of Marazion. The sunlight and shadow striking the windbreaks form the principal, horizontal axis of the composition. Making up the central, vertical element are the motif of a red dinghy sail and the beach dog. Although it amuses, the dog is not caricatured. With dry, 'hairy' strokes of the brush it is vividly characterised. Howard clearly retains some affection for *Beach Dog*:

'Chrissie and I decided to keep this picture, something I never did until she arrived. It would have been better to have done this when I was younger, because now I have to go to the salerooms to buy things back, sometimes paying over the odds.

'I usually start off the summer in Cornwall with a series of watercolours, then go on to smaller oils and only after that build up to the larger studio canvases. All this does of course depend on the weather. It can be very frustrating when one is constantly chasing after the light, wondering if it will be the same tomorrow – and it never is. That is probably why the English made such good watercolour painters. The English light is much more transitory than if you work, say, in the South of France. Working on the spot, I think it is often only possible to capture it in such a potentially quick medium as watercolour. But this does add an element of tension to the experience, which I thrive upon.

'One of the problems I find with pure watercolour is that one is sometimes controlled by the medium. On the beach you can't allow that to happen, because there are so many things you are involved in capturing, and at the same time you are also composing. Whatever people may say about Monet being simply an eye, simply recording, he and the other Impressionists were very conscious of composing. They composed by putting things in and cutting them out, painting them over – gradually cutting them back until they got down to the essence of what they wanted.

'When I'm on the beach, I have to be selective from everything that's moving and changing in front of me. Although people walking past, sitting down, getting up, excite me, I still have to finish with the composition that I want. For instance, in this one I had in mind the complex nature of the left-hand side, the very simple areas on the right, the relationship between the dog and the sail in the background, the relationship between the dog and the figure in the middle-distance, and then the complex area beyond that. It's not a question of sitting down and thinking of a composition. It's a question of instinctively feeling that a thing is right and leaving it in, then putting something in and knowing instinctively that it is completely wrong, and therefore cutting it out. So, in this watercolour you can see shadows of things that were there before. But finally, what is left is what I want to be left.'

One can indeed see the transitory leg of a sunbather who, for at least part of the duration of the artist's presence, was ensconced in the chair to the left. Howard's comments recall the problems associated with the sanger drawings in Northern Ireland, notably when he had to make a composition from two figures who were not depicted simultaneously.

While his methods might be mistrusted by a puritanical realist, Howard's inspirational recording method is a genuine attempt to get to the heart of the matter, to reveal the essence of his subject. He rightly cites the Impressionists, who, like all significant painters, were selective in their vision. The naturalist artist is not a camera. If he is, photography has dulled his effectiveness. His task is to reveal to the spectator, in their essence, truths that otherwise might remain unseen. We have all seen dogs playing on the beach, but this one is the quintessential beach dog, and Howard tells us more about his character than countless snapshots could.

Towards St Michael's Mount
Beach life is not the only aspect of the Cornish coast in Howard's repertoire. In recent years he has produced a body of work at Newlyn harbour, and some at Penzance, just along the coast to the north-east of Mousehole. This small panel was painted one morning, overlooking the docks at Penzance. Its particular effectiveness lies in the recession of a natural composition of shapes through aerial perspective, out across Mount's Bay.

The outline of St Michael's Mount, about two miles away, is veiled in early-morning mist. Although much further out than from Marazion beach, the change in the clarity of the Mount's depiction is largely dependent on different atmospheric conditions. The handling of the thin paint is economical and direct, allowing the muslin and gesso support to show through in places and emphasise the transparency of the suffused light. To capture the luminosity of a limpid morning, Howard was at his easel well before 7 am:

'I had seen the subject a couple of days before, in mid-morning, and thought how good it would look in the right sort of early-morning light. It is a natural composition, with the road cutting across the lower part, and then the eye being turned back in through the freighter boat alongside the harbour. Then behind that the *Scillonian* carries the eye further out to the distant St Michael's Mount.

'It was a beautiful morning – grey, slightly foggy, nothing staccato, all extremely soft. At first I was extremely disappointed with this picture. I went home about nine-thirty and went to bed, because I felt so miserable about the whole thing. It was one of those sensations – which I think all painters know – when you wonder what you have learned in the past thirty years, if you just can't put two pieces of paint together to re-create the sensation, to make the effect that you want. I remember how marvellously ethereal this subject was and I was aiming for something too high. I'm quite pleased with it now.'

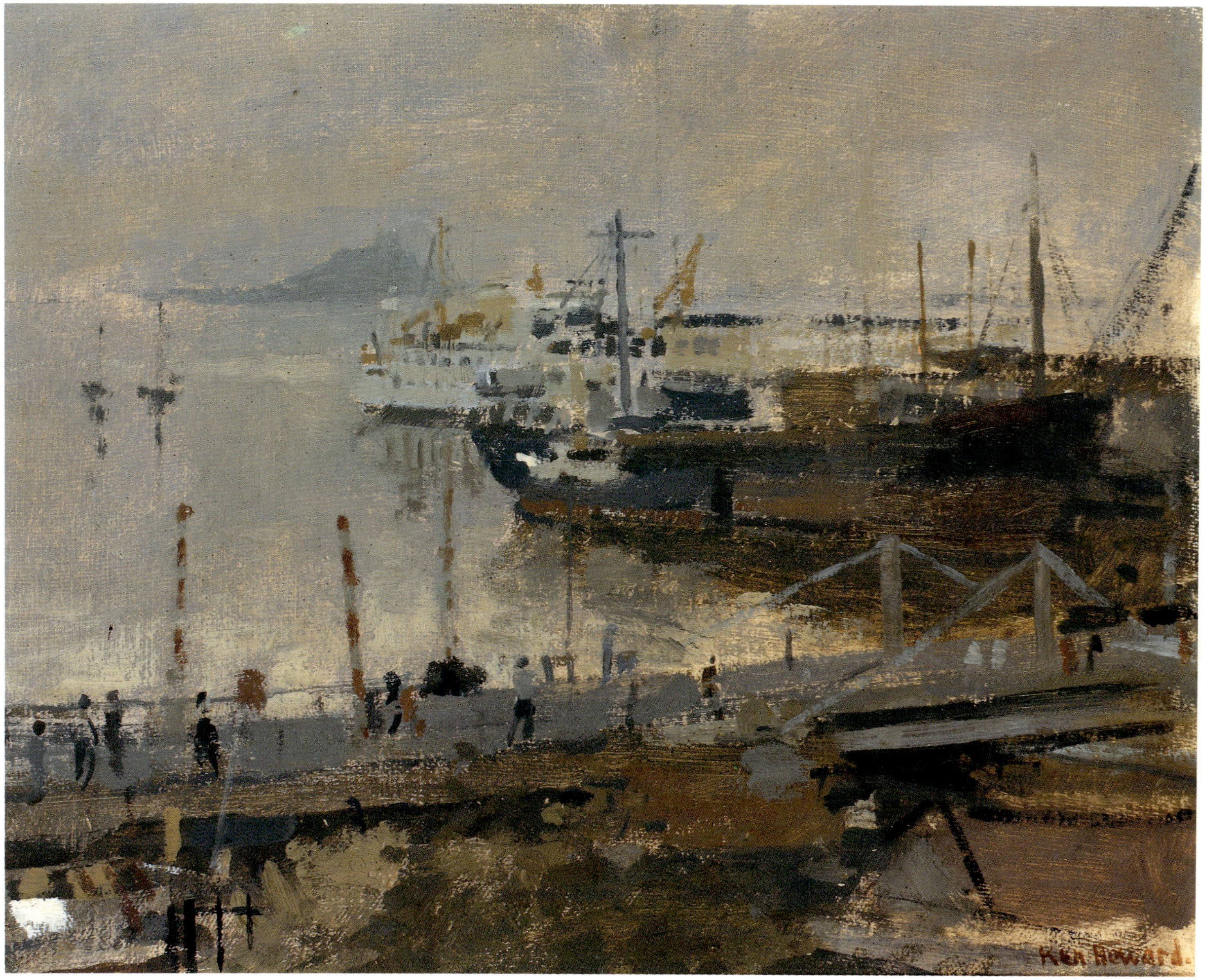

Towards St Michael's Mount
Oil on panel, 1986. 8 × 10ins.

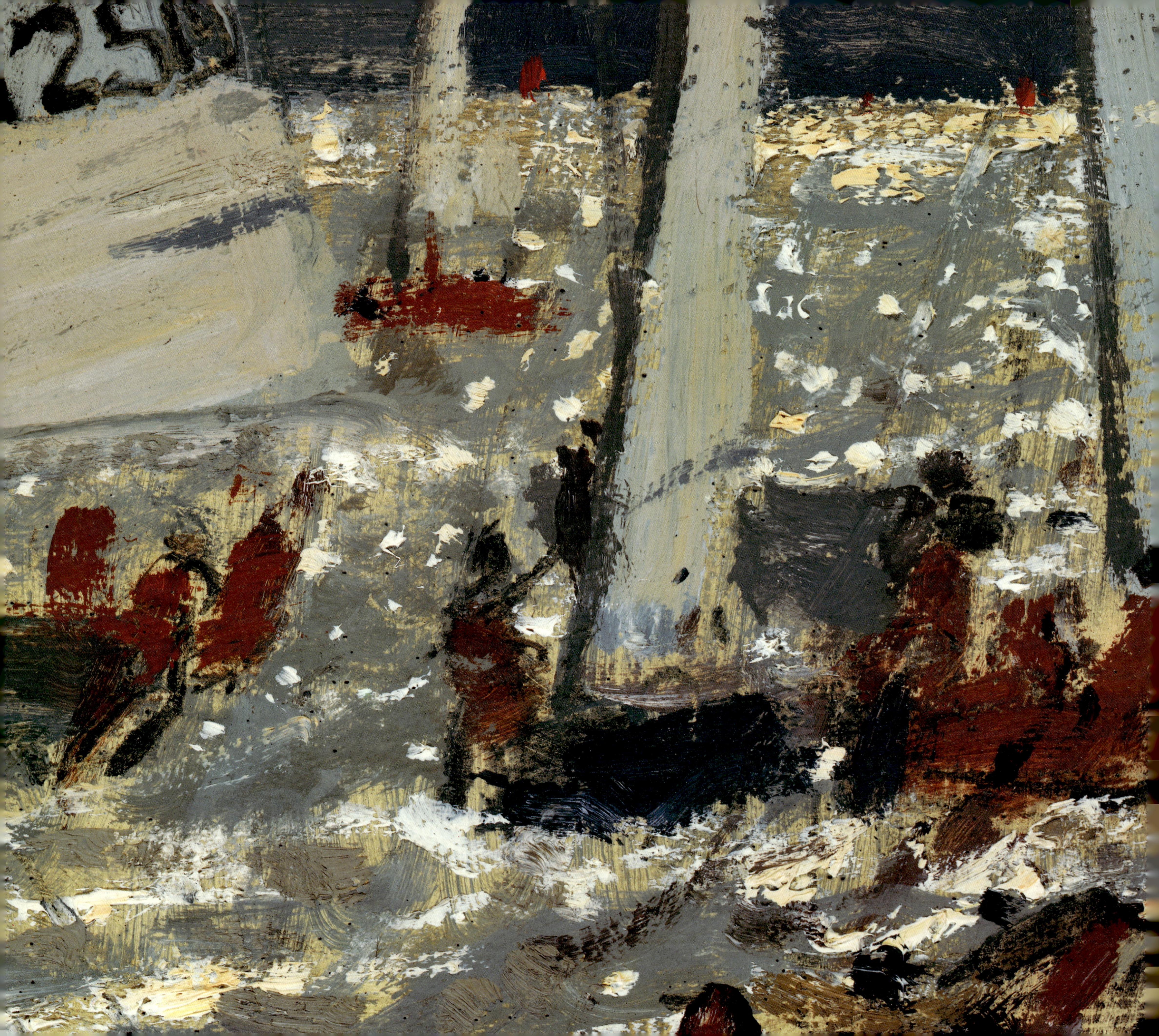
25

Racing Dinghies, Marazion

This very small panel is painted with almost frantic energy and excitement. Here, reproduced around life-size, every mark of its energetic brushwork is visible. Yet somehow this frenetic, dancing array of marks consolidates to form a believable and extremely active image. Seen in the enlarged detail opposite, the brush-strokes take on a freedom and life of their own, exploding in a glorious burst of painterly freedom.

'This is one of my favourite pictures. It was done almost instantaneously at the end of a day's painting at Marazion beach. I clearly remember being very tired by the end of that day. The tide had come in and I was packed up and ready to go home. As I walked back towards the car I suddenly noticed all the dinghies were coming in to be drawn up to the path where they are kept. I realised instantly that it was going to be an incredible subject in four or five minutes' time.

'I debated whether I had the strength to unpack everything, set the easel up and be ready for this moment, when it happened. But what was in front of me insisted that I did so. So by the time the boats were coming in and the people were jumping out and pulling them up the rocks, I was in full flood. As far as I can remember the picture took less than fifteen minutes. For this reason it is very spontaneous.'

Suggested rather than described, much of the image is left for us to read into it what we feel is, or should be, there. For example, the figures are each noted with one, perhaps two, strokes of paint. As individuals they are too broadly treated to make sense in the way those in the *Marazion, Evening* sketch did. In a sense these sailors are represented not literally, but in shorthand. Yet in their groups, and in the context of the animated brushwork around them, their urgent communal effort to pull down the sails and beach the dinghies is conveyed and understood. So too is the exhilarating rush of boats moving in to shore after an afternoon's sailing.

The whole scene jumps and sways before a bright late afternoon sun. The flashes and glints of light catching sailcloth and reflecting on metal are dominated by the dazzle on the water. This intensely flickering light, seen *contre-jour*, but with so little of the low-toned sky visible that the light seems to come from the water, is brilliantly mimicked by the broken, sparkling brushwork. 'What I would love to be able to do is paint a picture with this sort of verve on a much larger scale. Maybe it'll come – I hope so.'

Racing Dinghies, Marazion
(detail)

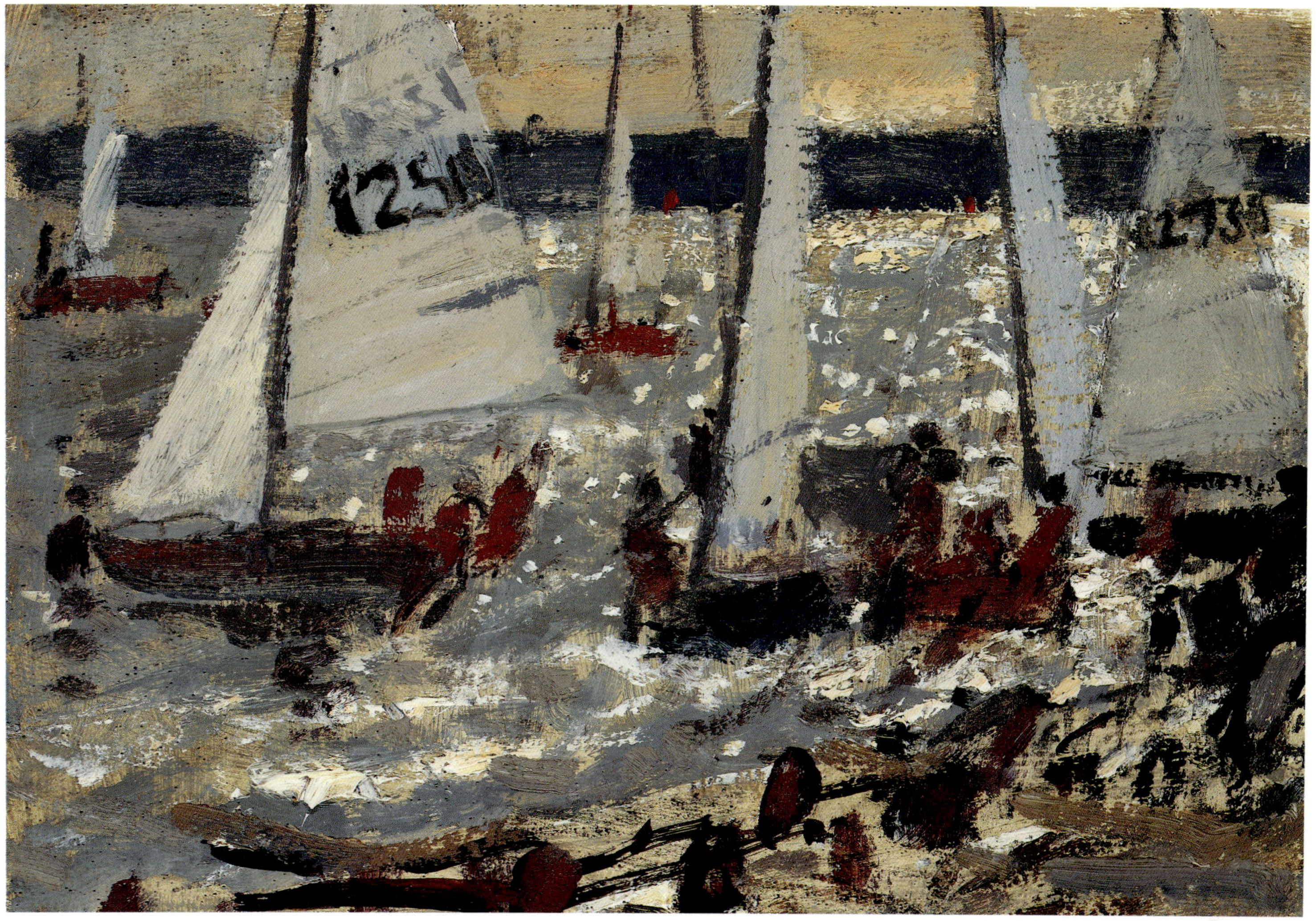

Racing Dinghies, Marazion
Oil on panel, 1986. 6 × 9ins.

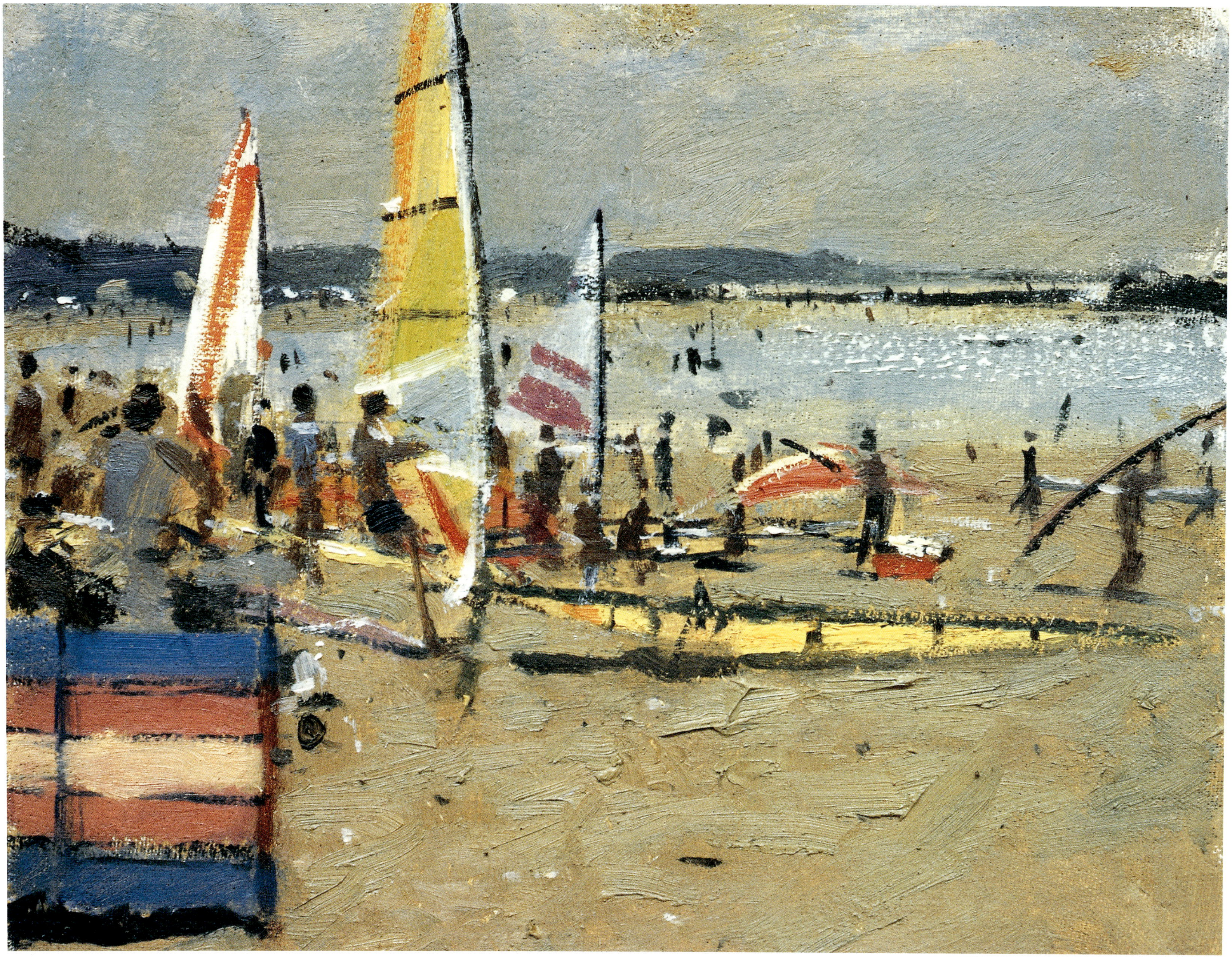

Windsurfers, Long Rock
Oil on panel, 1987. 8 × 10ins.

Windsurfers, Long Rock
Another of the freely-handled, small oil panels, this work was made at the Long Rock beach, on Mount's Bay between Penzance and Marazion. It is full of incident and pictorial interest, if less drama than the previous painting. The familiar interests are here – the windbreak catching the light and the figures silhouetted *contre-jour.*

The colourful world of windsurfing was introduced to the Cornish beaches not long before Howard started painting there and one can imagine that it formed part of the attraction. The coloured sailboards and costumes provide much visual interest, but for this artist the many-hued sails, acting as lightbreaks, are natural subjects. Too subtle a painter to over-exploit such a godsend, Howard integrates the sails into the overall effect of intense summer sunlight:

'It is the vertical lightbreaks of the windsurfers that appeal to me. When the men are setting them up, they stand on the beach to test their tautness. Even when they are lying on the beach the light cuts across the multicoloured sails. But if they are standing against the evening sun, the light absolutely blazes through them. They make a marvellous vertical contrast to the beach – going right back to my earliest roots, when I was so interested in the vertical and horizontal in composition. As I've grown older I've become more interested in the rhythms in composition, but I still have a strong feeling for the stability of the horizontal line and the soaring contrast of the vertical.

'I think it would be marvellous if Boudin were alive now. What wonderful beach pictures he would have made. Instead of women in black dresses with parasols, he could have painted windsurfers with their brightly coloured wet suits, the sunbathers in their beach wear, the surfers with their surfboards. I think he would have liked it.

'On the other hand I would have loved to be around when there were tall-masted ships in Newlyn Harbour, and the red sails of those fishing boats that you see in Stanhope Forbes's paintings. But in fifty years' time, I am sure people will look back and marvel at the life of today, and certainly at the bright beach life.'

Lightbreak, Sennen, Blue and Yellow
There are works that are judged as seminal in an artist's *oeuvre,* whether by the artist or another observer. These milestones are not necessarily masterpieces, although they often are. Neither are they necessarily works commenced with high or new aspirations in mind. Howard regards *Lightbreak, Sennen* – the first of his windbreak pictures – as a milestone. Although there is no compulsion for the spectator to judge it on anything but aesthetic merit, the artist's recollections of its making and the importance he attaches to the result are of great interest. They may also be valuable aids to our own appraisal of its qualities.

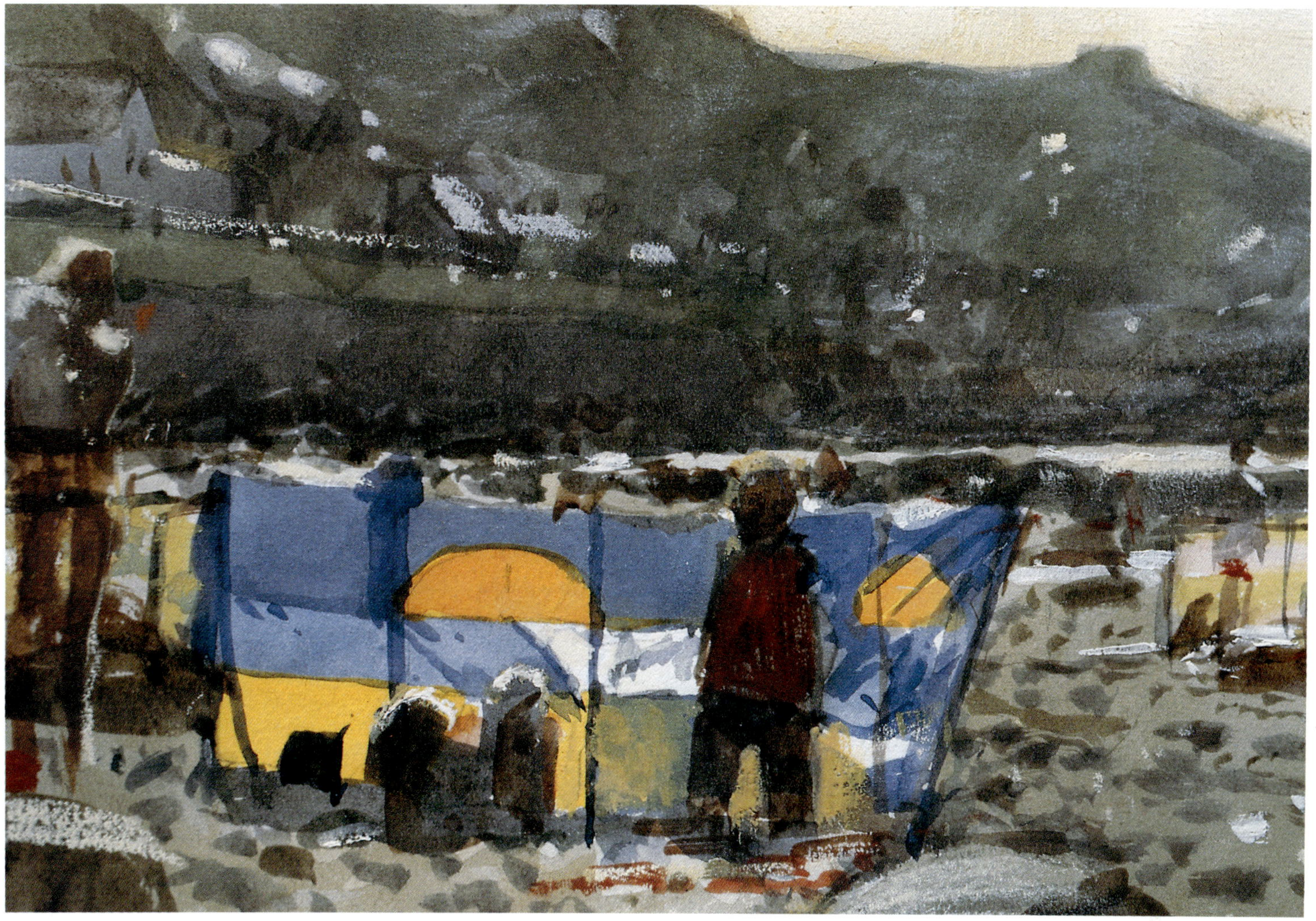

Lightbreak, Sennen, Blue and Yellow
Watercolour, 1985. 5 × 7ins.

'This watercolour is the work which I believe has gone furthest towards capturing the sensation of light which I want to achieve. Whether it's on the beach, in the studio, in Venice, in Newlyn, the essential thing that I've been involved with in the past six or seven years is the sensation of light. I would love to feel that I could make light come from the picture, rather than describing light. The really great masters did this – for instance Rembrandt, and Sickert too. Their pictures have an equivalent for the real sensation of light rather than just describing it.

'I have a long way to go, but this little watercolour actually gave me that sort of come-back – the light breaking through the blues and yellows of the windbreak, the figures leaning up in front of it, a silhouette of the figure at the bottom of the windbreak, the play of light on the windbreak contrasting with the Sennen cliffs in evening shadow. When I first saw this subject the light excited me incredibly, but I didn't like the windbreak itself. I think I'm something of a creature of habit and get used to certain images. This was to me a completely new one. But when you try something you have just seen, its unfamiliarity can make for a very exciting image.'

It is helpful to be able to study this watercolour at around its actual size. Within a simple composition, the brilliantly coloured windbreak, which so enthralled the artist, dominates our view. It has been described with flat washes of paint that show remarkable conviction for such an unrehearsed subject. The artist's rapture has carried through to the rest of the brushwork, which is rapid, broken and of mixed medium, as it splendidly conveys the distinctive dark, cold colours of the partly shaded Sennen Cove.

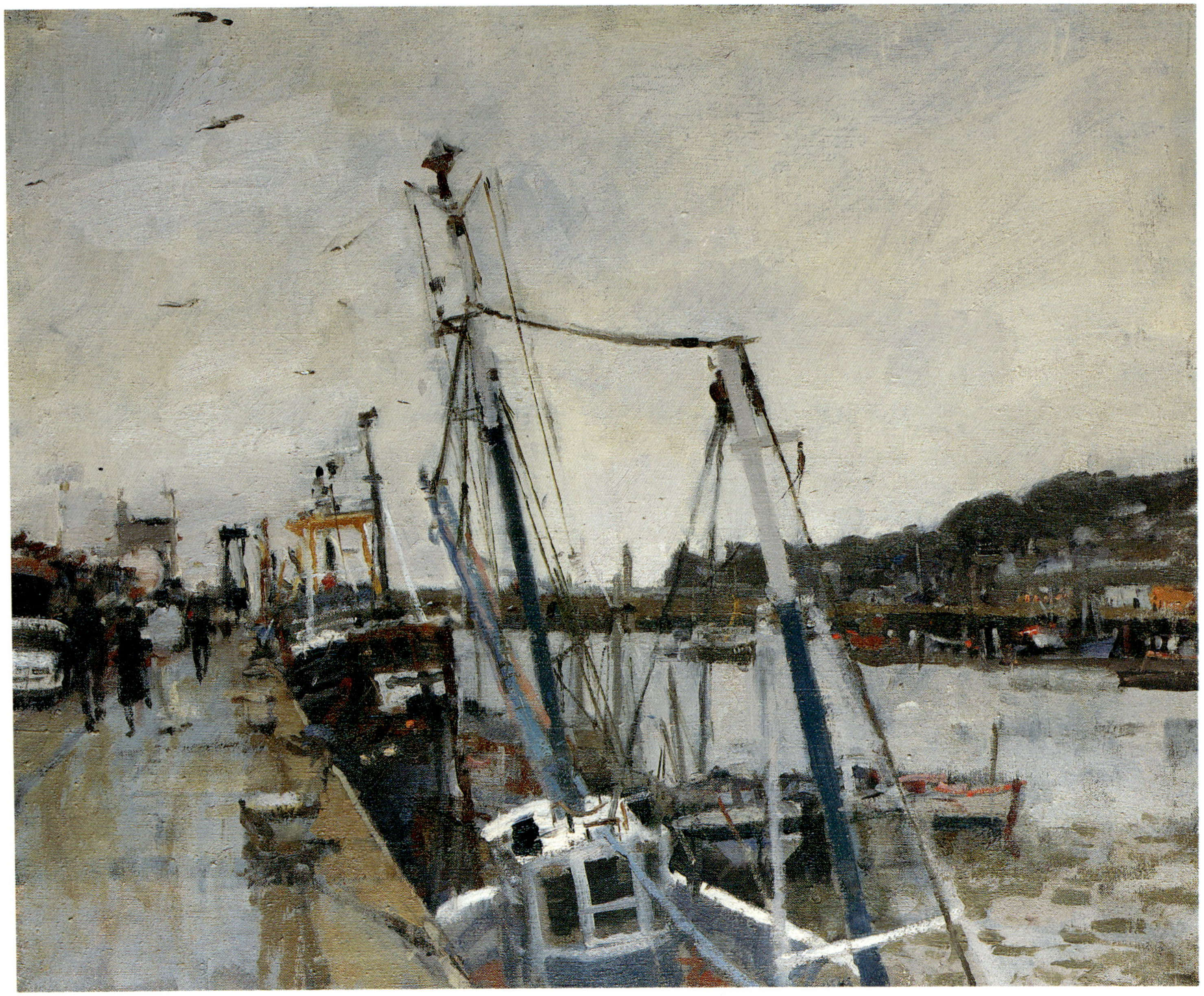

Newlyn, Low Tide
Oil on canvas, 1986. 20 × 24ins.

Newlyn, Low Tide
Travelling along the coast road from Mousehole to Penzance, one passes around the old harbour of Newlyn. Unlike Mousehole, Newlyn is still a busy fishing village. Although the harbour and boats have undergone modernisation, one can still recognise the place from the pictures of the Newlyn School painters, who congregated here in the late nineteenth and early twentieth centuries. On a blustery autumn day, the spirits of Stanhope Forbes and Frank Bramley walk the quays and sands. On their behalf, today's Newlyn life is painted by Ken Howard. Not being a natural seascape painter, he has over the years concentrated on the movement and bustle of harbour life.

'I do like to paint Newlyn and Penzance on silvery days. I love the architectural qualities and marvellous shapes of the boats, and their bright colouring contrasts well with the neutral greys of the harbour and sky. For me this subject lends itself to oil paint and I find that trying to do the boats in watercolour is very much more difficult. I can work on the beach or in the studio in watercolour quite easily and freely. But because boats are such complicated affairs I prefer oil, which can be scraped out and restated. It has the right consistency for the textures of the boats.'

Reminiscent of the pylons and telegraph posts seen in many earlier works, the leaning masts of the trawlers give a dynamic accent to the composition. The steep perspective is stressed by the receding lines of the quayside and the masts of the foreground boat. The forward mast rears up from beneath the artist's area of view. The sharp cut-off line at the bottom of the picture is a reminder that the realist painter selects a picture area which reflects his understanding of our natural angle of vision.

As a young man Howard tussled with the theories of Ruskin and his concept of an all-embracing vision, but seems to have emerged with a firm knowledge of the surrounding area we can consciously take in when focussing on a subject. Tests conducted on fighter pilots have shown that between 60 and 80 degrees angle of vision, the computer-generated images which they see on their visors change dramatically. At 60 degrees the images are described as being like pictures in an art gallery. At 80 degrees they are transformed to virtual reality, a panoramic scene of which the pilot is a part.

Sixty degrees is probably the sort of angle of vision most artists choose. This can be expanded or reduced for pictorial purposes – like fitting a wide-angled or telephoto lens to a camera – but on the whole the spectator tends to feel comfortable with the visible area that camera companies choose for their 'standard' lenses. For a painter of the natural world, this can be an important consideration, and Howard's intuitive sense of the correct angle of vision is one reason his pictures are so accommodating to the eye. In this work, the cut-off point is a true one and not simply a pictorial device. It does, however, contribute to the looming perspective and thus to the drama of the subject.

Sennen, High Summer
The most ambitious beach painting of the 1980s, both in scale and composition, *Sennen, High Summer* was worked and reworked in the studio over several months. Its composition was radically altered some four months into the process. To attempt to incorporate over fifty clearly defined figures within a single canvas must have been an immense task. That the result is such a fine achievement is a tribute to the natural resilience of an artist who now feels he works best in the spontaneity of the moment. Although the figures are spread right across the picture-plane, itself tilted upwards by the high viewpoint, the linking forms of windbreaks and parasols bind the image and form a subtle and satisfying composition.

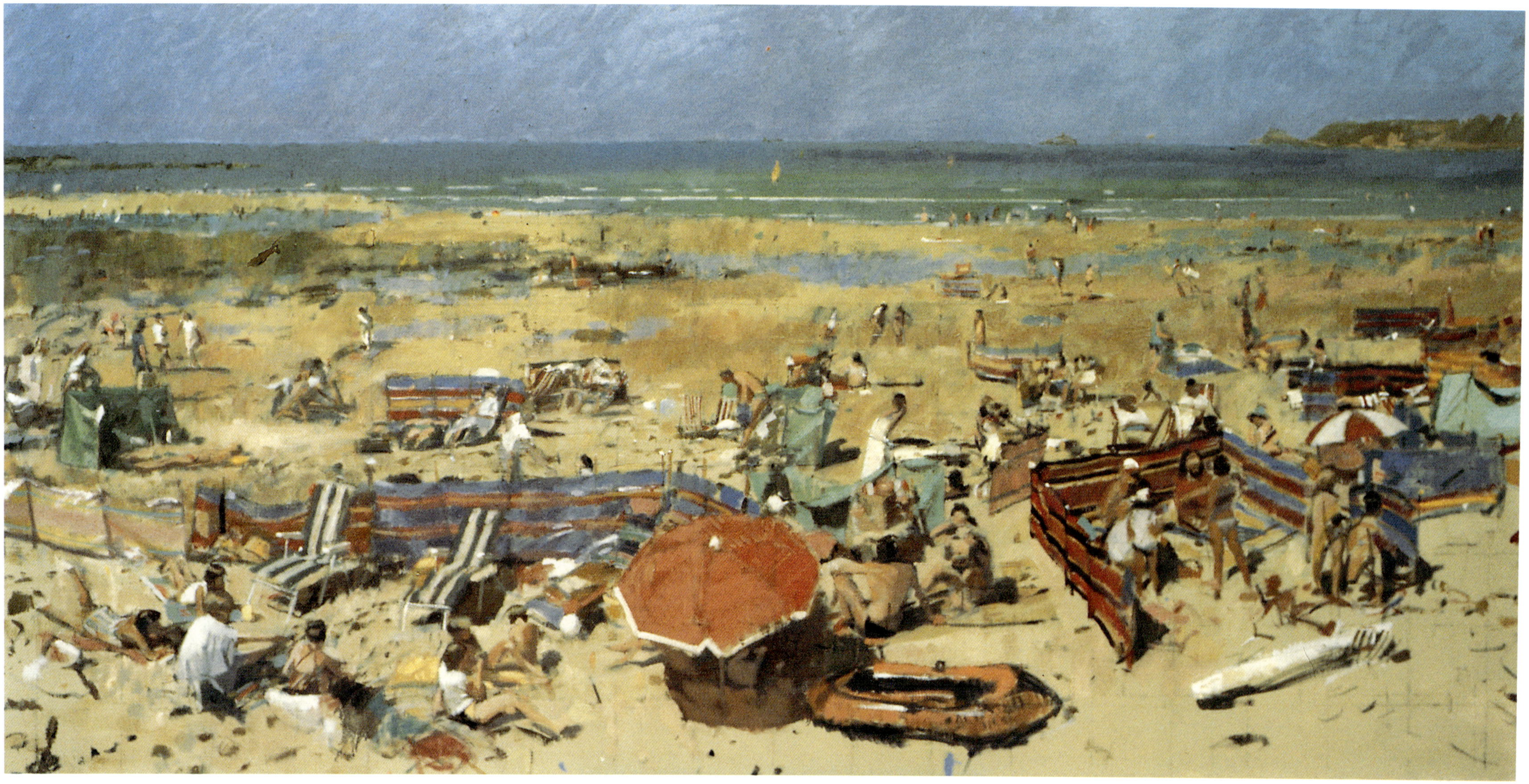

Sennen, High Summer
Oil on canvas, 1988. 56 × 112ins.

The two views of Sennen Cove illustrated thus far have been comparatively narrow-angled glimpses back from beach to cliff. Here the artist has chosen what is for him an unusual viewpoint – one which commands a wide angle of sight. This broad vista Howard has painted echoes the way we would take in the bright, spacious scene if we were to stand in the same position, gazing down on the scattered sunbathers. The artist is being true not so much to any scientific theory, but to the response the subject dictates:

'When I saw this subject from the cafeteria overlooking Sennen beach, I knew immediately that it needed a vast panoramic canvas to get the view. None of it was worked on the spot – I made studies on a series of small panels and also some photographs for reference. In fact, once you know that I used photographs, you can see the evidence. There are various figures whose movement seems to have instantaneously stopped, something that only happens with the camera. This is why I don't really like working from photographs. I hope that eventually I'll be able to paint a big picture like this without needing to lean on such things. In other words I would pick all the figures up from drawings. If you draw when the figure is moving you can only get the essential down on the paper, but you also get the suggestion of movement. You certainly don't get what I would call photographic detail.

'I like the sense of depth in the composition. Firstly all the foreground, then moving back to the great sweep of Sennen beach at low tide, then the sea and then right back to the far horizon. I tried to get much of the balance of the composition through the placing of figures, although the red umbrella in the foreground is the focal point that holds it all together. I wanted to take the eye on a visual walk through the figures, through the windbreaks, right down through the beach, down to the water's edge and then off and away.'

Although the struggle to complete the composition was a long one, it is arguable whether detailed drawings would have helped. Howard would not suggest it himself, but one feels that his long apprenticeship – drawing for doctors and directories, regiments and presidents – was enough drawing for this painter.

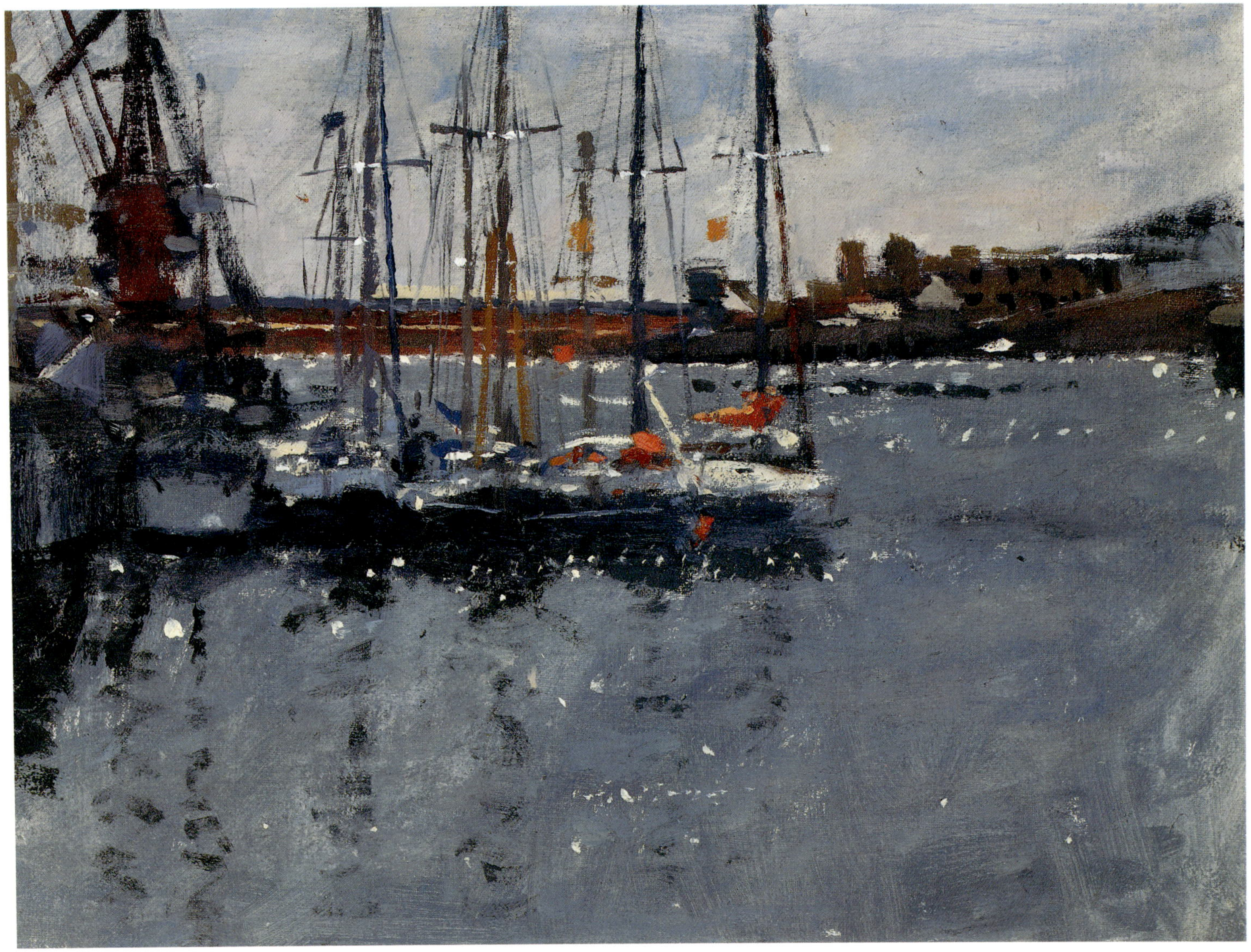

Newlyn, Summer Morning
Oil on panel, 1988. 8 × 10ins.

Newlyn, Summer Morning
This delightful small panel features the leisure side of Newlyn's boating activities, seen in the bright light of morning. In that it is a scene of buildings, quays and boats, painted *contre-jour* with light flickering on the water, it is reminiscent of the artist's Venetian work. Like the view from the Riva degli Schiavoni, this panel is painted with a restricted palette, the predominant blue only relieved by brief passages of red and touches of yellow. This essentially primary palette is characteristic of much of the artist's work in Newlyn harbour:

'When I'm painting indoors my palette is nearly always based on the earth colours. Outside, and particularly at Newlyn, I tend more towards the primaries. I think that a subject must speak to you and in many ways it will dictate the palette. I don't go to a subject with a set concept of the palette I will use, but over the years I have found that different subjects demand different palettes. Although I have used red and yellow here, the image I finished up with is still about tones of blue. In this respect, an advantage of oil paint over watercolour is that you can go on working at it to get a more exact tonal value, even in one wet. Although I do work tonally in watercolour, it is inevitably done more intuitively.'

This is the last of Howard's *plein air* panel paintings to be illustrated in this book, for we are shortly to enter the studio. These spontaneous paintings are invariably handled with natural fluency, as if they are the artist's true eyes. They are typically made independent of any planned composition. Even when they do relate to a studio canvas, they are usually such complete images that one hesitates to describe them as sketches or studies. This is undoubtedly how the artist intended them to be. It is no longer within the ethos of the man to throw away such an opportunity, to grant time to a picture that will never be seen by anyone else but him.

Sennen Evening II
'Because West Penwith is a small land mass surrounded by sea, one gets very unusual and beautiful light effects. This is the time of day I love most on the beach, when the sun is sparkling on the sea. It is at a time like this when it is most like Venice.'

Here indeed, offset against the highlights on the water, are the warm, mid-toned sky and the richly coloured shadows that were noted in the Venetian watercolours.

This studio-painted canvas shows the darkening mass of the cliffs to the south-west of Sennen Cove, set into the distance by aerial perspective that truly seems to be shaped out of light itself. The entire composition relies on the perspective of light – a light which almost envelops the limbs of some figures, as they walk into the sun's rays. One lightbreak provides a sharp accent of colour in what is a largely tonal arrangement of shapes.

The genesis of this image occurred one evening when, as the shadows lengthened, Howard had been about to leave the beach. Rather as he had spotted the *Racing Dinghies* at Marazion, here at Sennen he had suddenly realised the possibilities of an image he was about to participate in. Quickly gathering together his materials, he made a rapid watercolour of figures striding towards the sun.

Both the initial sketch and this resulting canvas provide a memorable and appropriate image with which to conclude the Cornish coast paintings of Ken Howard. It will be interesting to see how they are to evolve. It is perhaps the Newlyn series which the artist feels most clearly have potential for development. The beach paintings are already a major achievement.

Sennen Evening II
Oil on canvas, 1990. 40 × 48ins.

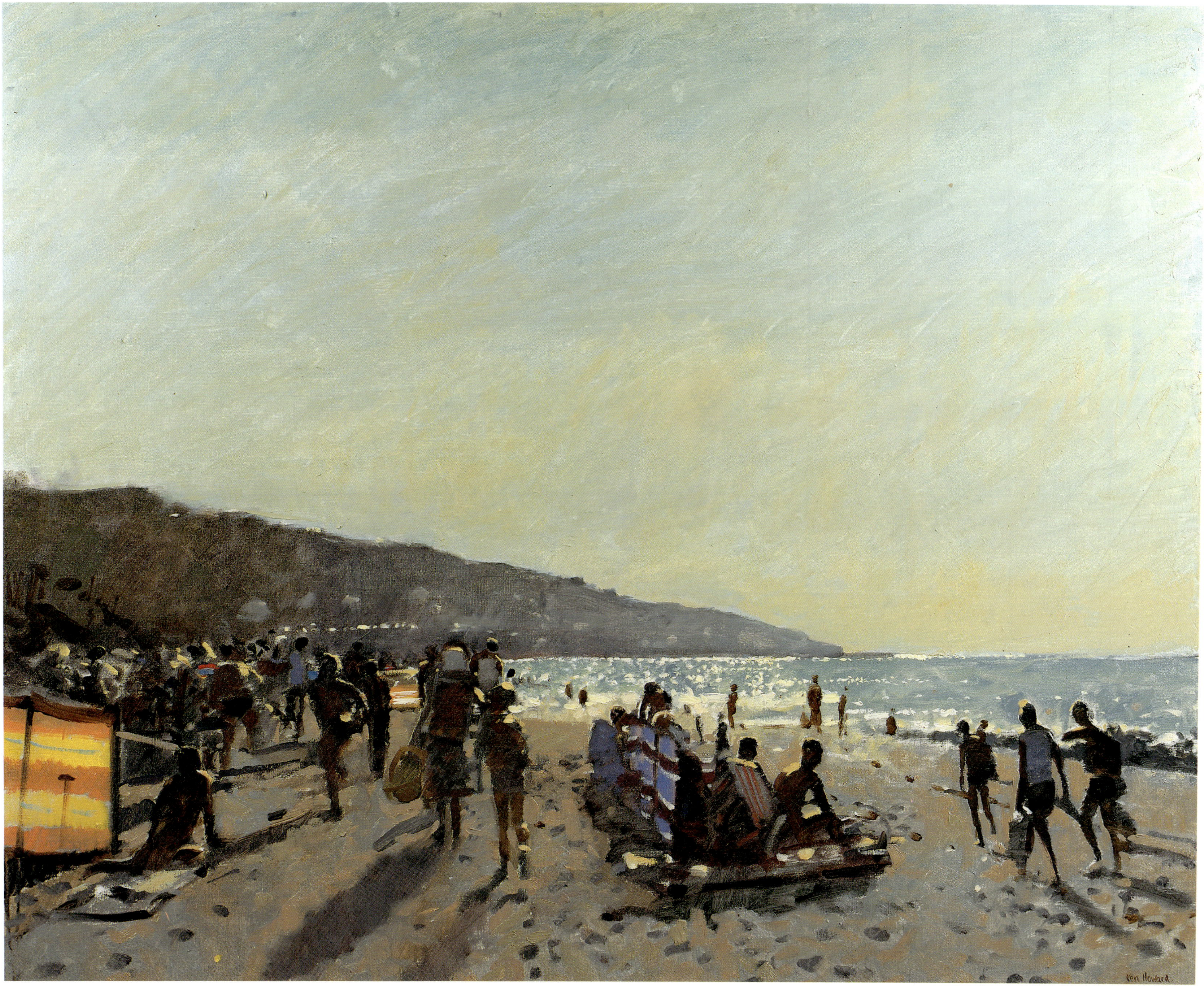
Ken Howard

The Studio

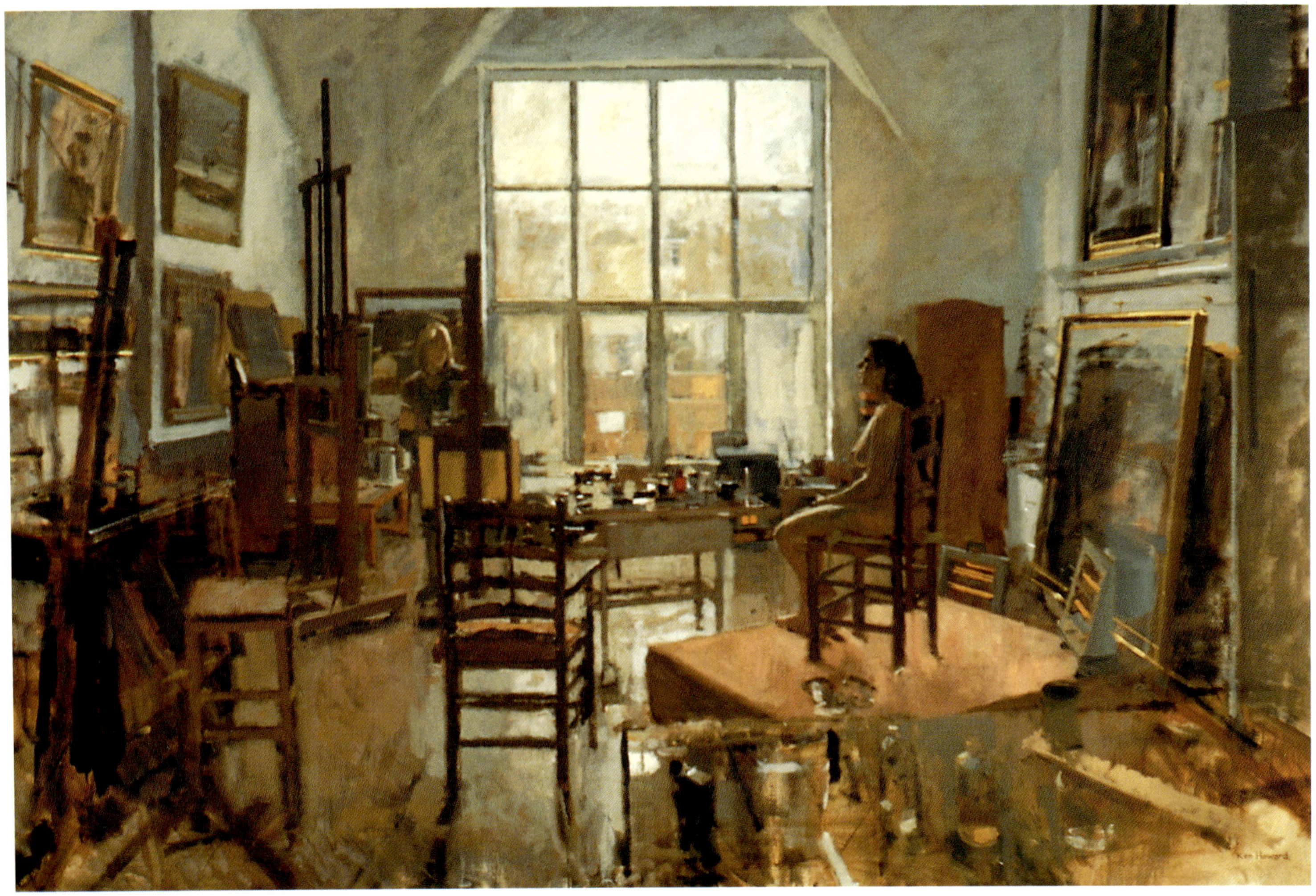

The Studio
Oil on canvas, 1980–1. 60 × 72ins (RA 1981, No 648).

The Studio
Ken Howard had been painting interiors at odd times over his career, but not as a consistent theme:

'My first studio picture was painted when we were set the subject of artist and model for our final-year set-piece at the Royal College. I painted it in the loft of my parents' home in Cricklewood. It was a small loft with a skylight in it, which we had converted into a studio of sorts. I later showed a picture of the Royal College life class at the Academy. After that I didn't paint another studio picture for a long time, maybe because I worked in such small spaces.'

On 1 January 1975 Howard moved into the studio at South Bolton Gardens. Although he now had access to, and made use of, a superb studio, he continued to travel widely on commission, finding new subject matter in countries from Cyprus to Hong Kong. He describes the recognition of the studio interior as a potential subject as a moment of revelation:

'Having looked at that studio for four or five years I came out of the bedroom one morning and suddenly saw it as a subject. I thought, why am I wandering around the world in search of subjects, when there is a whole world in here? It was as clear as that – and I began to paint.

'At that stage I used to work on the paintings much longer than I do now. I pushed them around and changed them about, building the composition as I went along. I would move chairs, bring things in, take things out – not only in the painting, but actually in the room. I came to see my studio pictures as interior landscapes, through which you can walk. Instead of walking amongst trees or past water, in my studio landscape you can move past ladder-back chairs and over shiny floors. You can explore areas that have got lots of little bits and pieces on them – in this case the foreground with all the turps and oil bottles.

'From the start these big studio pictures took a lot of pulling together. No doubt this is because my idea of a good composition has always been one in which each part works in itself, each part works in relation to each other part and each part works in relation to the whole. The bigger the canvas, the more difficult it is to make that work. With this picture I can remember labouring for days on the grey of the background wall, trying to get its tone to balance with those of the light coming through the window and the dark of the girl's hair.'

One of the first of the studio interiors, this wide-angled perspective from the back of the room shows Christa Gaa painting the model. It already bears many of the hallmarks of the series of canvases which were to follow. The 'interior landscape' is already conceived and expressed through the artist's instinctive understanding of the perspective of space. Linear and aerial perspective have already been noted in his work, but the ability to construct an absolutely believable space is most notably visible in these interior settings.

The spectator is immediately sure, not only of his own place in the room, but also of the exact positions of all the items of studio paraphernalia before him. To establish such a suspension of disbelief does mean relying on classical linear perspective, but only becomes convincing through the artist's skills in the disposition of shapes and the combination of tones. Although tighter in handling and composition than much of the later work we shall see, *The Studio* does point the way forward.

Self-Portrait at Oriel

The painting that won first prize in the 1982 Hunting Group Awards recalls major pictures of the artist's earlier years. It has the limited earth palette, the flat, centralised composition and forceful verticals of *The North Door, Westminster Abbey*, *Southall 2: Silver Morning* and *Ulster Crucifixion*. Looking forward, it also includes elements which would recur in studio paintings throughout the next decade: the finely observed foreground arrangement of jars and bottles, the reflection in the studio mirror and the view out of the window that brings the outside world into what might otherwise be the very enclosed world of the studio.

One senses that at this stage in his career, before election to the Royal Academy, the artist was still driven by the need to paint major pictures – literally masterpieces. This is one of them, and many months of labour were absorbed in producing this powerful and striking image:

'Knowing that the judging committee included a number of Academicians, I was greatly encouraged by the prize. But I am aware that I have a tendency to be too conscientious about pictures. They said that about me when I was at Hornsey, and when I started the studio pictures I was still overworking them. But sometimes a certain sort of toughness came out of this, and I think this picture had this quality.

'It was on the easel in the studio for a period of a year and I would have blasts at it, working for several days and then leaving it to dry, then having another go. If it were X-rayed there would be a completely different composition underneath. The mirror got smaller and smaller. To begin with it was quite large and there was none of the studio around, but gradually it was honed down. One of the things I admire about Giacometti's paintings is the way he makes the figures become more and more taut, shrinking and paring them down to an absolute state of tension. I would like to feel that sometimes I do that myself, pulling everything in and gradually tightening it up.

'I had an incredibly hard job getting the tone pitched correctly in order to get the sensation of the light coming from the window into the mirror. Looking at it in the mirror the room did seem very dark. Consequently I kept painting the tone of the picture too low, then bringing it up and getting it too high. Eventually I arrived at something like the balance I was looking for.'

The studio at South Bolton Gardens once belonged to that revered painter of London society, Sir William Orpen. It was he who named it Oriel, after the house in Ireland in which he was born, and he lived there until the day he died. During his occupancy he bought the studio next door and made one large space, although the dividing wall has since been re-erected. Ken Howard's studio is perpetually bathed in true, cool north light. Thus Oriel is ideal for the portrait painter, who needs a consistent, even light. The sun only enters the room late on summer evenings, in contrast to the warm, seaside light that floods St Clement's Studio in Cornwall.

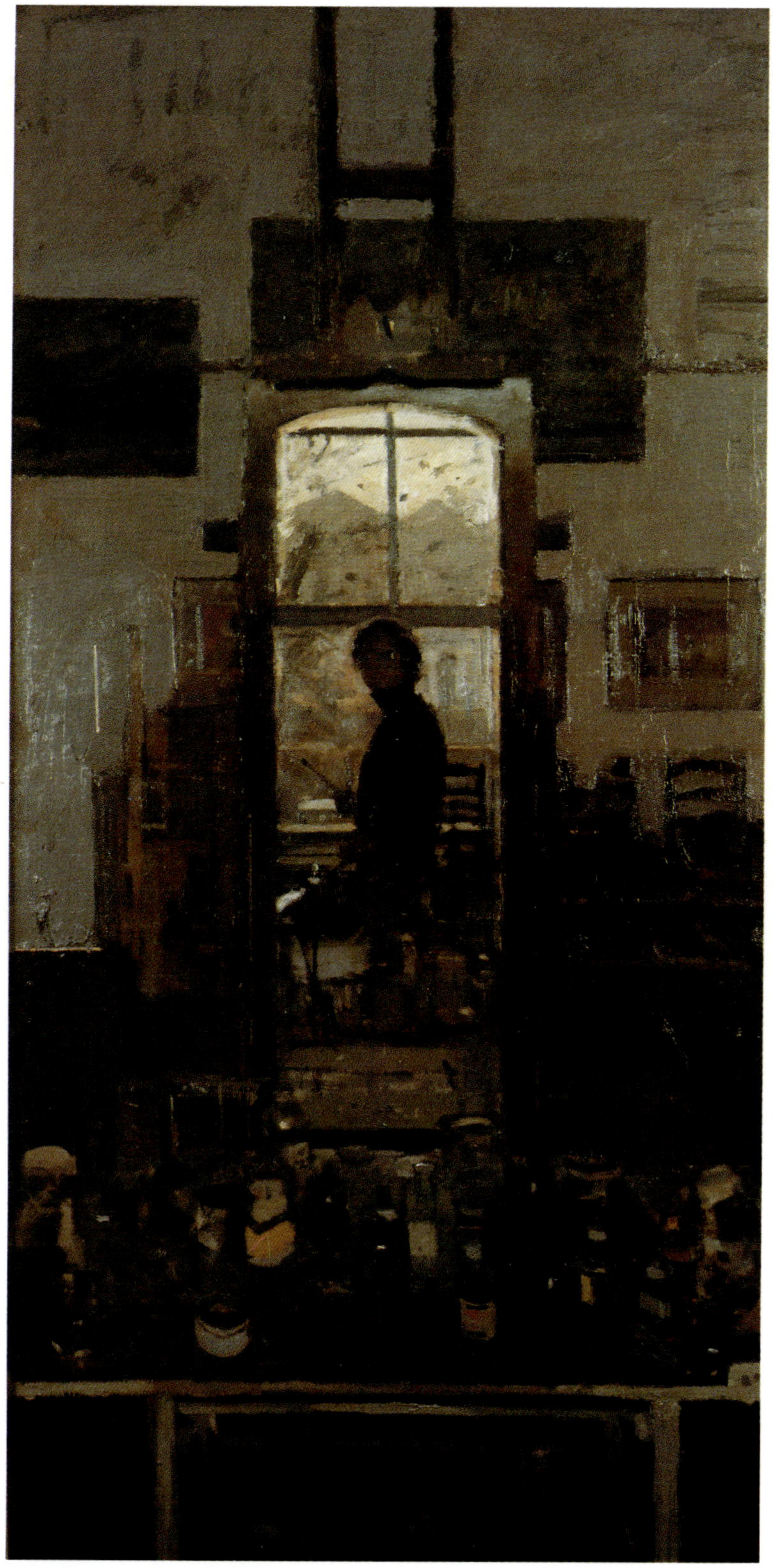

Self-Portrait at Oriel
Oil on canvas, 1980–2. 72 × 36ins.

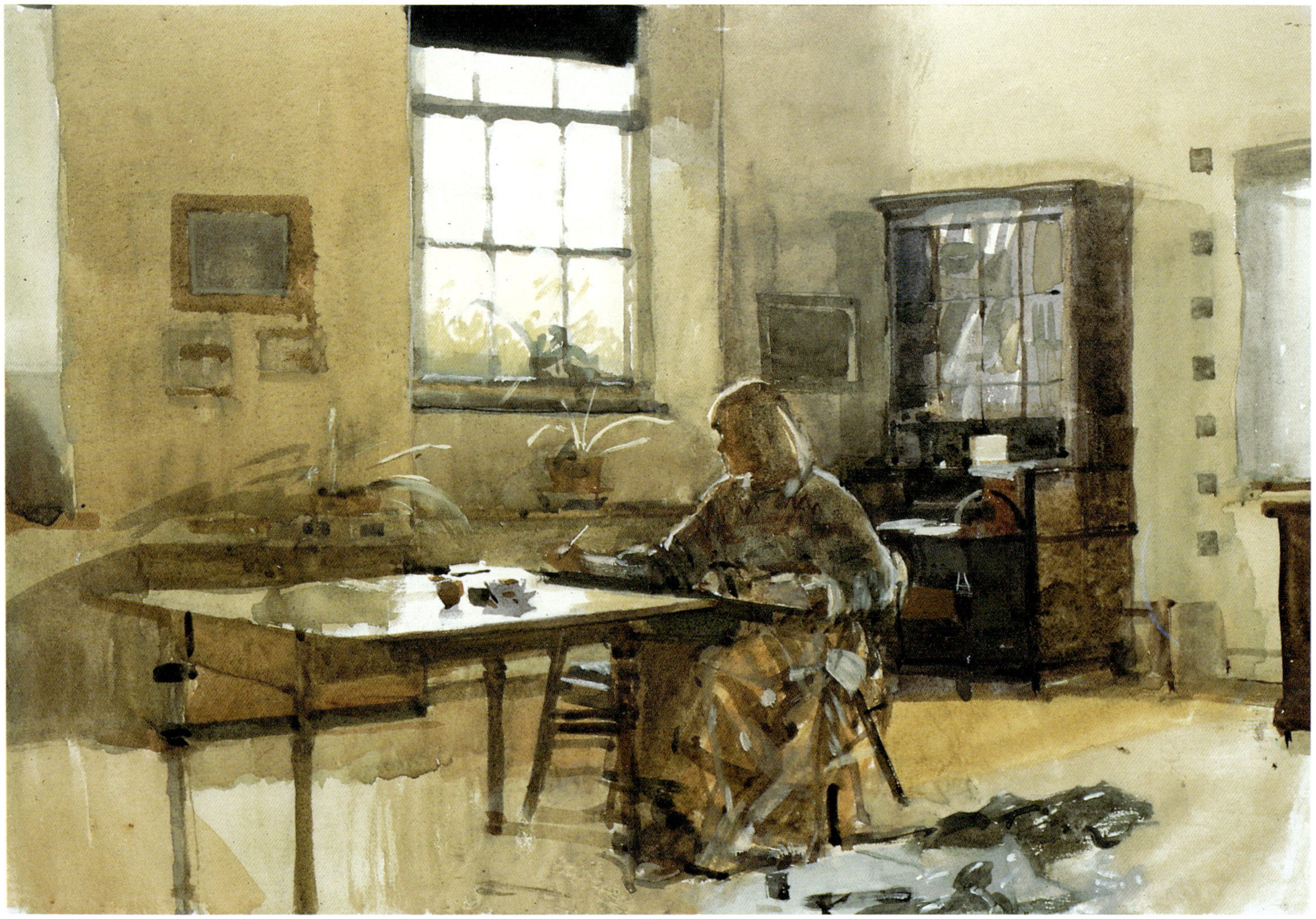

Christa Gaa at Mousehole
Watercolour, c 1985. 15 × 22ins.

Christa Gaa at Mousehole

Here the artist has employed the transparency of watercolour to capture the warm light suffusing the living-room of the house at Mousehole. Although the tonal range of the picture is quite wide, the washes have been lyrically, almost tenderly laid in, perhaps as a response to the choice of model.

Howard's close connections with the Cornish village date back to 1955, when his sister married a Mousehole fisherman. In 1961 his parents moved to the village. After they had both died he sold their cottage in order to acquire St Clement's Hall, which had come onto the market. Named after St Clement's Isle, which lies a few hundred yards off the coast, the new building had great potential for two painters.

The house had been converted from a school and the thirty by sixty feet village hall, now attached to it, had already been used as a vast studio. During its occupancy in the 1930s by the painter, George Lambourn, the studio was also sometimes used as a theatre.

Until the installation of central heating in the studio, Ken Howard and Christa Gaa worked in the spacious living-room in the winter months. South facing, this room receives a beautiful warm light, reflected off the sea. Not surprisingly the ever-changing light effects became the principal concern of many of the pictures Howard has painted, and continues to paint, in this room:

'You can almost see the light move around the room like the hands of a clock. This watercolour was done in the winter. Thus Chrissie is sitting painting a still-life with a blanket around her. I was pleased with the way I caught the sense of her. If you look closely there are no eyes or mouth, and only just about a nose. Otherwise there is just a bit of light catching the back of her hair, giving a certain halo around her head. But the basic shape of her head – that's Chrissie's head.'

Christa Gaa at Sampford Spiney

This canvas was painted at the Dartmoor studio which Howard had created from a derelict school house. Although they were eventually to sell up in favour of St Clement's Hall, he remembers that, on her arrival from Germany, Christa found the place to her liking:

'She fell in love with it straight away. The landscape was hers for a start – the rolling moor and always-changing skyline attracted her very much as a landscape painter. After the first year or two we really only kept the studio to paint landscapes in the winter, and I very nearly became a landscape painter again up on the moor.

'The studio itself was a lovely interior – not vast, but large enough for us both to work in. It had high, church-like windows. In this painting I was quite pleased with the scale of the figure to the interior – quite big but not too big. Like tone, scale is very important. In recent years I have felt less need to push figures around to get it correct – it seems more intuitive. But at the time I painted this picture I often had to work hard to get the scale.

'As with all painting, change one part and you've got to change the lot. Whether it's colour, tone or shape, every colour, every tone, every shape depends on every other one. Radically change one and everything else has adjusted to fit. It's similar with scale. I used to change the size of the figure and then end up changing the size of the entire interior. Sometimes I would work on a canvas so long that the painting became a sort of tortured surface and lost any appeal, any touching quality. Eventually I found that the crucial thing governing correct scale was the size of the figure in relation to the overall shape of the canvas.'

As well as getting the scale right, and hence the perspective of space, Howard's inborn ability to capture the look and bearing of a person has again produced a fine likeness of Christa Gaa.

Christa Gaa at Sampford Spiney
Oil on canvas, 1984–5. 40 × 48ins (RA 1985, No 613).

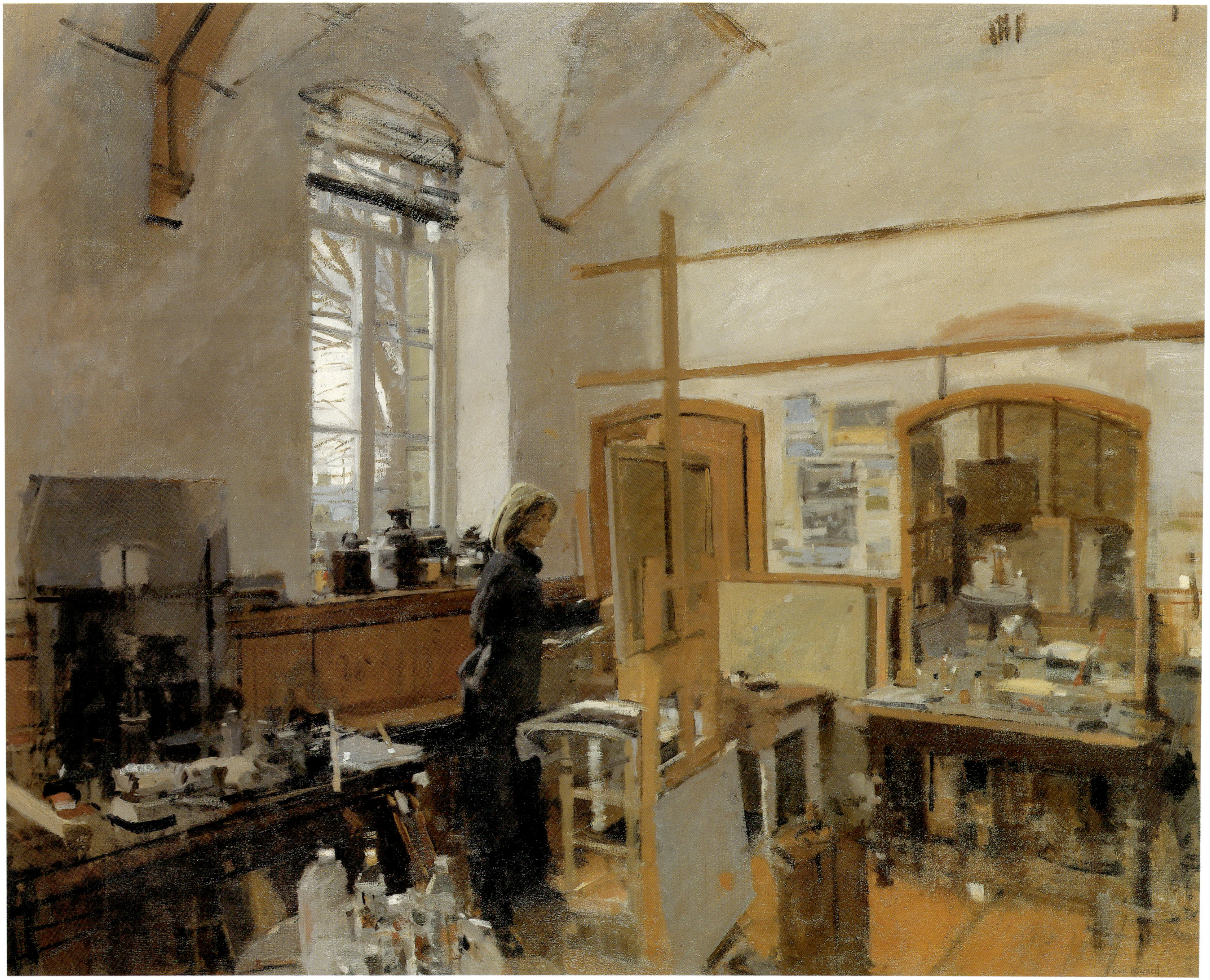

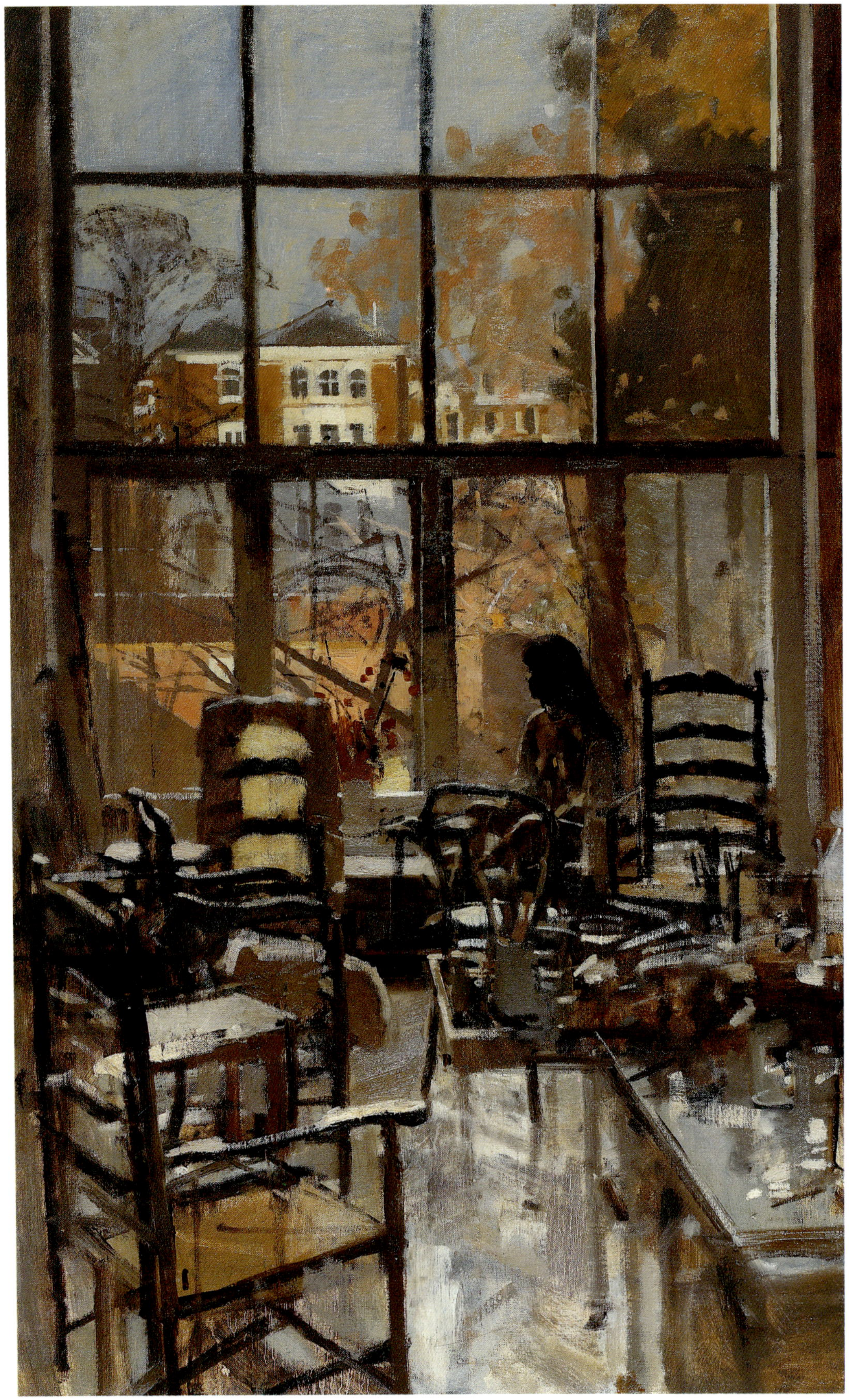

Winter Sunlight at South Bolton Gardens
The mid-1980s saw the growing use of the London and Cornwall studios as settings for the nude or draped model. Virtually without exception the model fits into and animates the studio interior in an easy and natural manner, as though she was always meant to be there. One reason for this is that Howard only rarely adopts the common practice of portraitists – painting the model and her surroundings on separate occasions. Just as he would not think of inserting an imaginary tree into a landscape, he generally manages to shun this convention, governed as it is by practical considerations. Thus the whole subject is always before him, each element having a bearing on the rest of the composition.

This painting of the London studio beautifully captures the cool, bright winter sun, as it glances off an assembly of chairs, catches the lightbreak of a silk shirt and casts a deep reflected light into the room. With increasing inventiveness, the many assorted items of studio artefacts and furniture provided an ever-varied interior landscape for the model to inhabit. Although the artist has said he would never dream of painting a studio without a figure, the sheer beauty of these interiors in the series of large canvases which were to follow is one of the pinnacles of his achievement.

This particular painting is something of a chairscape. The bright, sweeping brush-strokes picking out arms and ladder-backs are the dominant lights in the interior. They arrest our eyes only briefly, however, as we follow the model's gaze out to the sunlit urban scene:

'At this stage I used to glaze quite a lot at the end of the picture. Rather than use ordinary varnish I would often use a thin glaze – one of the transparent earth colours like raw umber, burnt sienna or burnt umber – which would act as a varnish and bring back the darks without being too varnishy. It also acted as a unifying colour, which helped just subtly to pull the tones and colour together a bit more, and knocked the edge off the highlights. I think highlights are very important because in a sense they bring the source of light down into the room. They're the reflection of the source of light, but obviously you can make them so light and jumpy that they don't fit within the context of the picture.

'Sometimes I would then work on the picture once more, as I did with this one. After the final glazing I heightened the outside view, bringing back the pure colour – probably because it is an outside view. One can't imagine an Impressionist picture being glazed – or indeed one of my beach paintings – because somehow they need that clarity of light which you get out of nature. In the interior the glazing brings out something of that atmosphere of being inside.'

Winter Sunlight at South Bolton Gardens
Oil on canvas, 1986. 40 × 24ins.

Saskia at St Clement's Hall
'I well remember when as a boy I first found this studio. I had cycled down from London to Land's End with two friends and we were just starting back home. We got to Mousehole and walked up the hill from the village. I saw old Lambourn, the painter who owned it, sitting at the back door of the studio looking like a latter-day Augustus John. All sorts of thoughts were going through my head and one of these was that I was going to do it, I was going to be an artist.'

This is one of the earlier St Clement's Hall pictures, painted within two years of the move there. The electric fire testifies that it was long before the introduction of central heating into the vast studio space. Howard was later to build a large balcony at one end of the room and over the years introduced considerable quantities of the familiar studio paraphernalia. At that time, however, the room seemed extremely empty and he divided the space into sections with temporary screens. Several sections could be set up with studio props and he would often be at work simultaneously on different canvases. Here the artist has chosen a simple composition in a warm alcove.

The sun floods in through the window, silhouetting Saskia's angular pose and catching her silk shirt. The shirt acts as a device to bring the light into the room and around the figure. There is also the lightbreak of a thin white sheet against the window, softening a light effect which is fully understood and subtly conveyed.

In a number of the studio pictures a clue appears to tell the observer something more about their theme. With his innate ability to get a likeness, Howard's models are always depicted as individuals – unlike the classical life model – and sometimes a visual reference to the model will appear. In this painting, the clue also illuminates the studio routine:

'Saskia was one of my first models when I came down to Cornwall. She was a sculptor and a very good model. There's a backgammon board in the front of this picture and Saskia, who lived in Greece for many years, is a very considerable backgammon player. At this time we used to start at seven in the morning, which I still do in the summer. We would break at ten and while we were having a cup of tea and a bit of breakfast we would have a quick game of backgammon. We still play, maybe once a month, and she thrashes me even though I think I'm not a bad player. If I didn't paint I think I would become a continuous backgammon player. Like with painting, I suppose it's a matter of always wanting to improve.'

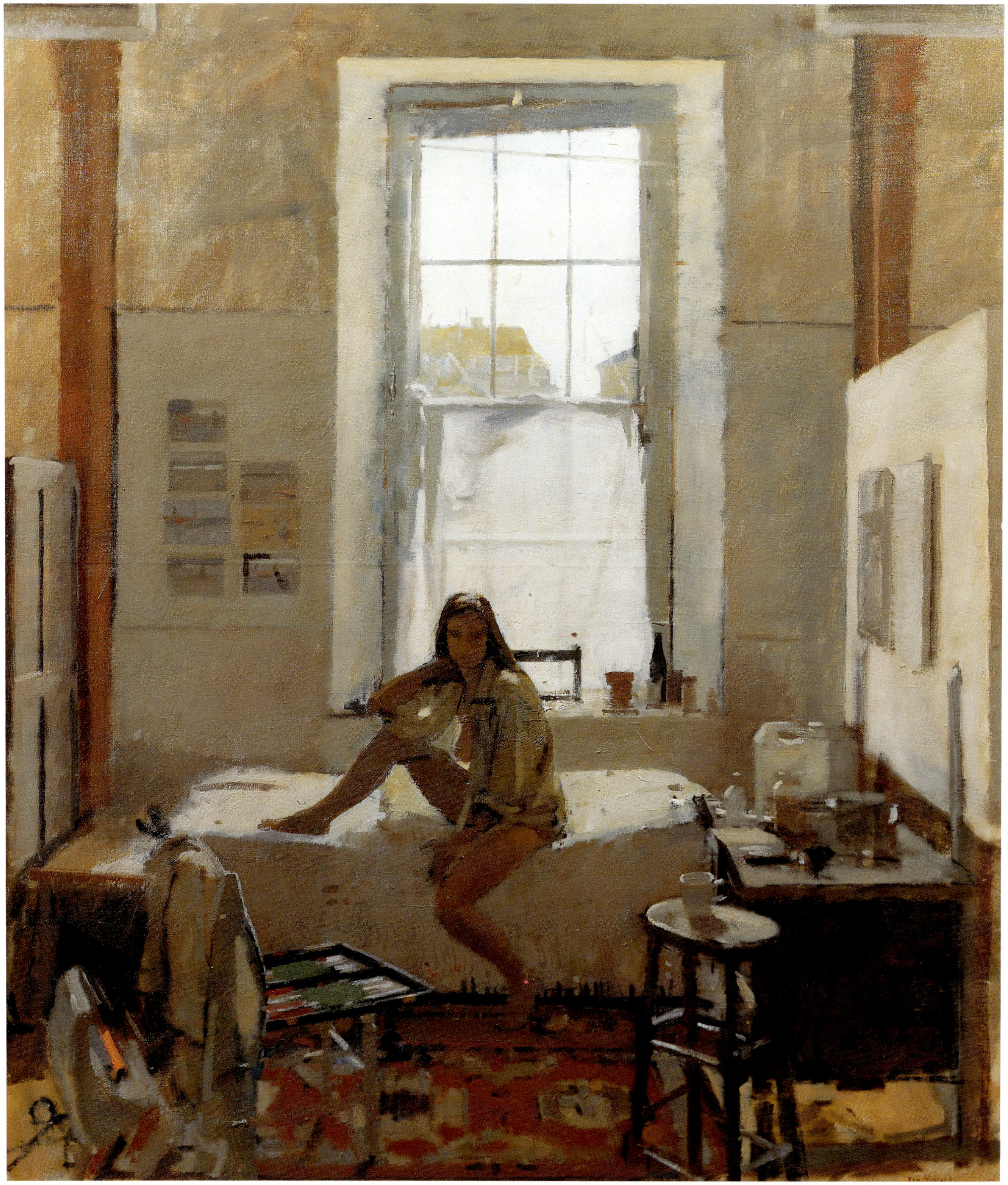

Saskia at St Clement's Hall
Oil on canvas, 1986. 48 × 40ins.

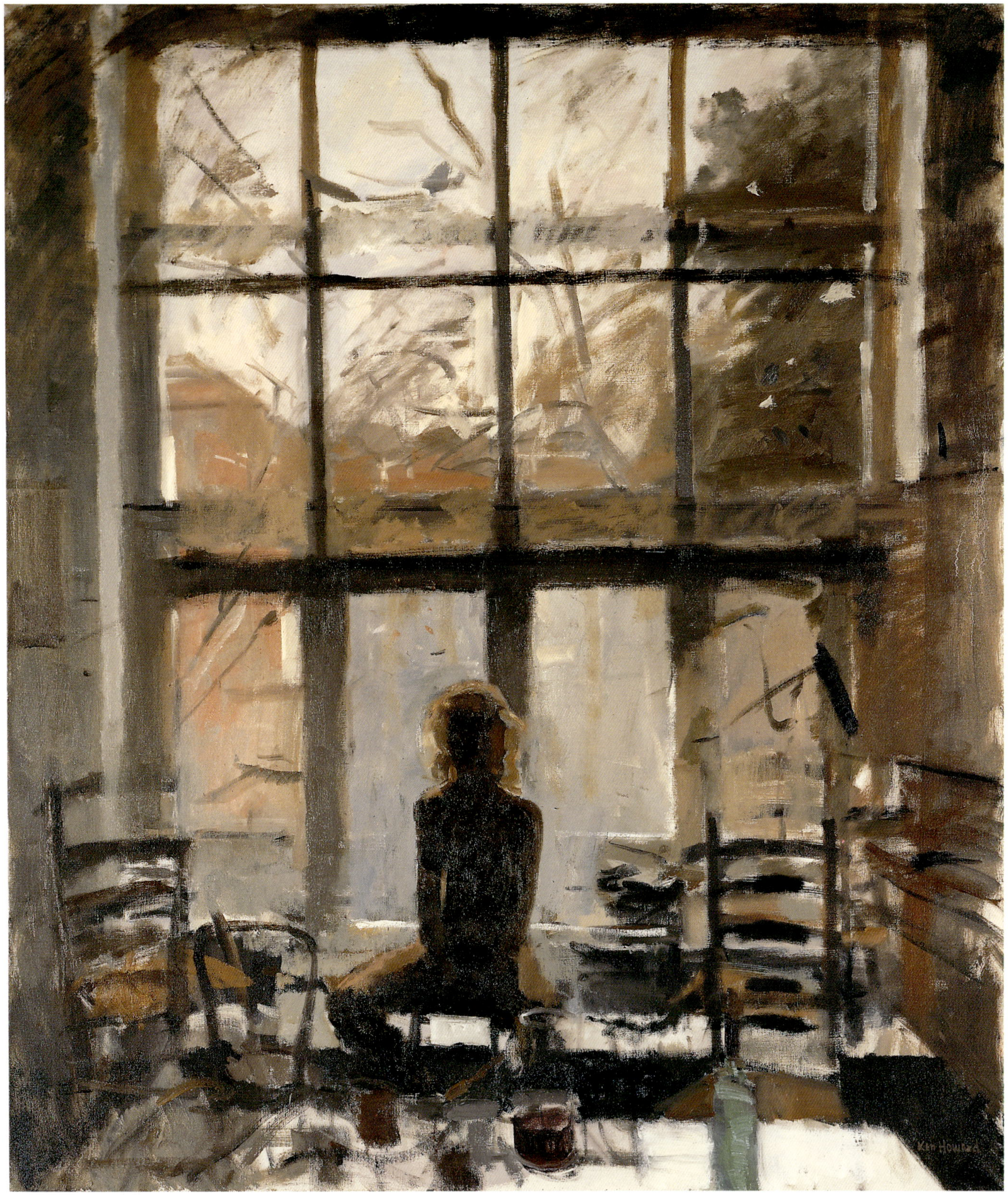

The Sparkasse Nude
Oil on canvas, 1984. 48 × 40ins.

The Sparkasse Nude

'This canvas of Marika at South Bolton Gardens was the first full-scale sketch I made for a large painting – that of *Marika and the Orpen Paint Box*. Marika is an excellent model, by profession a dancer, who I have worked with for a long time. A lot of my London models have been dancers. I think I use them because they can stand very well, which is not easy on a long pose. They also have a fantastic sense of movement and are generally relaxed in the way they pose. Even in this sketch I think you can see the way that Marika is sitting on a stool by the window is very relaxed and natural. It is just as if she is looking at you and talking to you while she is posing.

'In fact I'm not very good at talking when I paint and therefore I usually have music playing in the studio. In a sense music separates you from the model and from any involvement with her, leaving you to see her simply as a beautiful object. Although the model is very alive and full of movement, I like to keep that certain distance between us and to look at her rather as at a still-life.'

While the artist clearly responds individually to his different models, and portrays them as single characters, this notion of the dispassionate, objective painter is something he shares with Degas and Sickert. It is also in tune with the realist spirit of Howard's art.

Of the two canvases reproduced here, this sketch probably contains the more vivid likeness of the model. Even without knowing her, it is possible to feel her particular presence more strongly here than in the more formal painting. It is also plausible to speculate that she – or the artist, or both – might have sipped red wine from the carafe on the table. What could be seen as an anecdotal touch is more truly an example of the real life that is caught in Howard's direct oil studies. In the finished painting, the carafe settles into a still-life, or 'tablescape', in which the accompanying glass seems untouched.

The sketch is a *tour de force* of painterly brushwork. The equivalent in its way of the beach studies on panel, it conveys all the excitement of the artist's reaction to his *contre-jour* subject.

'I did it in one wet, straight from the word go, with a palette of earth colours. When it was finished I felt straight away that there was something about it, which very often a sketch has and a finished picture doesn't – to some extent like Constable's large oil sketches for his six-footers.

'I kept the canvas for some time. Then a friend who has a gallery in Basel wrote, suggesting I should send something to the Sparkasse Bank competition at Karlsruhe, which that year had the theme of a figure in an interior. I didn't think my work would go down well in Germany. But we were going over at the time, so I took this picture and sent it down on the train to a friend of Chrissie's in Karlsruhe, who would hand it in on the appointed day. I then forgot all about it until a couple of months later the phone rang, and Chrissie came in and said I had won the critics' prize – there was also a public prize – at the Sparkasse exhibition. If it had been in England, I think I would have been more likely to get the public prize than the critic's prize. But I suppose the sketch had a breadth about it that accorded with a German concept of figurative painting.'

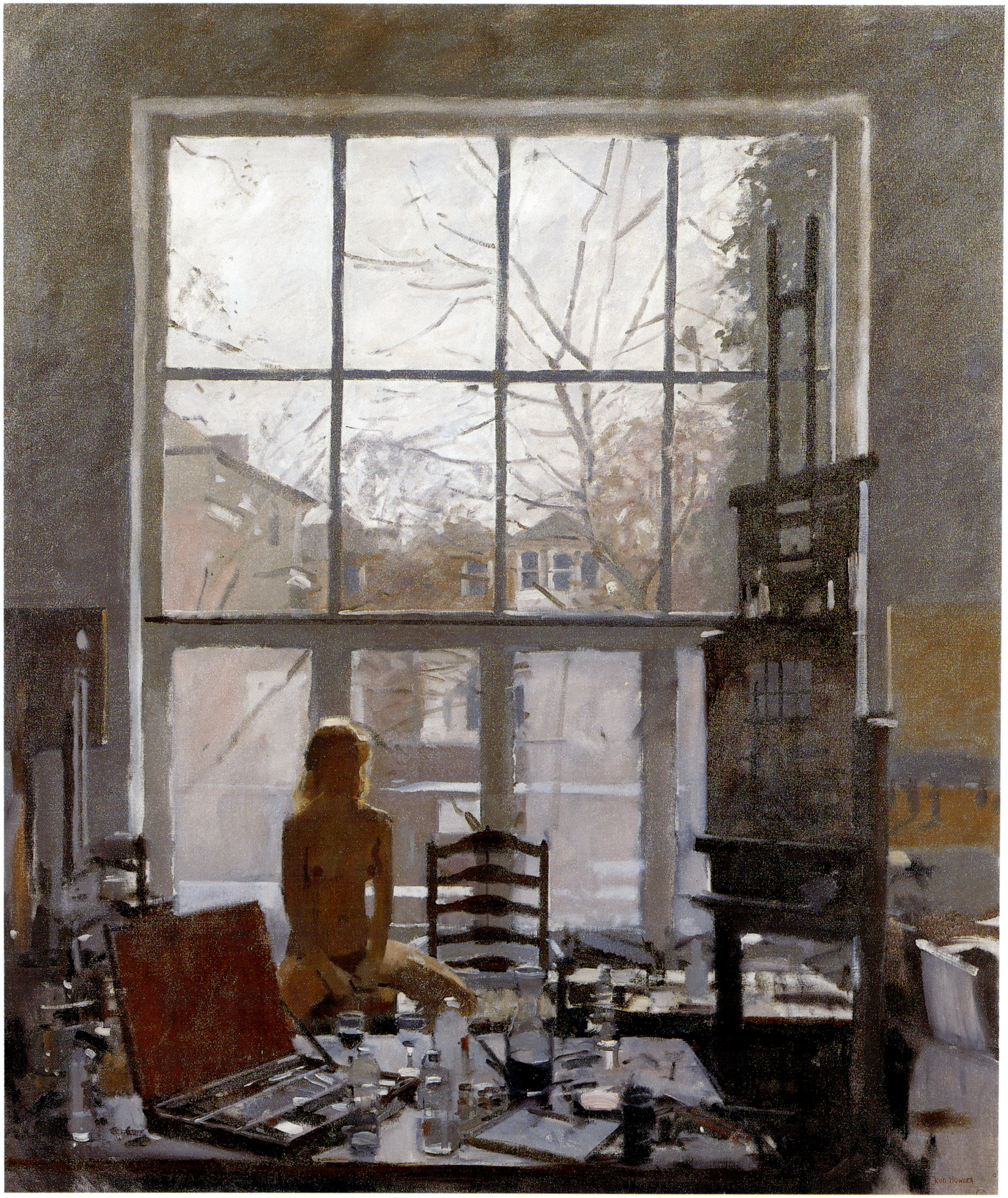

Marika and the Orpen Paint Box
Described in the 1985 Summer Exhibition listing as *Marika and the* **Open** *Paint Box*, this composition has been formalised and rearranged from the simple, almost artless conception of the sketch. In addition to broadening the angle of view and setting the model off-centre, Howard has included in a splendidly studied foreground 'tablescape' the open paint box of Sir William Orpen.

'The paint box is the one shown in a photograph of Orpen, that was reproduced in a book called *Mirror of an Age*. He is in the army, sitting painting in a French town, and this paint box is down by his side. It's a very beautiful box. It even has a brass plaque that reads "William Orpen, 8 South Bolton Gardens", and it's a great thrill for me to have it in the studio. I don't use it, although I suspect he might have liked the idea that it was still being used.

'In moving things around a bit, I made the ladder-back chair a key note and balanced Marika with the easel on the right-hand side. This is an example of the continuous struggle to relate the inside of the room to the outside. I was particularly trying to relate the tone and colour of the wall around the big window to the outside view itself. I was in danger of overstating the exterior to the extent that it would jump forward into the room. It sounds quite simple to do and I can never understand why it doesn't get easier. This is obviously a much more worked picture than the sketch, and I think a more subtle, better one.'

Marika and the Orpen Paint Box
Oil on canvas, 1984. 48 × 40ins (RA 1985, No 570).

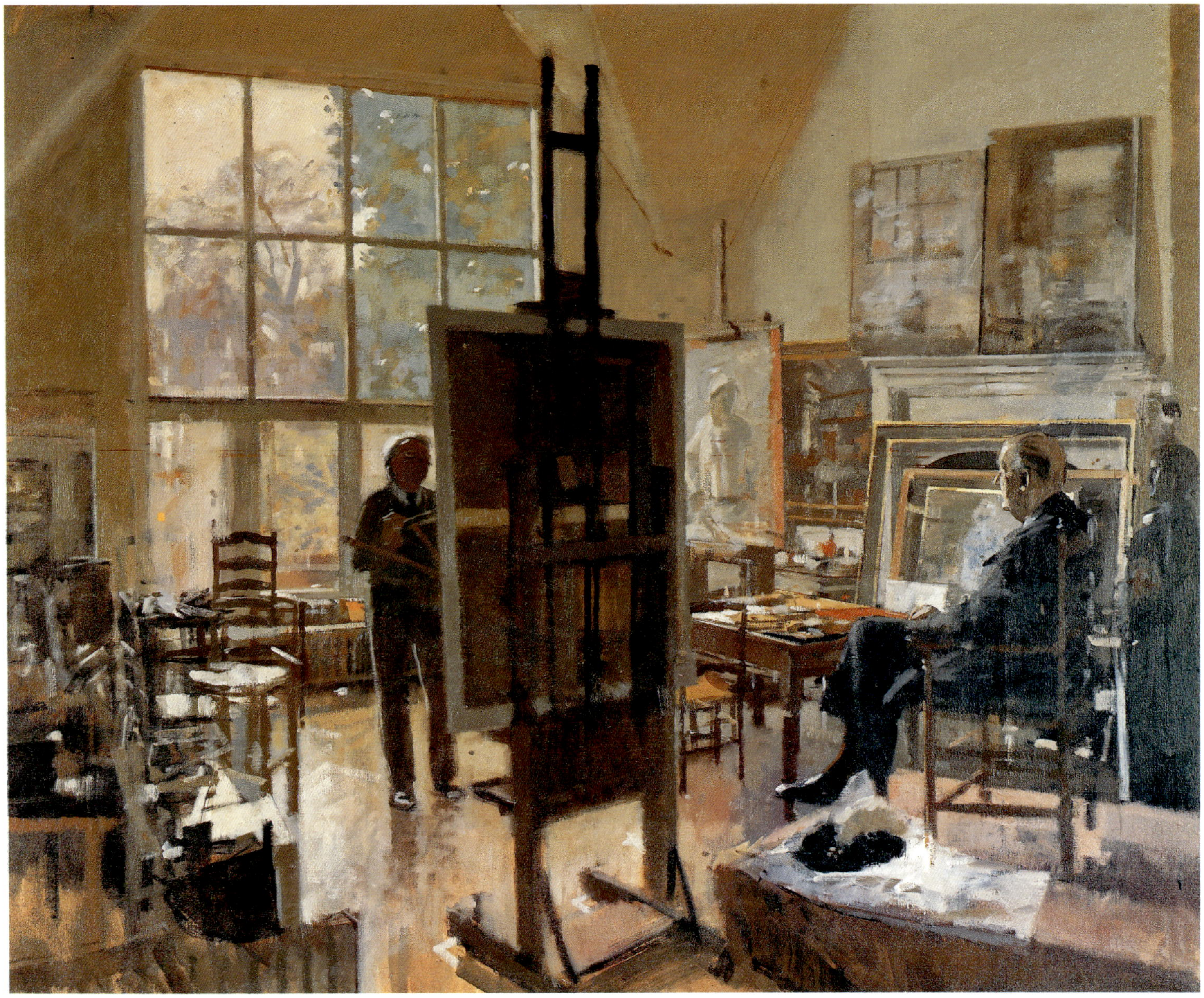

John Ward at Oriel
Oil on canvas, c 1986. 40 × 48ins.

John Ward at Oriel
Looking into the studio from the doorway corner, we find another painter at work with his sitter. In the earlier painting entitled *The Studio*, its author was clearly sharing the model with Christa Gaa, whereas here the artist is apparently an onlooker only. The stage has been commandeered by John Ward and his sitter, Lord Normanby.

'I was going to be spending most of my time away from London for a while, and John asked if he could use the studio to paint this portrait. I have enormous admiration for him and his art, and was delighted to agree. It was a great pleasure to watch him working while I was up in London. His whole attitude to painting is one of complete dedication, and he won't let anything come between himself and his work. I saw him go through the considerable struggle of making this painting. Unlike many artists today he uses no photographic reference whatsoever and just keeps working from the figure until he gets it right. As neither sitter nor artist objected, I painted a two-foot canvas of the scene and then the larger one you see here.

'I liked the idea of not being able to see the canvas John was working on – just him standing behind his easel. I think it is interesting to make the eye go round and through things, under tables, round easels, behind figures. It's a matter of being able to give the sense of space through which the eye can travel.'

Here the artist is describing his own conception of what has been described earlier as the perspective of space. Although it is described as space, this is not a vacuum between objects. It is visible, dusty air – believable space, through which the spectator knows he could pass. It is as if this tangible air as much moulds the shape of objects as the other way round. The suspension of disbelief is so strong that one is almost surprised, as one might be on entering the studio itself, to find another artist and sitter have entered the intimate world of Ken Howard's studio.

'When the picture was finished I was rather pleased with the likenesses. Lord Normanby did indeed buy the smaller canvas from me. I was keen to exhibit the larger picture at the Academy, but he is a modest man and preferred me not to do so. So I was glad that it still found a good home through Dudley Dodd of the National Trust Foundation for Art.'

Homage to Sir William Orpen RA
This bravura account of Orpen's portrait of *Le Chef de l'Hotel Chatham, Paris* is to be seen sitting on an easel in the background of the picture illustrated opposite. The young Ken Howard copied the old masters voraciously, but, given the acknowledgement to Whistler and Sickert in *The Red Parasol* and *Pax Tibi*, such direct

reinterpretations of another artist's work are comparatively rare in more recent years.

All artists are influenced to varying degrees by the discoveries and successes of their predecessors; if not, there would be no development in painting. More than some, Howard consistently and enthusiastically talks of his debt to the painters he has admired. He could pay no more public homage than to make specific and generous reference to men such as Sickert and Orpen. A postcard of Orpen's *Chef* was prominently included in the tablescape in Howard's 1984–5 self-portrait of the same title, illustrated in the first chapter. Clearly Orpen's striking image was on the artist's mind at the time:

'I suppose the ghost of Orpen has haunted me ever since I came to Oriel. I've always been very conscious of him as a painter. I don't think he was a great master, but there have been very few portrait painters with his panache. I feel you can be sure when you look at an Orpen that it is as near the absolute essence of the person as it was possible to get. I think drawing is at the root of it, and Orpen was a fine draughtsman.

'My slight obsession with Orpen came to a head when I was elected to the Academy and saw the big Orpen Diploma work of *Le Chef de l'Hotel Chatham, Paris*. I decided then I would like to do a version of that picture. I didn't particularly want to start looking round for a similar model, but just decided to use a similar composition. One day, however, I was in the Academy restaurant and noticed one of the boys working there, who had wonderful dreadlocks. He seemed just right for the picture, so I asked him to sit for me. I've always been fascinated by Negroid features – when I was at Hornsey I made a number of studies of a friend of mine who became a well-known portrait painter in Barbados.

'This boy had a marvellous head, and the colour of his skin against the white chef's clothes and the shaded white walls of the studio was fantastic. To follow Orpen's picture, I put a pork chop and a bottle of wine in front of him. After about ten minutes he began to look unwell, but said he was feeling all right. Another ten minutes later the sweat was beginning to pour off him. I asked if he wanted to sit down. He said that he was afraid that if I didn't take away the pork chop he would faint, as he was a very strict vegetarian. As soon as I'd done that he was fine, and I had to paint in the pork chop after he had gone.'

Despite this incident, the painting is a harmonious, broadly brushed tonal study. It is handled with a freedom and confidence which reflects both the artist's excitement in his subject and the strength of purpose that the homage provided. This happy combination of imperatives has produced one of Howard's most ravishing images.

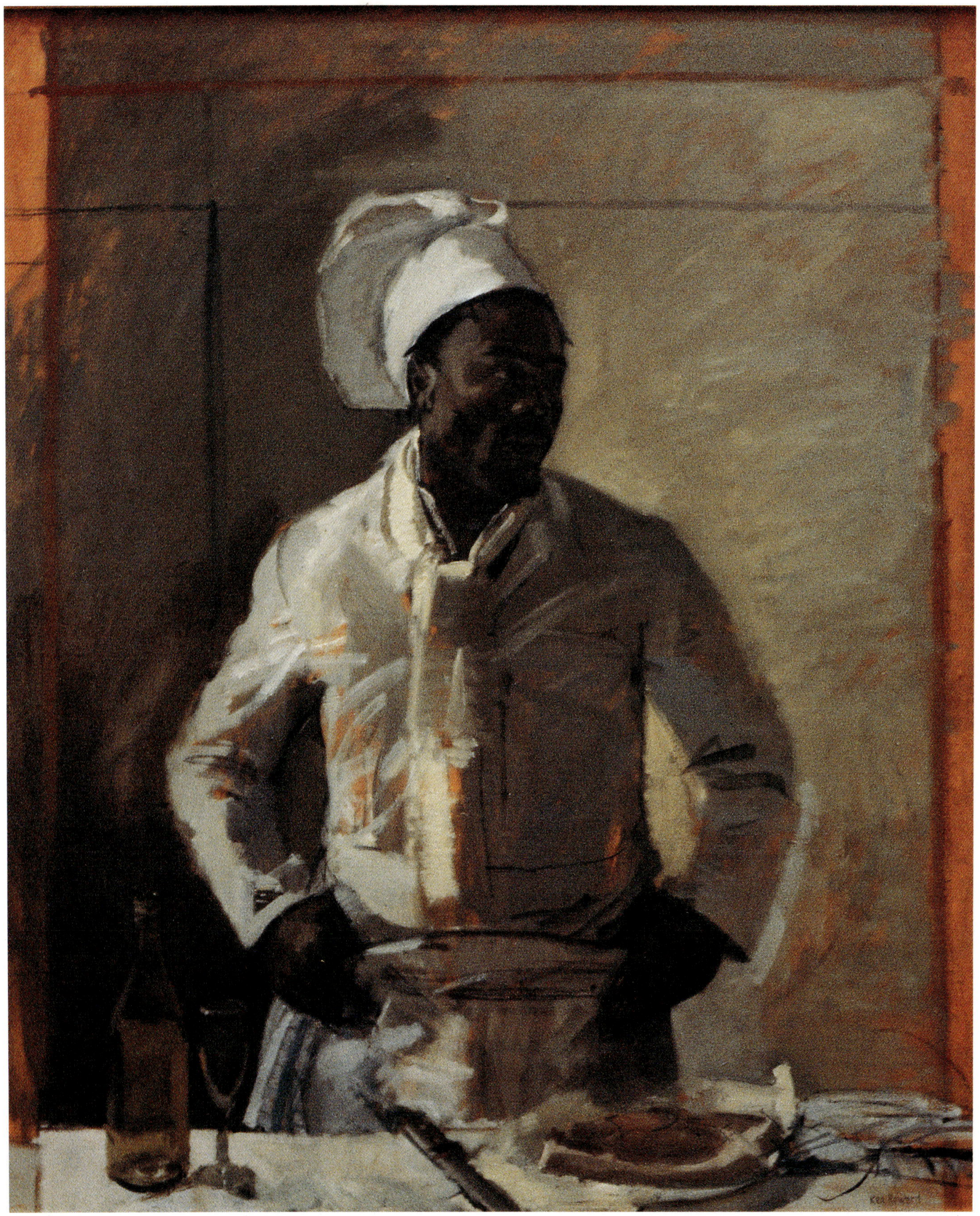

Homage to Sir William Orpen RA
Oil on canvas, 1985. 55 × 44ins (RA 1986, No 600).

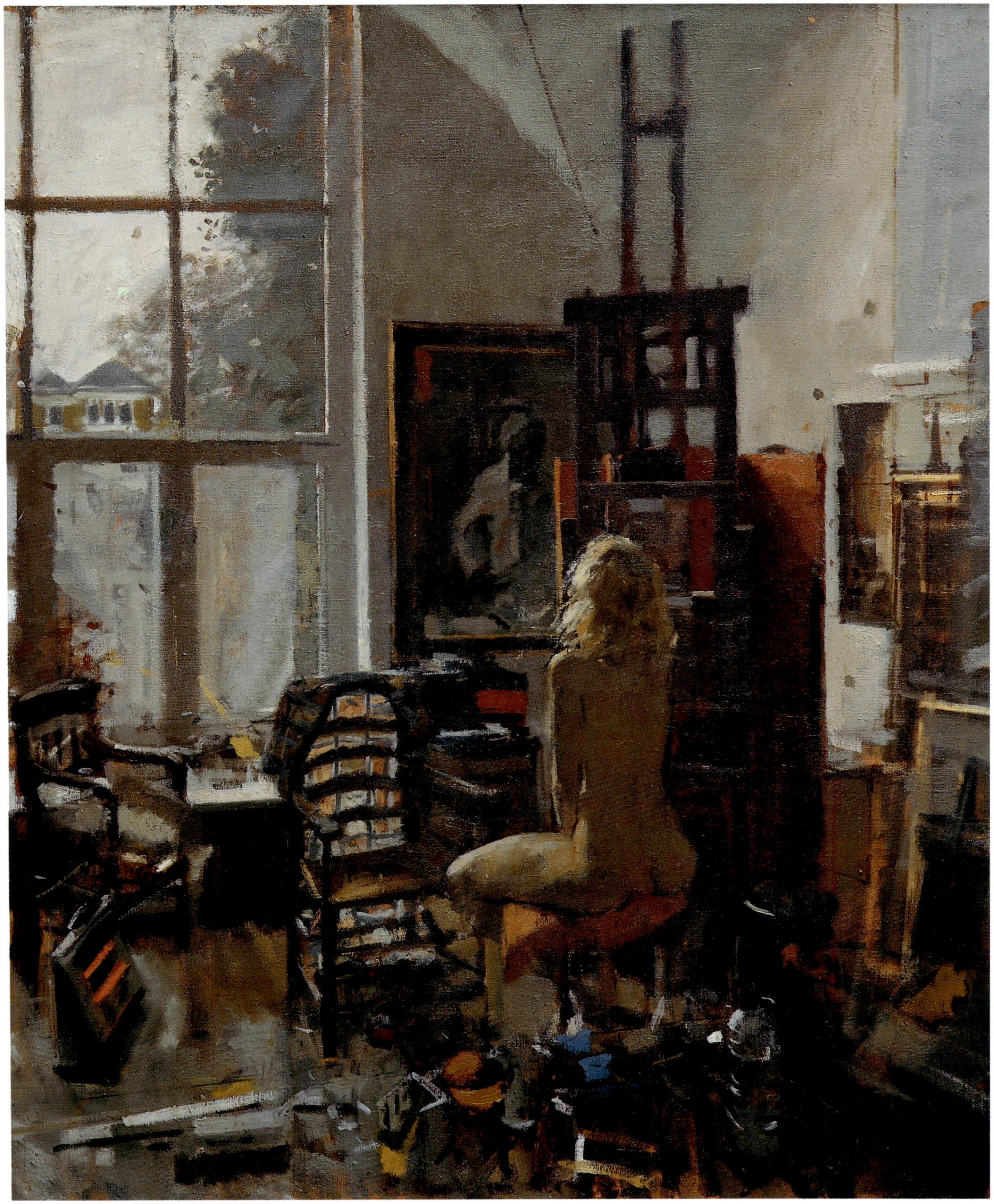

Marika, Le Casque d'Or

The *Homage to Orpen* is now off the easel and on the wall abutting the window at South Bolton Gardens. This rich, sensuously painted canvas, of Marika looking towards the light, bears another title with associations.

'When I was a boy I saw a film called *Le Casque d'Or*, which starred Simone Signoret. Like many of my contemporaries I fell madly in love with her and I have never really forgotten that. The light in the London studio is much more diffused than in Cornwall. But when the figure is seen against the window, one still gets this light coming through things, like the silk shirt on the chair. Marika has got very fine blonde hair and one time she came to pose for me at the studio. I thought the light shining through it looked just like a halo or helmet of gold around her head, so I called the picture *Le Casque d'Or* in memory of Simone Signoret.'

Bathed in glowing light, which brings out the colour in the studio clutter, the model and her surroundings are painted with soft, attractive brushwork. Marika looks up from the heated studio towards the sunlight outside, as if – one might feel from her alert, dancer's posture – in revelation. She sits in a pose similar to that adopted in the *Orpen Paint Box* and its sketch.

'This was a case where I just could not be satisfied with the pose of the figure. I changed it three times – from facing me, to side view, to back view. The same effect was there on the hair all the time, but the pose didn't feel right. I know people think of me as a rather logical painter, but I do think that sensing that the figure is right is crucial to me.

'I don't usually have such difficulty getting the figure into the right position and to the right scale in relation to everything else. But I do have a problem sensing that the figure is facing the right way in relation to everything else. I can't analyse it to find the right pose. It finally has to be sensed as right.

'Obviously one can be taught composition and perspective and use that experience in one's work as it becomes part of one's language. But in the end sensing what is right is what matters. I don't think one should apply theories to paintings – in that way I am not a particularly logical painter. But often, if I analyse a picture once it is finished, I find that it will break down into the principles of the golden section, for example.

'I am sure there are common proportions that run through many things that people recognise as being beautiful or ideal, in terms of composition and design. I imagine the Greeks found these proportions in nature and then made the mathematical analysis. I don't believe they simply applied a mathematical theory to art. Such theories are only useful to the painter if he has absorbed them into his language.'

Marika, Le Casque d'Or
Oil on canvas, 1985–6. 48 × 40ins (RA 1986, No 134).

Valerie: 8.40, July 20, 1987

As *Le Casque d'Or* catches particular qualities of the Oriel light, so this painting grasps the character of the brilliant early-morning sun of the West Penwith peninsula. The canvas is broadly painted, the fabric of St Clement's Studio almost sketched in, as the artist turns his attention to the sharply defined light and shade at the centre of the composition. Valerie gazes into the morning sun, as though symbolising the intensity with which Howard is himself drawn towards the source of light. Otherwise the model's function is as formal as that of the palette that has carefully been placed to catch the sun's rays. This acts as one vehicle for the study of light moving over and through objects and across the picture.

It has been seen that Howard paints the sunlight at all times of day, but that when painting outdoors he favours a low sun – into which he will commonly face as he works. The only opportunity he has to work in this way in the studio is while the morning sun pours in through the road-side windows of St Clement's Studio.

'Valerie was a model I used for some years. She was very natural. It is a great help when you get to know a model well and she feels natural and unselfconscious when she comes into the studio. In the summer the model comes at seven. At one time I even considered asking them to come earlier, but I thought that was pushing it a bit. So we work from seven until ten. That gives me the full day outside and gives the model the full day, having earned some money in the morning. Early on a summer's morning the Cornish studio is absolutely magical. The sun rises right outside these east-facing windows, and it absolutely floods in. The great painters of light, like Turner, would have revelled in this studio early in the morning.

'I seem to have gravitated towards high, spacious studios. Oriel is very high, although not very big, and this studio is large in every direction. It is a bit like a landscape, because the ceiling is like a great dome of sky. In this composition I was forcing the model further and further towards the bottom of the canvas, revealing more of the space above. When I'm too old to go out and paint, I imagine this studio being my landscape. It would be big enough and varied enough and have enough things going on in it, to keep me as fascinated as a landscape.

'At this time I quite often included the time and sometimes the date in the title, because light is rarely, if ever, the same twice. I see something in the light one morning that I may never see again. I will probably never be there in the same conditions at that precise time and date another year. If you like, it brings home Monet's idea of stalking a subject through different conditions of light.'

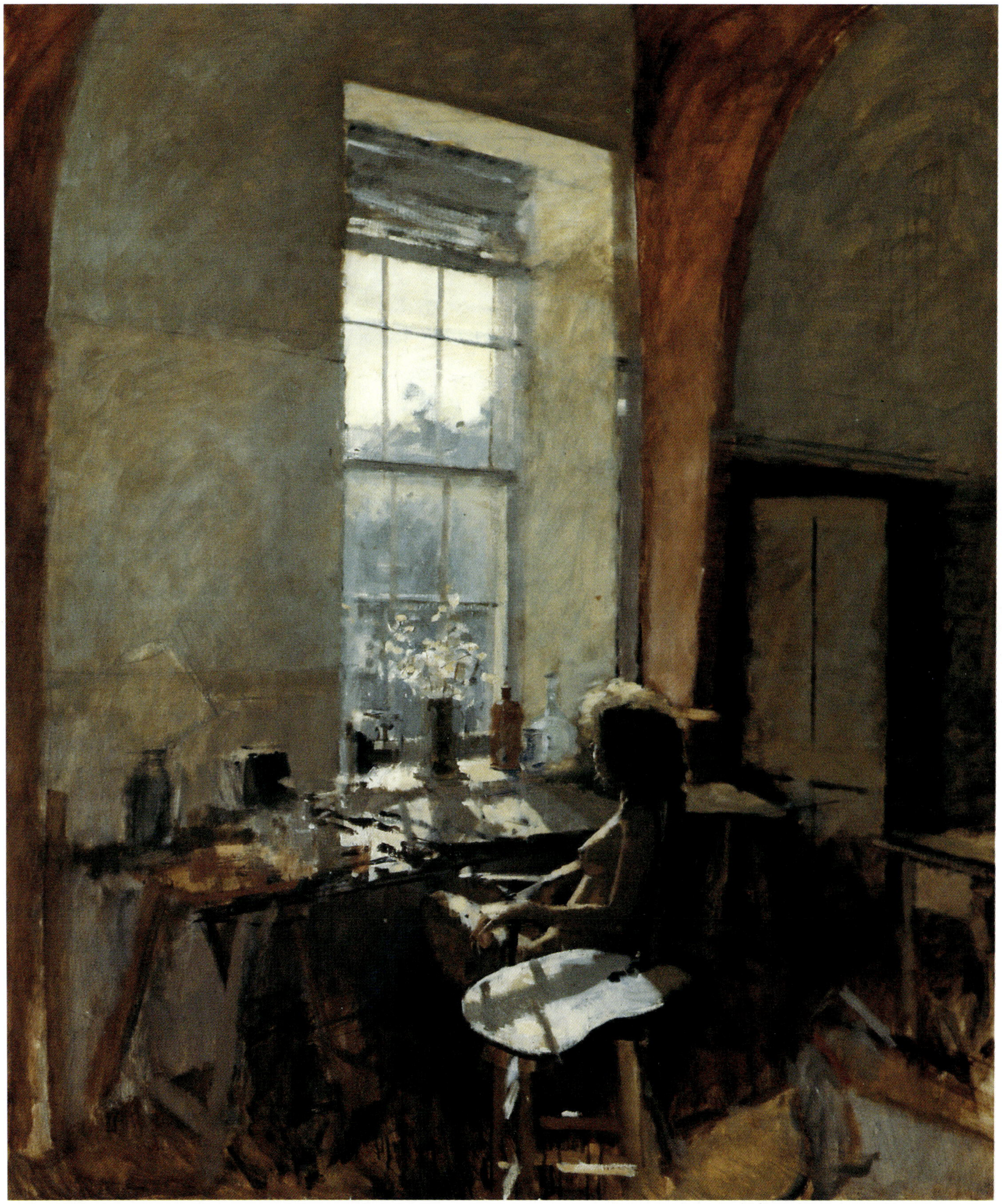

Valerie: 8.40, July 20, 1987
Oil on canvas, 1987. 48 × 40ins (RA 1988, No 976).

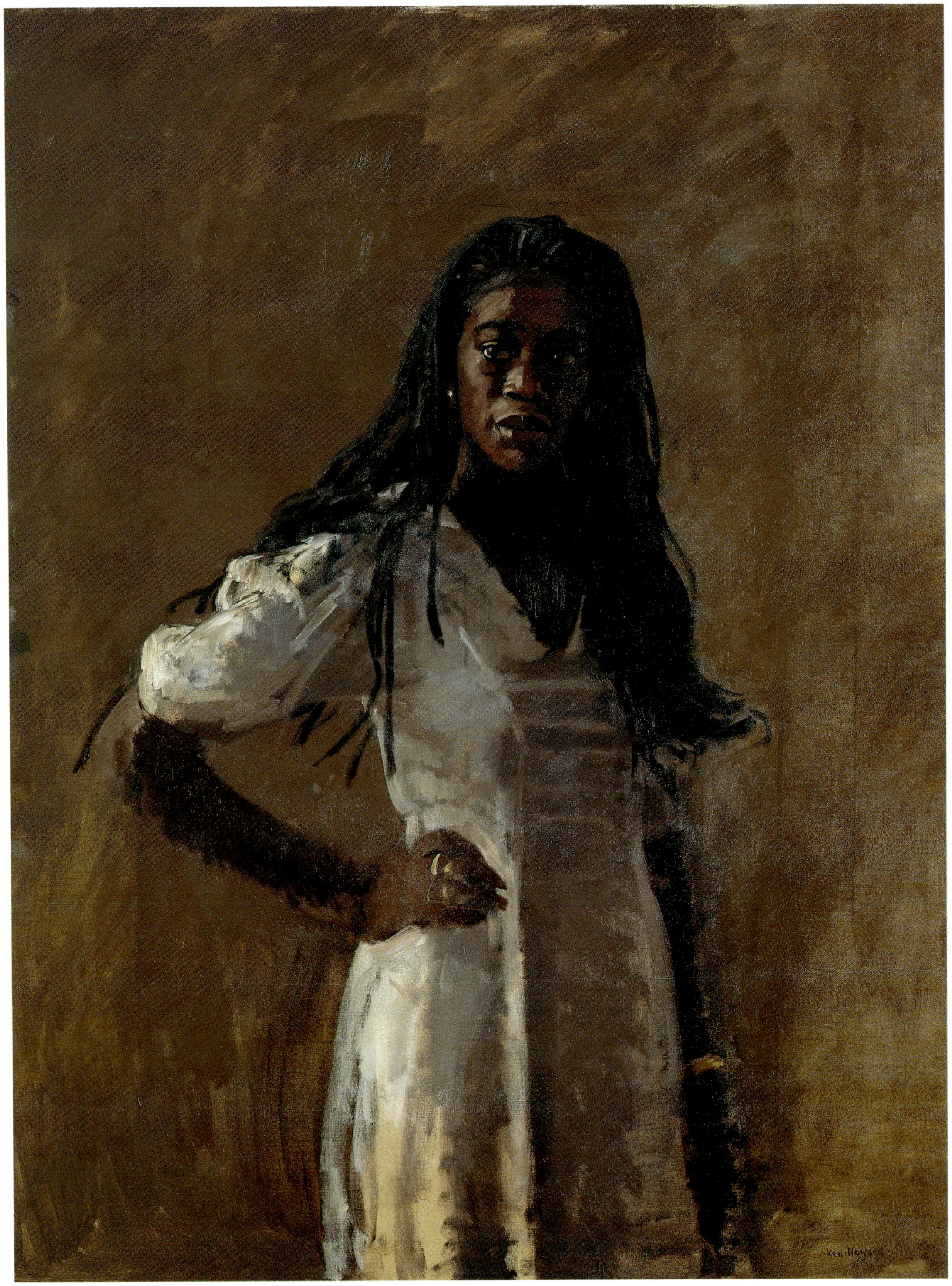

Malreth

'After painting the *Homage to Orpen* I decided also to do a picture of a black woman. I was driving back from Cornwall one time and picked up a student at Bristol. He had splendid dreadlocks and, as we were chatting on the way up to London, I mentioned that I had just painted a fellow who looked rather like him. I told him I was now looking for a female counterpart. He said he had a sister called Malreth who sang in a jazz band and was very striking, with long dreadlocks.

'Eventually I got in contact with Malreth. She agreed to pose for me and turned out to be a very beautiful woman, with a fantastic head. She was an incredible person, who spent all her spare time working both in a club for the homeless and a youth club, as well as singing in the band. This was all on top of a full-time job.

'I painted her twice, not initially being terribly satisfied with this, the first picture. But it appealed straight away to its present owners and that helped me to see more what was right about it, less what I thought was wrong. I like it when people immediately say that's the picture I want. I love the immediate reactions.'

It is quite possible to understand that this simple image would have a sudden impact on its new owners. Its directness is enhanced by the artist's effective technique. While treating less important areas of the figure with appropriate breadth, he has worked up the shoulder, hair and face to achieve a sculptural quality that emphasises the model's features. This concentration on a sitter's head through the intensifying of the paint's plasticity is a technique employed by artists from Rembrandt and Velázquez to Gainsborough and Sargent. To each of these men's art *Malreth* owes some debt, but the result is singularly Howard's own achievement. Like the *Homage to Orpen* it is a tonal study, a harmony in earth colours and white that would also have been worthy of Whistler, yet it is too a contemporary, challenging image of considerable power.

Malreth
Oil on canvas, 1986. 48 × 40ins.

The Picture
The composition of this picture is a bold expression of the interior landscape which Ken Howard has described. Nearly half the canvas is taken up by the simple vaulting of the dome-like ceiling of Oriel. If it were like an exterior landscape, it would probably be the kind painted by the artists of the Norwich School, with a large grey sky and the odd windmill and barn relieving the flatness of the terrain. All the familiar landmarks of the South Bolton Gardens studio are there – easels and canvases, a ladder-back chair and a foreground tablescape – all concentrated in the lower third of the picture. Around and above is space, described almost tangibly in what is a complex horizontal and vertical perspective.

Central to the composition are two figures, one nude, the other clothed. They are separated by their state of dress and physical distance, and also by the difference of the worlds they seem to inhabit. The model, Christa Gaa, belongs to the studio and is at ease in it, her gaze looking inwards towards the picture on the easel. The man, seated in a hunched pose, is also studying the picture, but is from the world outside and so his presence here is an ambiguous one:

'Chrissie hadn't got so involved in her own work at this time and was able to do some modelling for me. The figure on the right is a friend called Pete Archer, who now lives in Amsterdam. I conceived the painting with two figures of some sort, and had started by getting Chrissie to stand where Peter is, so that I could see the relationship of the second figure to the interior and to the nude in the chair.

'One day, when Chrissie was out, Peter came to the door and asked if I was busy. I told him I was painting but he could come upstairs and talk while I worked. I realised I had my second figure. He came up and sat in the corner and posed and talked – and I painted him. But the two figures were never in the room together.'

It is rare for Howard to paint any subject incomplete, but needs must, and the *Sanger* drawing and the *Red Parasol* painting show that he can do it when the situation demands. Yet, once we know this and the history of the picture is clarified, the disassociation between the figures if anything becomes greater and more interesting.

The whole interior is illuminated by a diffused, white light. Most of Howard's South Bolton Gardens pictures are painted in the winter months, when Cornish beaches lose some of their charms, and when most of the trees that shade the studio window in summer are bare. It is hard to think of any other painting in which the cool, northern light that envelops the studio is so keenly observed. This is an intriguing and rewarding painting, and an ambitious composition.

The Picture
Oil on canvas, 1983–4. 72 × 60ins (RA 1984, No 806).

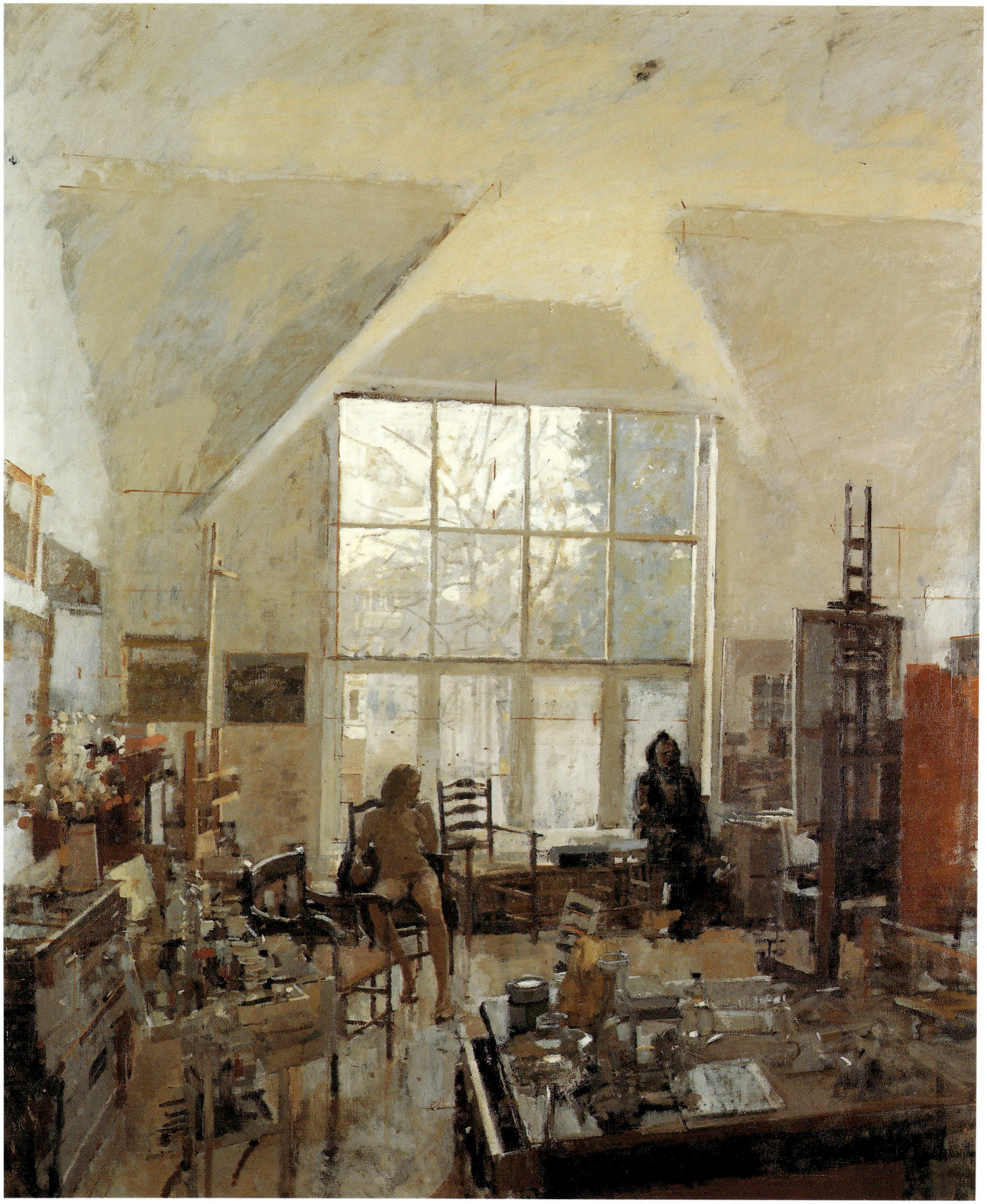

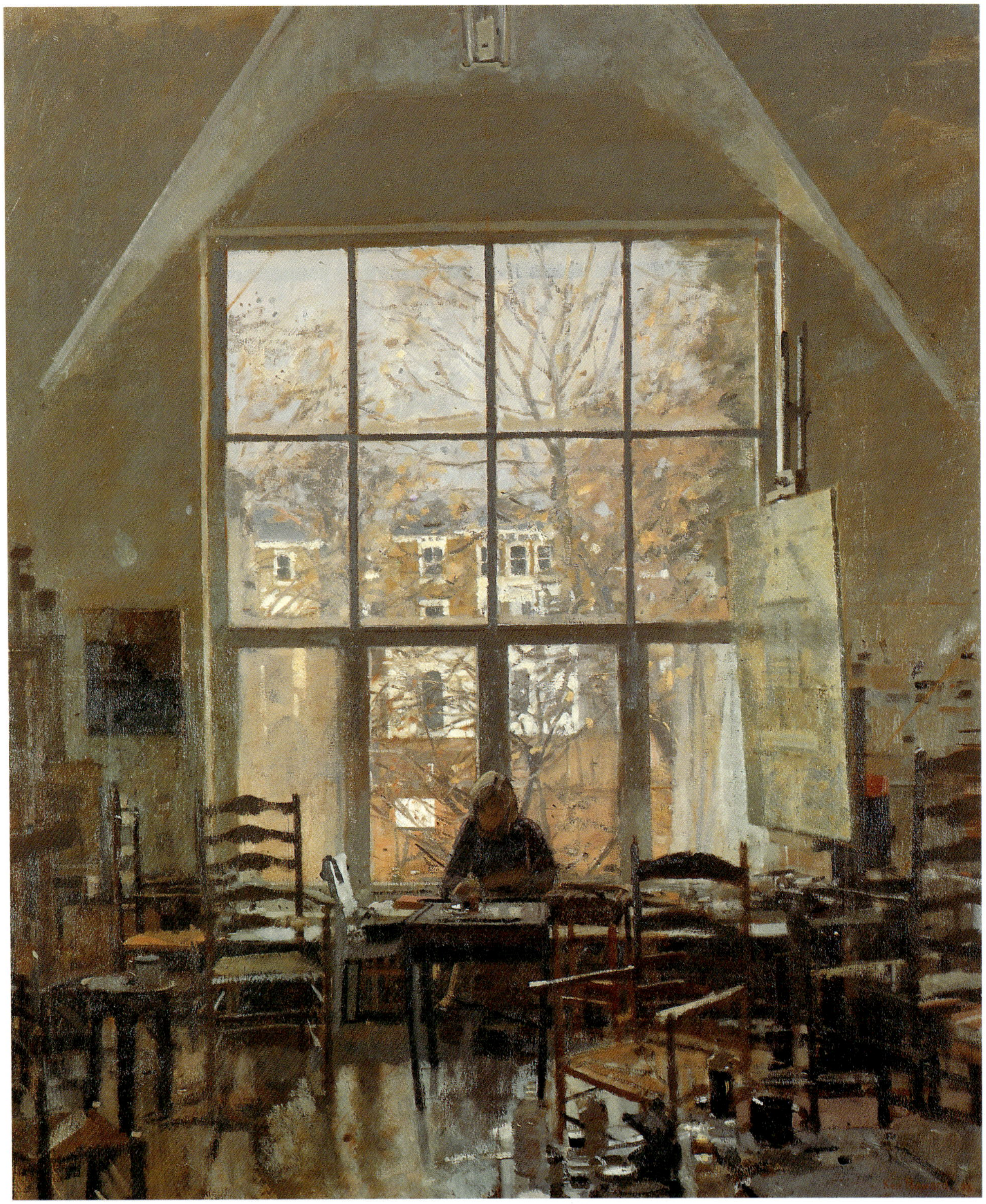

Interior at Oriel
Oil on canvas, 1982–4. 48 × 40ins (RA 1984, No 793).

Interior at Oriel
The late autumn sunlight creates an entirely different light in the studio from that of the previous picture. The light is warmer and less diffused, shadows and silhouettes are intensified and reflections on chair arms heightened. The apparently random array of chairs almost floats over the floor, on which the reflection of the window has blurred the surface. Beyond the lively activity of chair-backs is Christa, intently painting a still-life and positioned like a figure in a stained-glass window. Way above her hangs the majestic ceiling vault.

Again one is reminded of the cathedral paintings of earlier years. Static and noble, this symmetrical arch provides a fixed reference point for the composition and returns the eye back towards the scene below. It is a pleasing arrangement of horizontals and verticals, and a striking image, with possible religious overtones. As the artist explains, the final picture was only arrived at after much soul-searching:

'Originally this was a back view of Chrissie sitting on the floor looking out of the window. There was a lot of golden colour outside the window and I felt the picture worked extremely well. I hadn't yet been elected to the Academy and when the time came to send in to the Summer Exhibition, Bernard Dunstan came round to have a look at what I was going to send. He said, don't send that one, because it could be said to be sentimental. This was such a shock to me, because I really loved the picture and I couldn't see it was sentimental. But I did believe in Bernard's attitude, and that if he could see that, others might too.

'I looked hard at the picture and finally decided that he was right and I must re-state the figure. So I posed Chrissie differently. I went through four different poses and the picture gradually disintegrated until it had nothing to do with what it had been originally. Almost in tears I scraped off the last figure and threw the canvas into the corner of the room, intending to paint over it. It sat there for about eight months and I never really looked at it.

'Then one day I came into the studio and Chrissie was sitting painting by the window. As I walked through the door I immediately saw a subject. As she was going to work there for some time I decided to paint her. I looked round the studio and found I was short of a large canvas. So I went into the corner and rummaged around, and dug out this old battle-worn, half-destroyed canvas. The window and the upper part of the canvas were still intact. I put it on the easel and painted in Chrissie, reorganising all the bits and pieces, because they depended on their relationship to the figure. I did all the new lower part in one wet and knew very quickly that I had a picture that worked. And this is still one of my favourite studio interiors. I sent it in to the Summer Exhibition the next year, the first after I was elected.

'Despite the happy ending, I do sometimes think after a painful struggle like that I couldn't go through it all again. I think artists can be difficult to live with when a painting is going badly. Yet if you live with the right person, as I do, they help you through it. But it is important that they don't help too readily, because these problems are a necessary part of growing as a painter – of going into the mire and coming out again.'

Valerie: 9.20, August 11, 1987
This is one of the series of summer morning paintings of Valerie at St Clement's Studio. The artist would work on a number of canvases on the same morning, moving from one to the other as the sun rose. Completely altering the composition from one picture to the next – unlike Monet in his series paintings – Howard produced a remarkable record of a morning, or rather a series of mornings, in his Cornish studio. We have already seen Valerie at 8.40 am, looking out of the window, as the raking light outlined her body. Here, some forty minutes later, the light seems a little more diffused and a bit gentler as it illuminates the honesty by the window. But the focus of the simple arrangement of vertical shapes is the splash of light that catches the model's hair:

'I was very interested in the halo of light around her head – rather like Marika in *Le Casque d'Or* – and the way the light is cut off from the table by the model, yet goes through the bottle and jars. By the time I was painting this series I had come to realise that getting the sunlight was what I really wanted to concern myself with in my painting. It was a very good summer and every morning I had this incredible excitement as the light came into the studio, cutting through and round the model.

'When I feel I am getting to grips with this sort of subject I begin to believe I really am a painter. Unfortunately, most of the time I feel convinced that I have failed, but just having that good feeling every now and again gives me the strength to go on during the bad days. It is on mornings in the studio, with images like this, that I now and again get the feeling I have something of my own to say.'

This particular image does indeed say a lot about his art. In its single-minded concentration on a subtle light effect within a simple, broadly brushed tonal composition, *Valerie: 9.20* is quintessential Ken Howard. The splendid airy rooms, the complex arrangements of furniture and jars, are the glorious trappings of the studio pictures. But here, with Valerie standing in a characteristically natural pose behind an apparently un-arranged tablescape, any sense of artifice is absent. We are seeing the pure expression of the artist's raw, urgent response to visual phenomena that excite him.

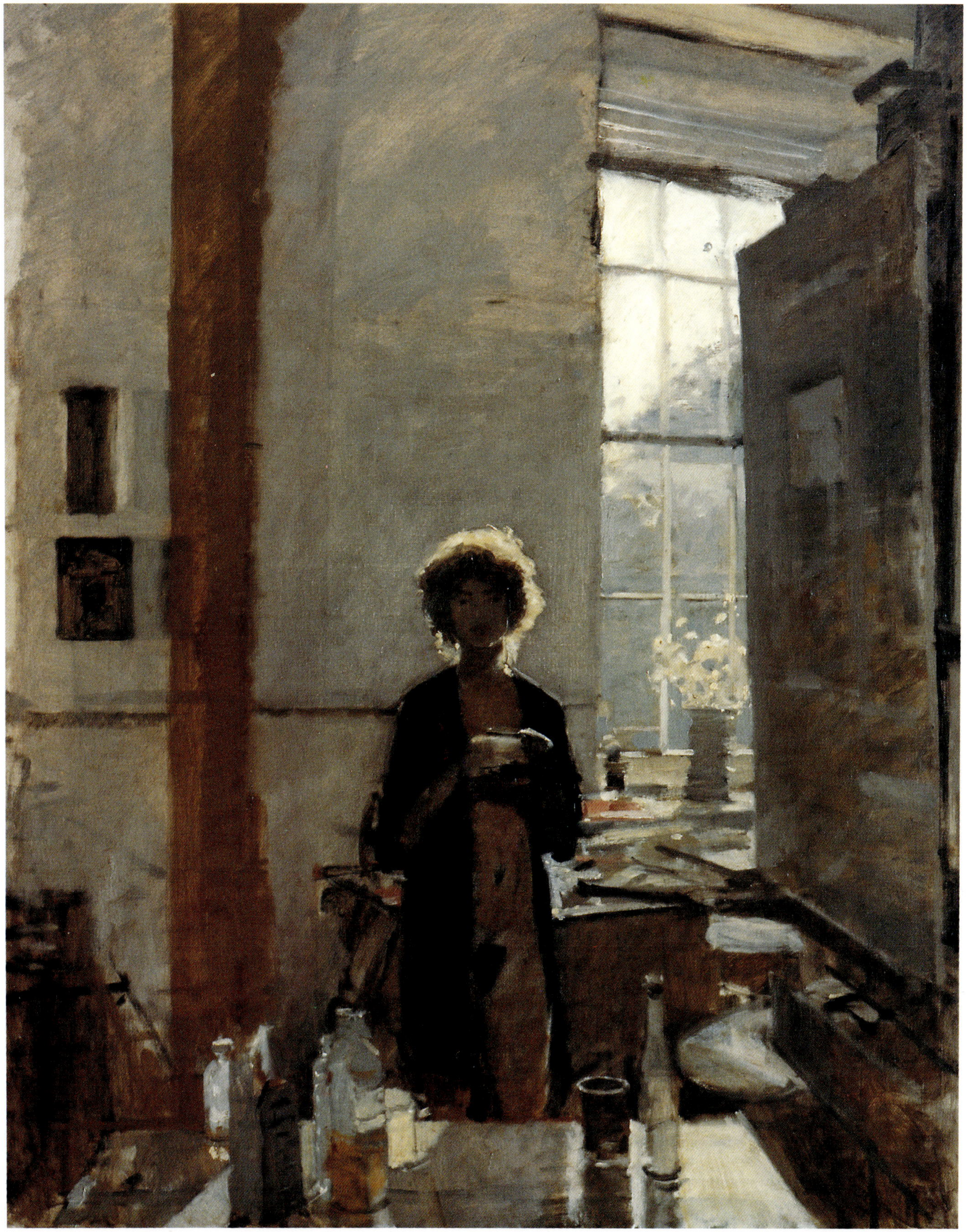

Valerie: 9.20, August 11, 1987
Oil on canvas, 1987. 48 × 40ins (RA 1988, No 69).

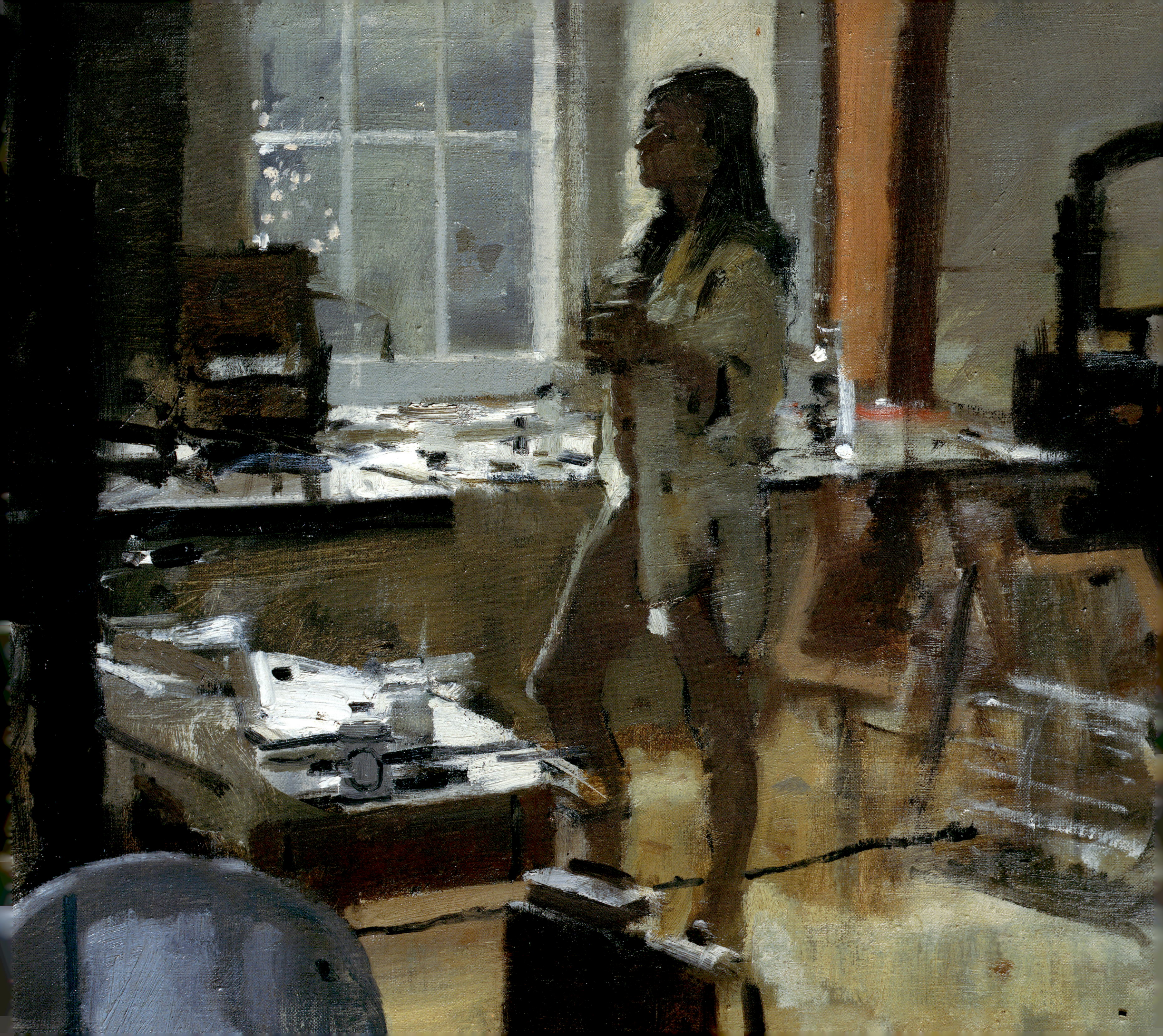

Saskia Resting
Looking back over his career, to the dark days at the Royal College and to the times when commissioned work seemed to be strangling his development as a painter, Ken Howard's present facility with the brush would appear to have been hard won. The fact remains that the most fluent of his recent paintings look absolutely effortless.

The at once generous and economical amassing of a heady mixture of wet and dry brushwork is synonymous with the artist's work. As he has explained, these glorious passages of paint are not always achieved without hard, and sometimes tortuous effort. Yet, as on the beach, there are happy moments in the studio, where the immediacy of his reaction to the subject brings forth a vital and spontaneous brush that has few equals.

The gorgeous textures and summary notation of the handling of *Saskia Resting* are revealed in the enlarged detail. Each brush-stroke seems to have a definite purpose and in every passage of paint the brilliant technique is laid bare. Nothing superfluous has been allowed to intervene between the artist and the planting of the image onto the canvas. We might feel we can sense the ease with which he has brought the picture to a pre-determined conclusion. This was not quite so:

'I was going to do a painting of Chrissie standing, looking at a canvas that you can't see the front of – rather like John Ward looking at his portrait. I knew Chrissie didn't have much time, so I decided to use the model to set up the composition. I was doing another painting of Saskia and while she was having a cup of tea during her break, I asked her to stand, looking at this picture, in order to get the scale. As soon as I saw her standing there I realised it worked compositionally. I abandoned the picture I was working on and painted this one, working on it for about two hours.

'I was dissatisfied with it and didn't feel it was coming together. Chrissie came into the studio and I said "I'm going to go on with that painting and get it right". She said "It is right". Only then could I see there was nothing else to be done. She has a marvellous ability to see when my paintings are ready, and I'm afraid I often do not.'

The artist's occasional urge to over-finish some of his most deliciously free paintings can be forgiven, especially if one bears in mind his prolonged development of freedom of handling in the face of an inbred work ethic:

'When your technique or way of seeing develop in a certain way you've got to follow that path. I am glad that in my youth, however madly I wanted freedom of technique, I realised it was wrong to think – like so many young painters – that I could decide to be more free. You cannot decide to be free – that is just an affectation, a mannerism. You find freedom through discipline over many years. I just had to keep on working at pictures until gradually, naturally, I began to be able to summarise something – to put something down broadly or simply. That can only come with experience.

'Perhaps one can liken painting to the craft of the ballet dancer. If a ballet dancer hasn't done all his practice at the bar before he goes on the stage, he won't be able to express himself. He might be able to give an imitation of being fluent, of being in command, but very quickly it will become obvious that he is not. Whereas, if he has done his practice over the years, and over the days before the performance, he will be able to go out onto the stage and truly express himself.'

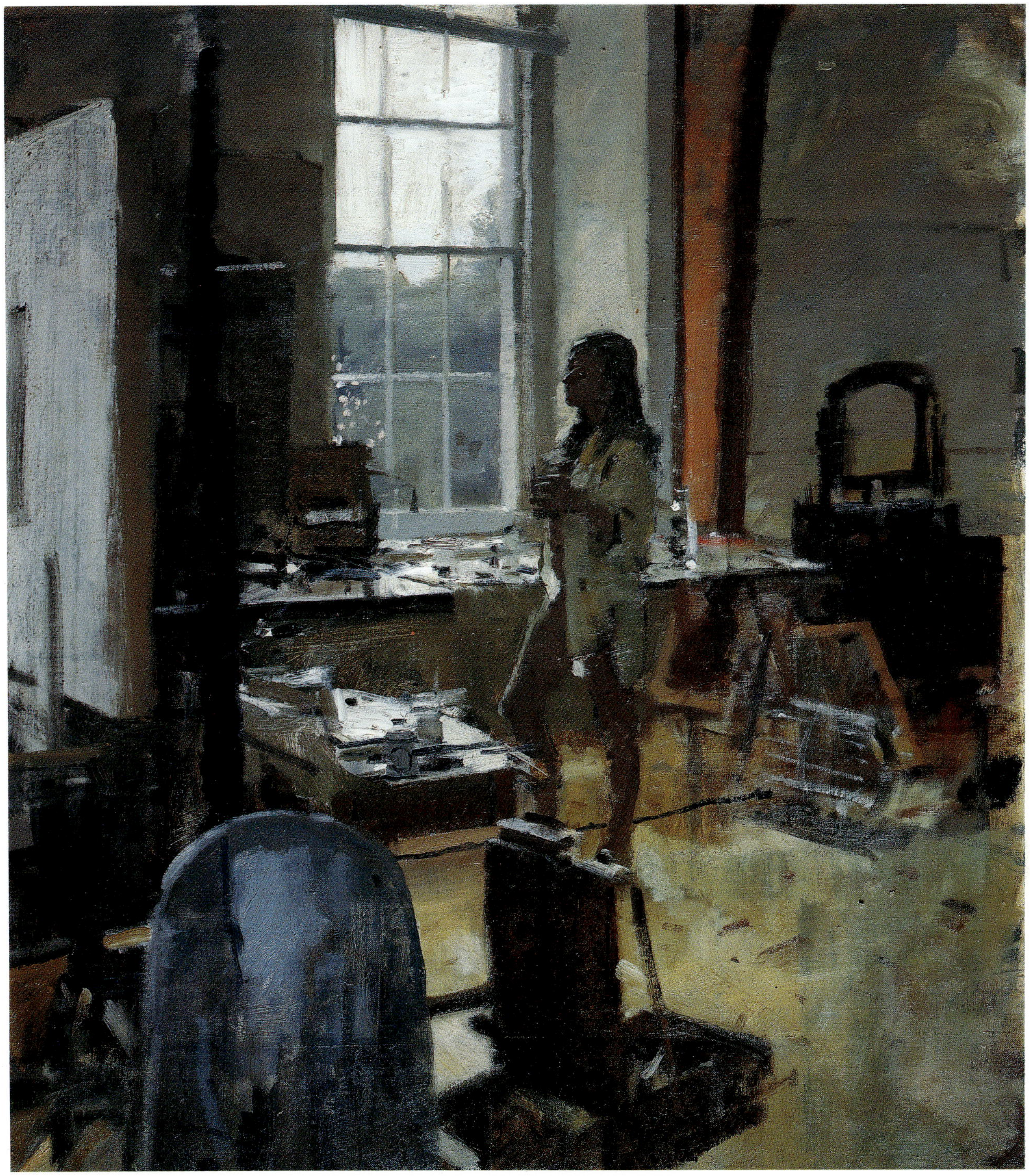

Saskia Resting
(detail)

Saskia Resting
Oil on canvas, 1986. 30 × 25ins.

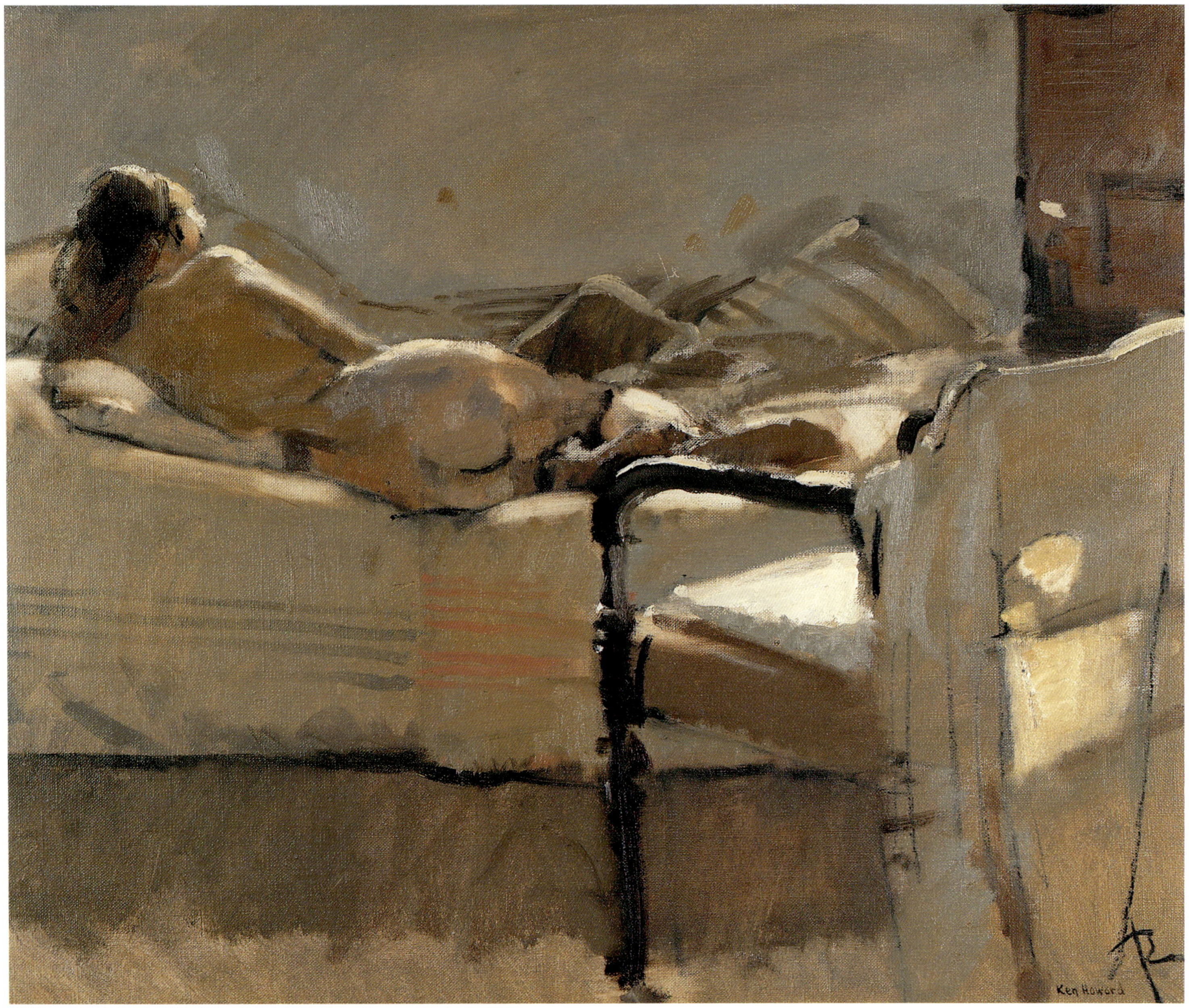

Saskia
Oil on canvas, c 1985. 20 × 24ins.

Saskia
Painted in warm Cornish light with a restricted, light-hued palette of delicate creams and pinks, this is at first sight one of the least complex of Howard's studio compositions. Its very simplicity is its charm. This simplicity is achieved with an arrangement of flat areas of thin paint, which form a satisfying arrangement of shapes. The composition these shapes form is finely judged, creating the right tautness over the picture-plane. It may appear totally natural and effortless, but the disposition of patches of light and shade has been selected with subtlety and sureness.

The simple form of the couch throws into relief the sinuous outline of Saskia's body and thus reveals the sensitivity of the artist's drawing. Although this is not one of the most deliberately 'drawn' of his nudes, it is a good example of how telling and effective his economical use of line can be. Such economy comes with years of practice and intense observation and is not earned by many. What is remarkable about this skill is that it is possible for a drawn or brushed outline to convey a sense of volume within, which is just added to by any modelling. Clearly the drawing has to be tight enough for the observer to understand that the line is able to contain this volume. Ken Howard recognises the importance of this concept:

'When I was drawing as a student I used to think of the figure as almost having a knot in the middle of it. From this knot strings ran out to all parts – the head, the hands, the feet, the knees, the elbows, the breasts. In doing the drawing one was tightening that knot so that all the pieces of string got very taut and the whole figure had a tension, all pulling towards the inside.

'I think I am less conscious of this concept now, although I hope it remains in my drawing. My compositions might appear much looser now, but I would like to think there is still a lot of tension in them. I hate nothing more than pictures I feel are floppy and loose – the figures structureless and looking as if they've been boned. I like a figure to look as if it's got a structure to it and a composition to look as if it's got a tension to it.'

This composition pays homage to Velázquez's celebrated *Rokeby Venus*, in the National Gallery, London, if only for the reversed pose of the model:

'From my youth I had greatly admired the Velázquez painting and I decided to do a sort of latter-day version. In my view painting only develops through building on what's gone before – adding another brick to the wall, as it were, to make it grow. Therefore I don't have any qualms about basing paintings on other people's pictures. This is different from direct copying, which I haven't done since I was very young. I often make notes in sketch-books when looking at pictures. When you stand and look at a Rembrandt, you only see it to a degree. But if you start to scribble in a sketch-book, it starts to reveal itself to you through the process of analysing it with a pencil. The process of drawing is a process of seeing, a process of revelation.'

Melanie Resting
This view of the studio at South Bolton Gardens is taken from a similar position to the monumental canvas, *The Picture*. Not being an upright canvas, the dome-like ceiling receives less emphasis, but the sense of space within the studio dominates the model, who is almost an incidental part of the landscape of furnishings. A warm, green light filters through the verdant trees outside the large north window and fills the space, defining as it does so the orientation and arrangement of the complicated interior landscape:

'Because of the north light, the London studio is a very controlled area in terms of tone. There is always a known and consistent difference in tone between the foreground chairs and the background chairs. I don't think much of working to rules. When I've studied Boudin's pictures, for example, I've seen that a boat in the middle-distance is as dark as a boat in the foreground. But it doesn't matter – the sensation of that boat, in relation to what is around it, is right.

'Rather than work to rules, I try to get the sensation of what I am seeing. Usually it will turn out that the

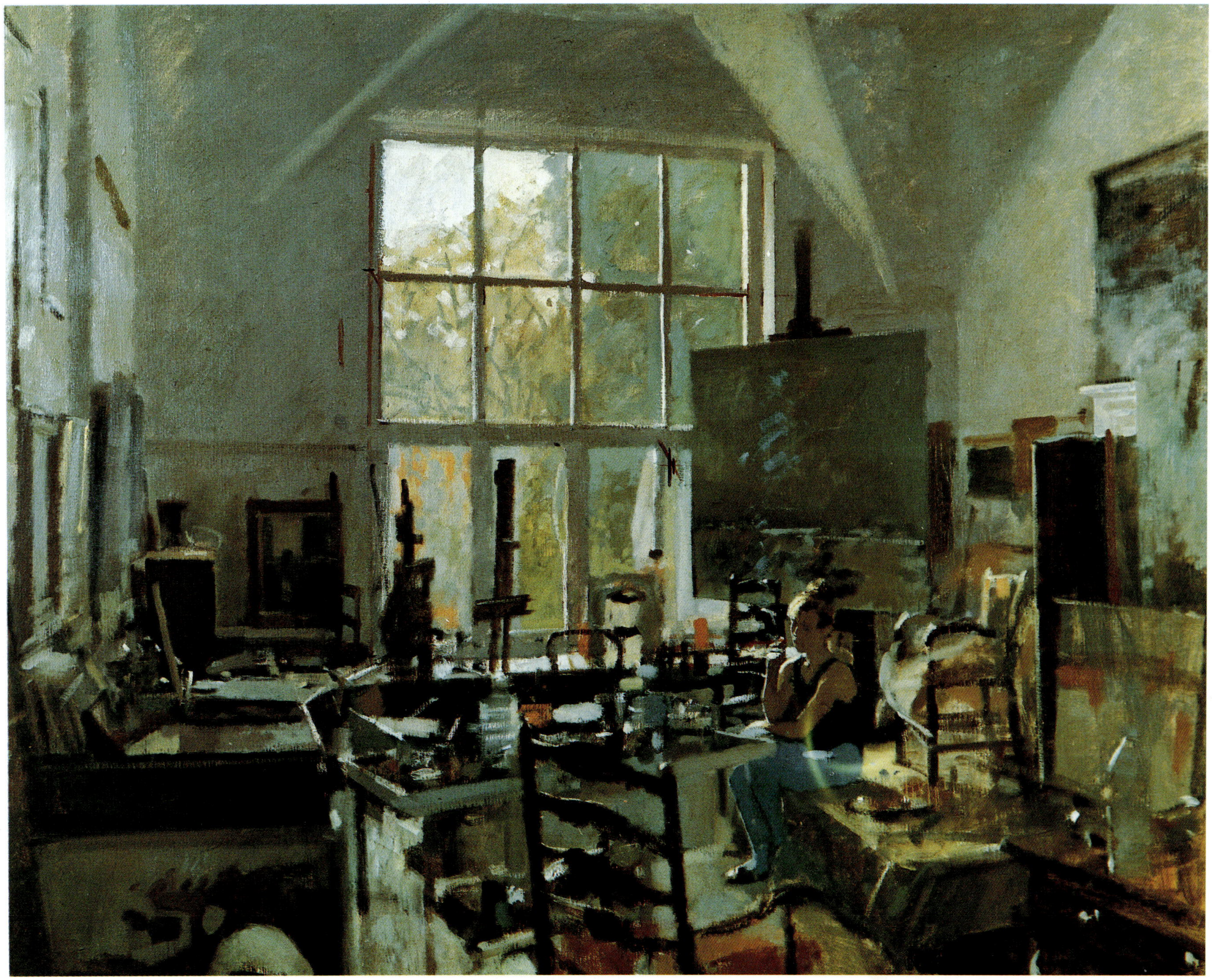

rules do apply, but they have not dominated the creation of the image. In the London studio the rules do apply and work very well, because of this even light. Consequently I am encouraged to paint all the clutter here. I paint what I see, not what I know, and it usually seems to work out. In Cornwall, on the other hand, the light in the studio is always changing, and the rules don't seem to apply very often.

'Melanie was a dancer and did some wonderful poses in a leotard. I saw the subject when she was resting, having a cigarette. I thought it was a big subject and put the picture I had been working on aside. As students we were often told that you shouldn't allow yourself to see subjects like that and start painting with the finished picture in your mind's eye. We were told you should discover it in the process of making the painting. I never believed that and I still don't believe it.

'Once you have seen the painting in your mind's eye, you have got to get it down on the canvas. Obviously you run into problems and you solve problems. You sometimes enter into terrible battles and can't resolve what was in your mind's eye. You can't get an equivalent on the canvas for what you've imagined. But you have to have the imagination – the image initiation, as it were – about what a picture can become.'

Melanie Resting
Oil on canvas, 1986. 40 × 48ins (RA 1987, No 1044).

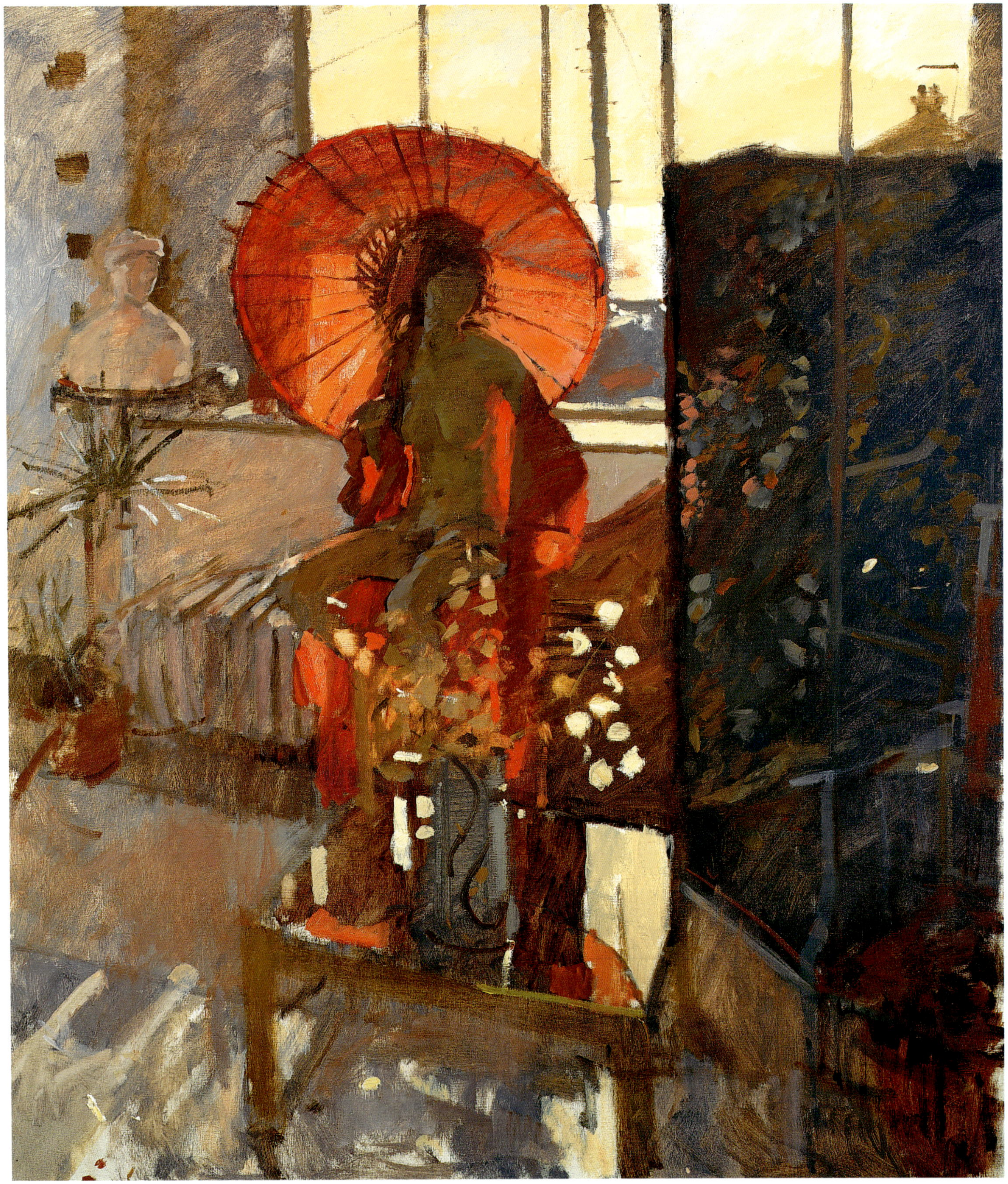

Red Lightbreak

We move again from the subdued, penetrative light of South Bolton Gardens to the brilliance of the morning sun, flooding over the sea and into the living-room of Howard's home in Mousehole. The tempo is further raised by the vibrant accent of the red parasol and kimono, which are the subject of the painting.

'It might seem pretentious to call a picture *Red Lightbreak*, but this stems from the experiences with the windbreaks on the beach, with the light breaking through them. I had already had shirts acting as lightbreaks in studio pictures, but I wondered how I could really bring the stimulus of those brilliant windbreaks into the room. I started by trying to get the light coming through kimonos and then suddenly it dawned on me that parasols would be the ideal equivalent of the windbreaks.'

Here the high sun strikes down onto the sea, turning it into a surface of brilliant light, against which the parasol is seen. As with the windbreaks, its stiffened, flat material catches the light head-on, creating a blaze of colour. In the foreground, the reflection on the table, and the leaves of honesty picking up the direct sun, carry the light further down into the room and towards the observer.

The red of the parasol is so intense and dominant that the artist was unable to make out the model's face, and consequently her features are almost obliterated. Lower down, the sun shines through her kimono, bathing her left side with an incandescent red light that is quite beautifully described.

'I got the model to hold her arm up to get this effect, which is quite miraculous. I remember I had a similar effect in a painting I was doing in the main studio. After the model had gone Chrissie saw the picture and said she thought the colour was over the top – it just couldn't be so strong. I sat down in front of the red kimono, which was hanging on a stand, and rolled up my trousers. The light wasn't even coming from the back, but was bouncing off the kimono. Chrissie just looked and said she could scarcely believe it – what I had painted was absolutely true.

'I am not much of a colour theorist. I paint what I see. But this is an example of very strong light creating the complementary colour. Of course there is an enormous amount of red light bouncing back and forth – onto the screen and the wall behind the parasol – and the picture takes on a pink hue, which helps to unify it. Being against the light, most of the figure isn't affected by the red, except inasmuch as the eye, wanting balance, looks for a contrast with the red and finds green. She really did look green.

Red Lightbreak
Oil on canvas, 1988. 48 × 40ins.

'I think red is a difficult colour to use, because you have to get the tone right. Because it is so hard to get the right intensity of red, there is a danger in concentrating on getting the colour and letting it fall out of tonal sequence with everything else. I've been learning how to use it. In these parasol paintings my palette really did start to widen, almost for the first time. I found I was starting to use oranges and pinks that I had never used before – at least not indoors. It was the only way I could paint what I was looking for. With this subject I feel at the very height of excitement.'

The artist's excitement is vigorously displayed in the free and liquid handling of this large canvas. It is as if he has raced against the disappearance, perhaps for ever, of that particular light on that particular subject – and won.

The Red Kimono I

On a similar scale to the previous canvas, this very beautiful picture has by comparison the look of a carefully composed set-piece. Painted in winter sunlight, it has more an atmosphere of reverie than the raw passion of *Red Lightbreak*. Even though a little of the intense excitement is missing, it is more than made up for by luscious brushwork and superb colour.

If Howard is by inclination a tonal painter, the parasol paintings and others that follow strongly suggest he is also a colourist. It is not simply the handling of the strong red. It is the manner in which the red, and the more muted fabric of the Aesthetic Movement harp chair, combine in juxtaposition against the blacks, yellows and other colours around them. Black can be a colour, and certainly is when used as the painters of the Venetian High Renaissance and seventeenth-century Spain used it – often set against reds, golds and flesh tones. Ken Howard has now found he can use his favourite blacks, greys and earth colours to set off the chromatic intensity of his new palette, and a true colourist is emerging.

Muted winter sunlight shines into the room, its coolness emphasised by the white of the parasol, which stands out as a highlight against the Mousehole hillside. Again the disposition of objects in the room enables the light to be brought down through the composition and towards the spectator. Looking at the controlled arrangement of furniture and props, one might pause to wonder quite why the model is sitting in the room with her parasol aloft:

'This was one of the first kimono pictures. When I started painting them my son-in-law thought it was strange to put such figures in a room in Cornwall, and I began to doubt what I was doing. But when Chrissie saw what I had been doing she said this was nonsense – there are no rules about what excites you visually.

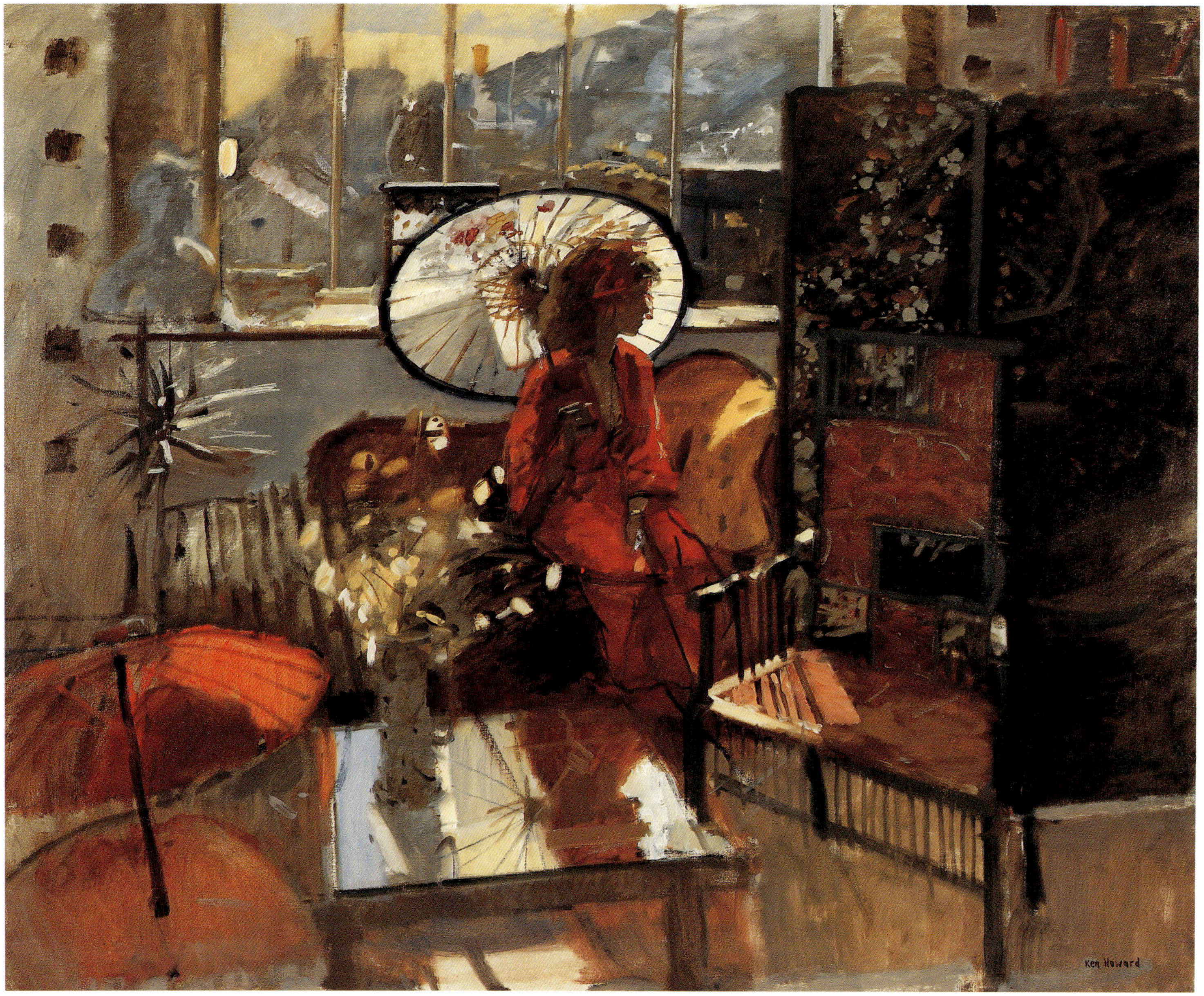

'At the time I was very interested in Whistler and – perhaps consequently – in *chinoiserie* and *japonaiserie*. One Christmas, Chrissie saw a Chinese box that she liked. I went back to buy it for her and in the same shop I saw a rather clapped-out screen. After Christmas I bought that as well, and then the screen and the box led me to think about kimonos – and then parasols.'

Such trappings are the stuff of many great paintings. The studio props of Rembrandt or Titian, and of course the Japanese borrowings of Whistler, are adequate precedents for an unashamed eclectic like Howard. Yet what is crucial is that it is the painting, not the props, that are the artist's true concern. The artist's genius must and can carry off almost any arrangement of objects, as long as the arrangement excites him and suits his needs. This is exactly what happens in this and other parasol paintings. As Christa said, there are no rules, but this last rule of hers only applies if the painter is good enough.

The Red Kimono I
Oil on canvas, 1989. 40 × 48ins (RA 1989, No 1122).

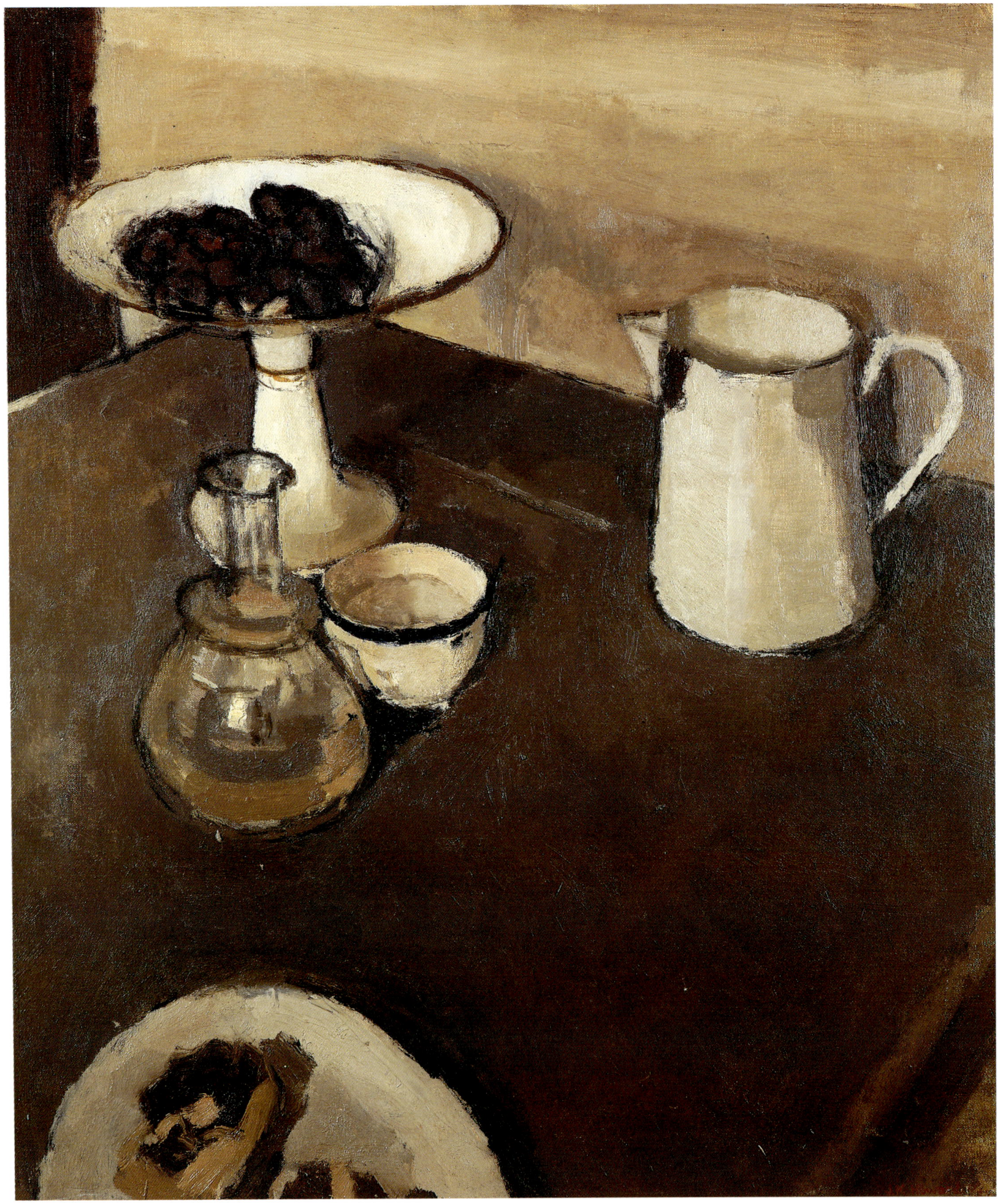

Still-Life

If anyone needed reminding, this is where Howard was before – before the explosion of colour, before the studios and the beaches, before Northern Ireland and the City churches – a tonal painter.

This picture came onto the market recently and its rarity value, as one of his relatively few still-lifes from previous decades, was appropriately reflected by its price. Reproduced here, it is way out of historical context, but the comparison with the example opposite of the still fairly infrequent still-lifes of recent years is instructive of how far the artist has travelled.

A painter who responds strongly to the human presence and the glories of sunlight might find still-life rather small beer. Yet if the weather is bad or the model hasn't turned up, an artist of Howard's resources and dedication will find an alternative:

'Most days I do feel I must paint. I just love using paint. I don't mean by that I sit down and paint just for the sake of it – I can't see any point in starting a painting unless I'm touched by something. This initial idea – the imagination of what the picture will look like – is absolutely crucial. If you've got your eyes at least half open, you will see potential subjects all day as you walk around – but it's only some of them that can be seen as pictures. Although I am not a still-life painter to any great degree I do sometimes see a picture in a still-life, or even want to set one up.'

Being as interested in formal composition and the abstract relationships of flat shapes as he was at the time, it is not surprising that Howard should find the qualities he was seeking in this frugal arrangement of vessels. This was also a period in which he was deeply affected by the art of the Italian painter of still-lifes, Giorgio Morandi, and indeed by the work of the Kitchen Sink realist painters of 1950s England. The extremely limited palette and flat, even lighting reflect both sources of influence. The simple, near-abstracted volumes of the objects echo the table-top paintings of William Scott, who would lift the table surface up to become synonymous with the picture-plane. The way the vessels are, on the other hand, almost carved out of space, suggests the impact of some of Morandi's more hard-edged pictures.

The result is perhaps eclectic, but when seen in the context of the railway yards and the later cathedrals, its formality is stamped with Howard's own personal style. This has much to do with the artist's carefully wrought brushwork, which brings light and reality into what could otherwise have been an exercise in modernist pattern-making.

Still-Life
Oil on canvas, c 1957. 24 × 20ins.

Spring Light, Mousehole II
Beside the solidity and seriousness of the early *Still-Life*, this recent painting of the Mousehole living-room window ledge seems positively vaporous and light-hearted. Instead of the weight of pottery and enamel, the principal interest of this still-life is light, drenching living plants and blooms. The familiar honesty also appears and, with the daffodils, acts as a brilliant lightbreak.

With the artist looking at an angle to the sun, which is obscured to the left, the direct light is, for all its brilliance, almost hazy. He has not been too dazzled to be able to see reflected light and detail in the shadows. The misty, veiled effect that results is most subtly conveyed and is instantly recognisable.

'I saw some daffodils in the room once, and the light was blazing through them. I realised this sight was more of an expression of light than I have ever seen in any single object. The *contre-jour* effect of the greys of the village in the background threw up the transparent yellows as the sun caught the daffodils. I painted several versions of the subject in that first spring. I have done one or two since, but never with that same initial excitement of discovery.'

This canvas is painted with delightful freshness and one senses the newness of the experience. That Howard could not continue convincingly with the subject in subsequent years does suggest he had taken from it all that was available for him and that those precious moments are now gone.

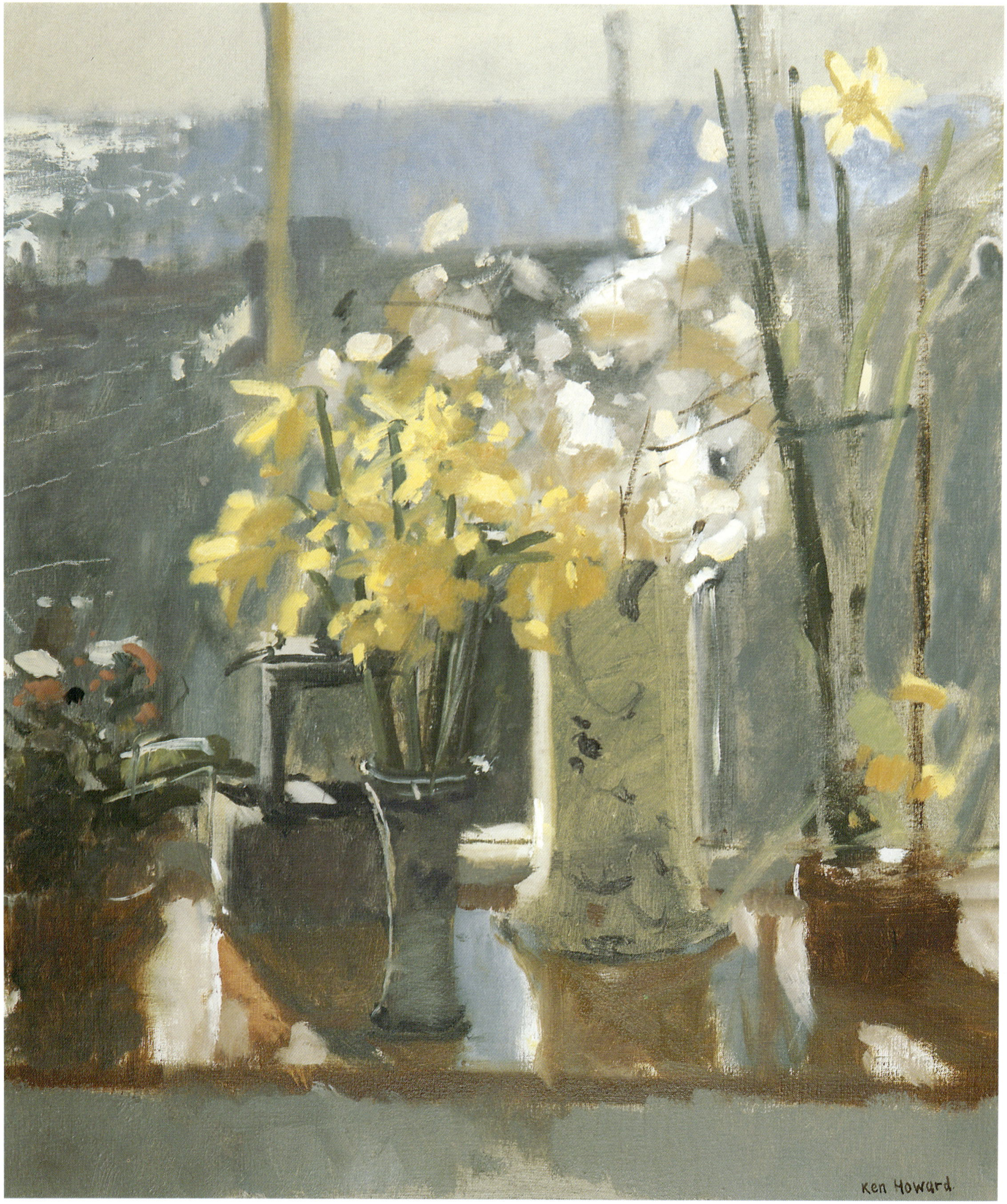

Spring Light, Mousehole II
Oil on canvas, 1989. 24 × 20ins.

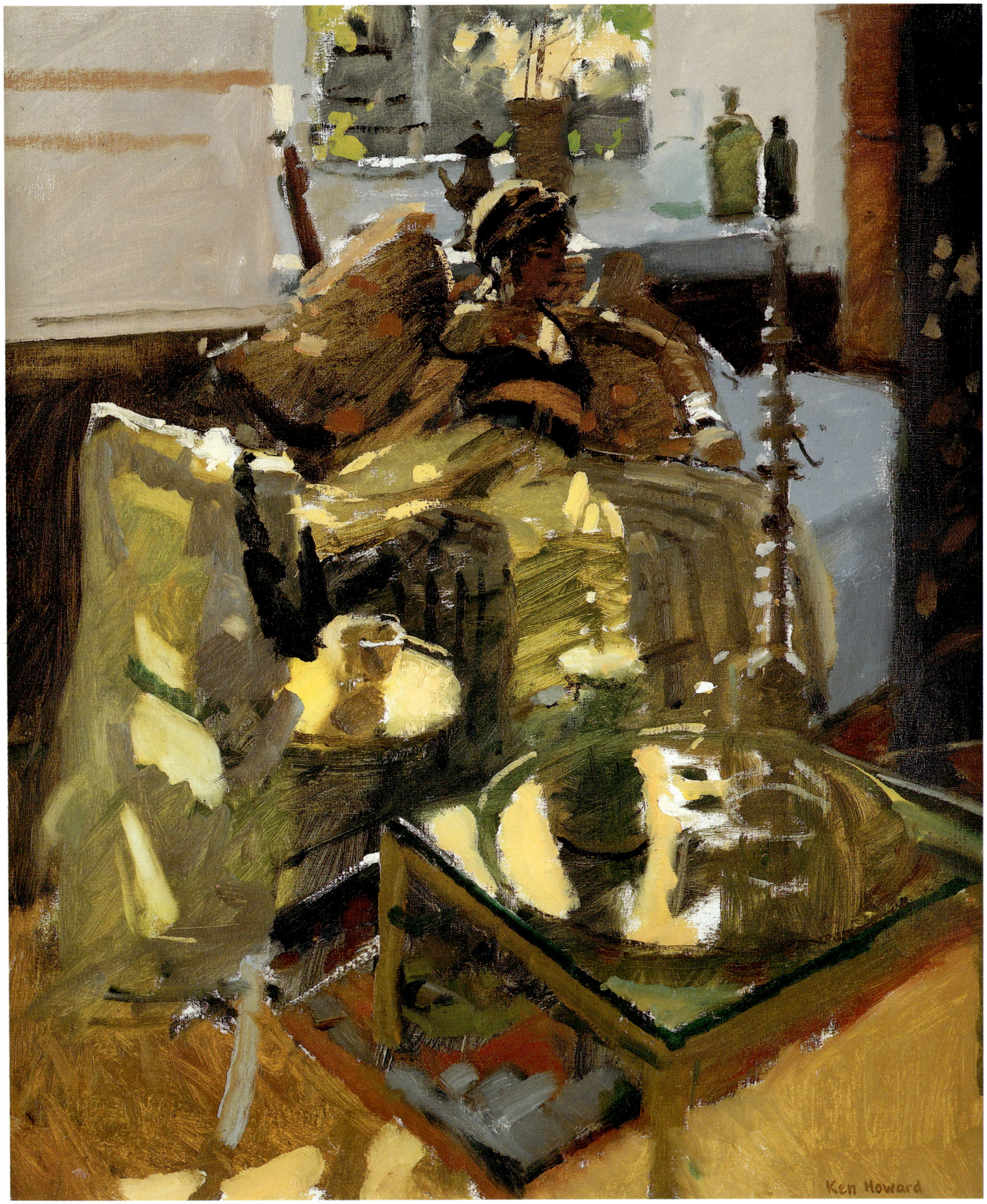

The Yellow Culottes
With his recently brightened and broadened palette accommodating the yellow of the daffodils, it was a logical step for Howard to capture the warm summer light of West Penwith on yellow and gold fabrics. As he did with the *Red Lightbreak*, he has again given full vent to his excitement at the sight of sun on fabric, in this vigorous small painting of his model, Lorraine, in her culottes. In his keenness to get the image onto canvas, the personality of the model has been subsumed in the explosion of colour and splashes of light.

This fairly recent canvas, though small in scale, is perhaps indicative of the way Howard wishes his art to go. The palette is broad and bright and the handling is more fragmented than before. Rather than describe the subtlest reflections of coloured light with a unifying hue, he has given each separate surface the equivalent, in oils, of a watercolour wash. This takes the form of a relatively even application of near-pure colour onto a ground that is white, rather than the habitual earth-coloured grounds of his earlier studio paintings. These flat shapes are summaries of the variations of light and colour falling onto the surfaces.

The technique and palette are reminiscent of Matisse, as is the Mediterranean richness of the subject. Indeed the lineage of the *'odalisque's'* attire and pose stretch back through Matisse to Ingres' and Delacroix's Arabian-inspired Orientalism. More opulent and lush than the Whistlerian kimono pictures, this relatively brief flirtation with the Orientalist tradition reaches a zenith in the majestic painting known as *Lorraine and the Yellow Culottes*:

'Lorraine had a marvellous range of clothes, which she started bringing up to the studio. I found that the paintings were beginning to become less of just the model in the studio and more of an exotic interior, with lots of eastern fabrics and objects. In the larger picture you can see the rug on the bed, and pinned on the wall behind Lorraine is a large bedcover, both of which I got while trekking in Nepal. Then on the table there is an Omani coffee pot I watched a man in Niswa make, while I was working there for the Omani army, and beside it a Nepalese copper pot. To the right of those is a hookah I've had since I was very young. In all it's a sort of record of my travels.

'And then there are Lorraine's wonderful gold trousers. At this time I was beginning to clothe the figure more. It started off with models having their robes on. I liked the way the fabric both wrapped around and revealed the figure. As Lorraine had all these lovely bits of frippery – funny things like clown's trousers – I started painting them more and more.

'With all the exotic colours, my palette continued to widen. I originally started to introduce red, then I

The Yellow Culottes
Oil on canvas, 1989. 24 × 20ins.

found that through the trousers I was beginning to use yellow. It wasn't very long before I found myself using green, and then the green and the red produced my blacks. Essentially I was starting to work in the studio with my outdoor palette. I haven't yet fully understood how to use it indoors. Every now and then I go through a terribly depressed patch, when I think I've lost the ability to use it and retire back into my earth palette again. But now, more and more quickly I find myself drawn back again to the wider, more primary palette.

'I think you have to grow into colour, like you grow into freedom of handling. When I was a student I saw a lot of good tonal painters who suddenly caught colour. They imposed colour on themselves, rather than it developing naturally, and their work never grew organically from then on.'

Lorraine and the Yellow Culottes

The chair is removed, the bedcover pinned up and the higher Cornish sun cuts less of a swathe through the composition. The overall effect is more luxuriant and the rich colouring resonates across the canvas. The dominant red of the bedspread, juxtaposed with vibrant accents of yellow, green and black, could be Venetian. The glorious, free brushwork hints at late Titian. This is a colourist's painting, and surely one of the most ravishing of all Howard's studio pictures.

The clothed model's face, although lit from over her left shoulder, is more clearly seen and portrayed than in the majority of the artist's paintings of the nude. The latter are characteristically seen *contre-jour*, clothing the naked woman with the mystery of light. Often the light effect will silhouette a particular movement of the limbs, or a twist of the body. Clothed, the model becomes less a beautiful object and more a portrait sitter – and the artist appears to feel more inclined to turn the light onto her face.

The effect of sunlight on the side of the model visible to the spectator has another purpose. While the kimono paintings exploit the quality of light shining through fabric, here the artist wants us to see clearly the inherent brilliance of the culottes and the sensuous contrast with her skin of Lorraine's black top. Like the paintings of black stockinged models which similarly study this juxtaposition of colour and tone, the effect is if anything more sensual than the dispassionate, and by comparison more anonymous, nudes. It is almost as though the life class has become more the class of life.

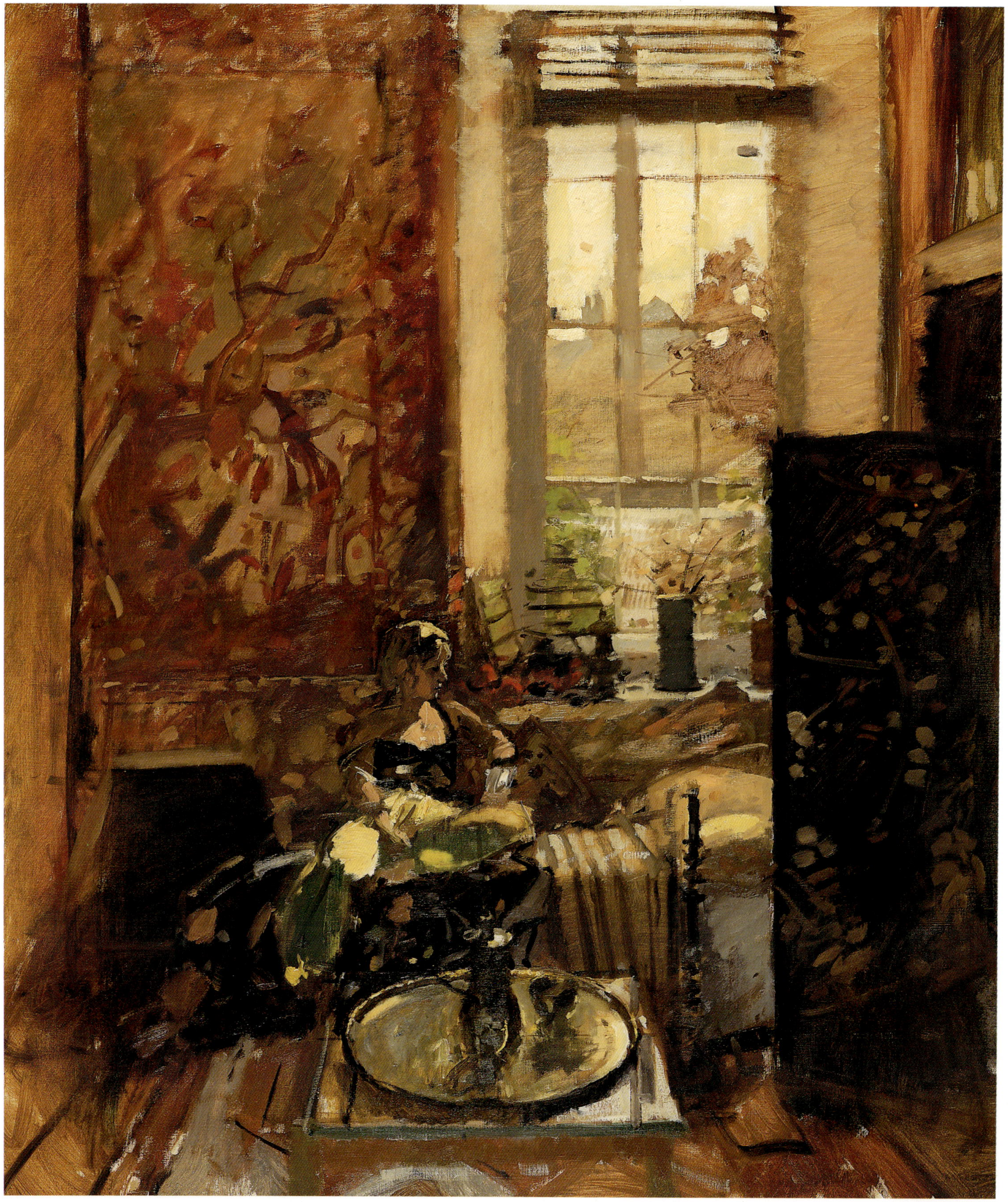

Lorraine and the Yellow Culottes
Oil on canvas, 1990. 48 × 40ins.

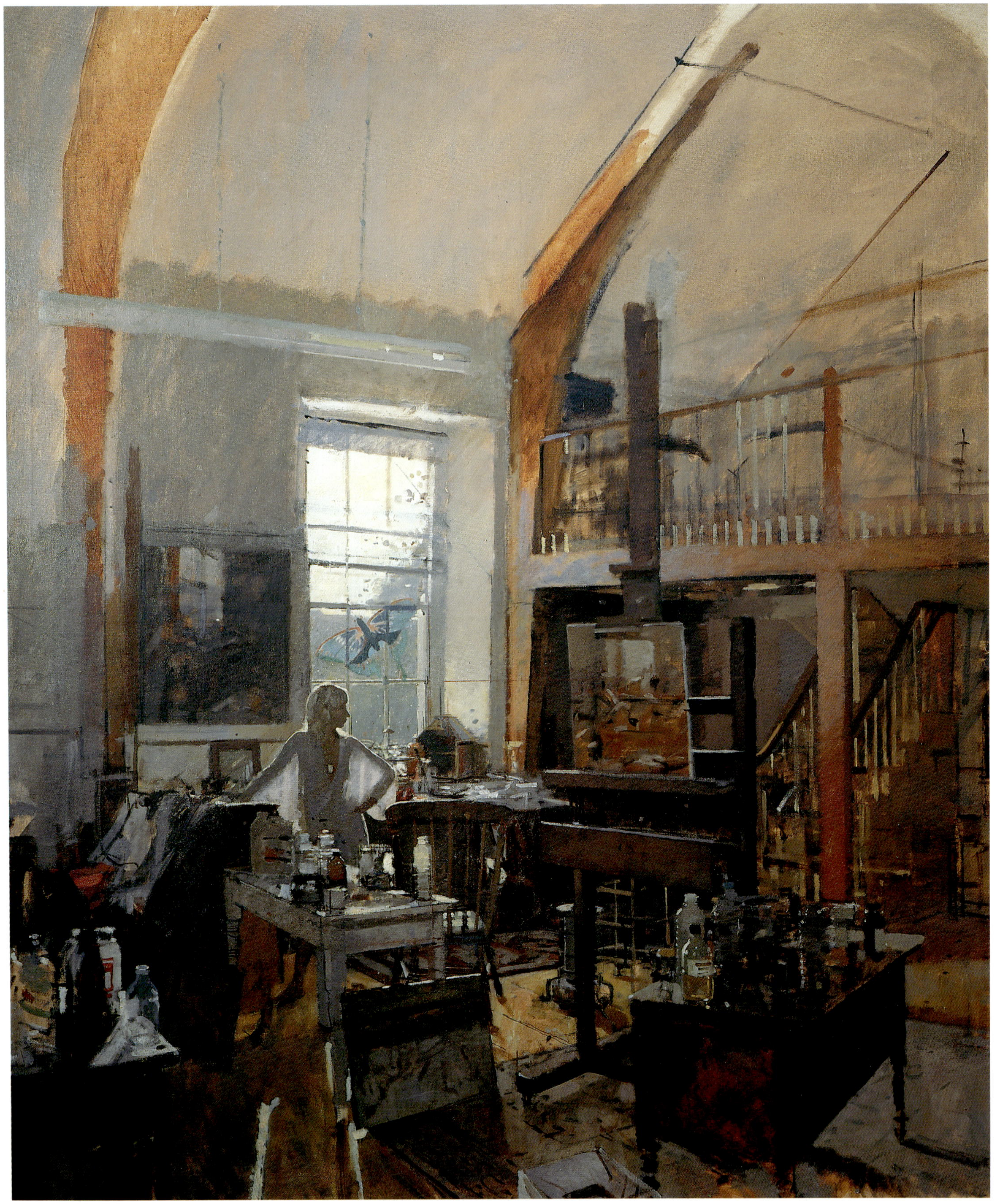

Morning Sunlight, August 1988
This is one of the most open views Howard has made of his vast studio space. He has already stated that the shifting variations of light in St Clement's Studio make him less sure of painting the interior landscape than he is at Oriel. We have indeed noted that he has tended to choose a window alcove to set up his model, initially perhaps for warmth, but no doubt also because the total landscape was too extensive for his purposes.

This large, formal, and highly finished painting resolves successfully the problem of depicting the studio clutter against a strong eastern light, without it all sinking into *contre-jour* shadow. The jars, bottles and furniture are all seen with a stunning clarity, right down to the individual sheen on different woods. The artist's sensitivity to the particularity of light is once again revealed with breathtaking lucidity. To confirm this we only have to compare the tablescapes with the different effects on any of those from South Bolton Gardens. The model's clothes have become a lightbreak once again and largely obscure the bright and potentially dazzling area where the direct sun enters the room. Thus the transparency of the cloth is emphasised, and at the same time the eye is given complete freedom to explore the crisp and detailed shadows of this splendid canvas.

'When I painted this I was beginning to work from time to time on a larger scale than my usual 48 by 40 inches. I was very much into the idea of taking the eye for a walk around the studio and felt that if I was going to do this in the Cornish studio, it should be on a large scale. This is one of the first pictures I did after I had the balcony built. In a way I suppose I wanted to celebrate the balcony, and so made it quite an important part of the composition.

'This very large interior also shows Lorraine, who is very small. She has a butterfly tattooed on her back and when she first posed for me this idea of the butterfly really got hold of me. I used to constantly paint her back, and I even acquired some paper butterflies to include in pictures. In this painting I got rather carried away with this idea of a butterfly, and of the light shining through its wings. A butterfly kite in the window catches the sunlight and so does the robe she is wearing, so that with her arms out it almost looks like a butterfly's wings.'

Through Whistler's prominent use of a Japanese inspired butterfly as his monogram on paintings and prints, the stylisation of the insect became something of a symbol of the Aesthetic Movement. While Howard's knowledge of the one on Lorraine's back was a matter of chance, his interest in the butterfly's diaphanous wings continues his exploration of the lightbreak. His use of the kite is probably a direct homage to Whistler.

Morning Sunlight, August 1988
Oil on canvas, 1988. 60 × 50ins (RA 1989, No 1128)

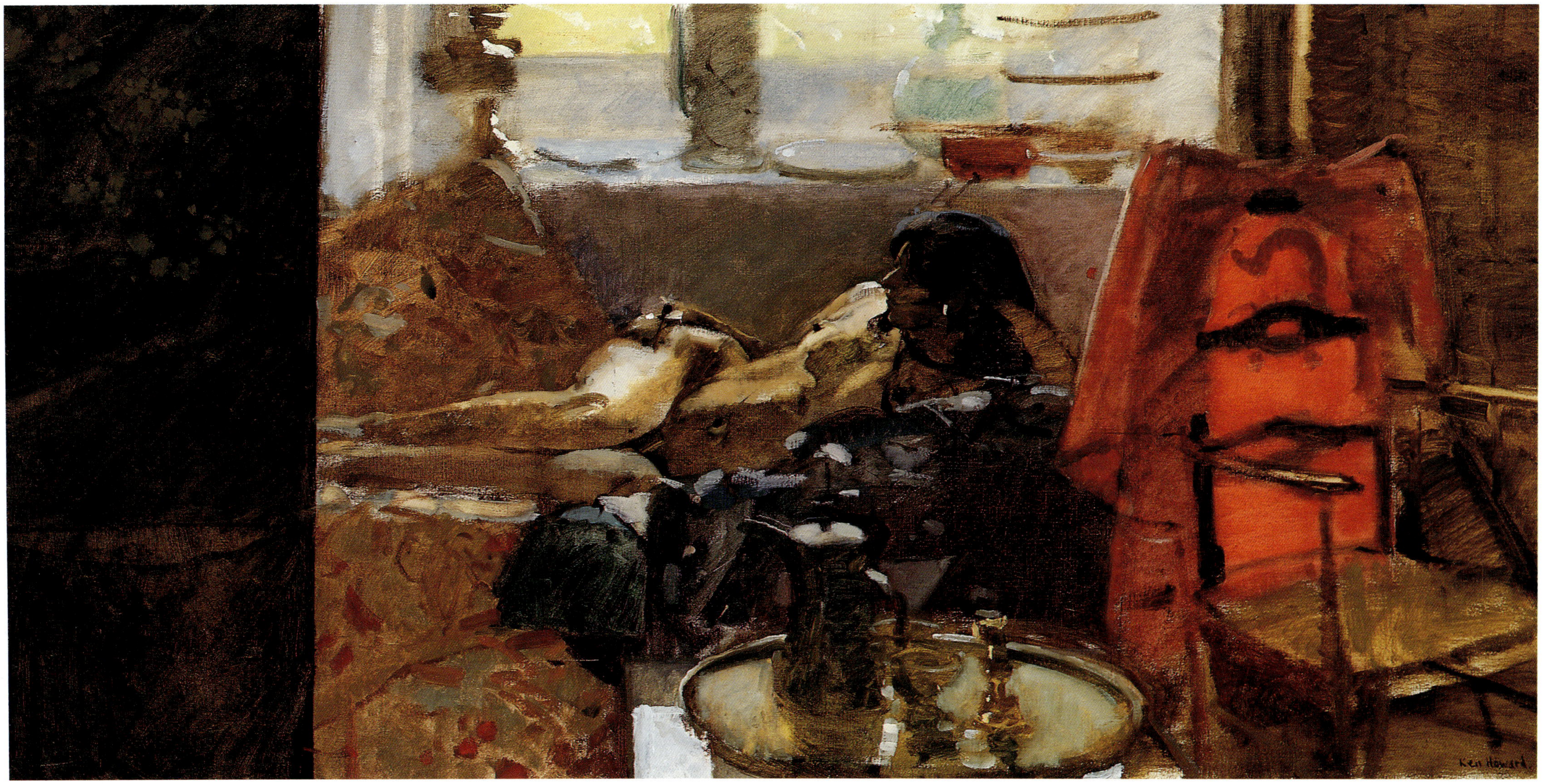

Sarah Allongée
This recent painting, made in the Mousehole studio, is a further example of the artist's ever-evolving freedom of language. The red lightbreak from the kimono paintings and the rich colouring of fabrics and artefacts from the Orientalist phase are combined in a geometric composition that owes more to Japanese design than it does to hard-edge abstraction. In truth, like the work of any consummate eclectic, the painting owes much to many and nothing to anyone. Howard's personal language has reached such an advanced state of development that he can incorporate influences and ideas from other painters, in depicting a subject he has painted hundreds of times before – and produce something new:

'In this painting I was working to keep a contrast between transparency and opacity, something I've been trying to do ever since I first started painting the sunlight. I try not to let the darks get too compact. That is Chrissie's term for it and I know exactly what she means – the paint becomes compact and there's no air in it, no space. Consequently the darks become just dull and heavy. If this happens, the only way you can rescue them is by glazing over, making them very dark but removing the solidity. *Sarah Allongée* has in it a lot of transparent colour. It's a studio picture which is in a way a balance between the earth palette and the primary palette. I let quite a lot of primary colours into it, but there was still quite a strong earth base.

'The double square is one of the canvas shapes that I've come to like very much. And I love the idea of breaking it up into very simple areas first of all – the screen on the left cutting off a whole section of area of view, and then allowing the eye to go past it to the figure lying on the bed.

'Sarah was one of my best models of the last year or so. She had a marvellous way of relaxing as she was posing, and seemed to quite enjoy the process of modelling. When I do these relaxing poses I don't like very strong sunlight, because then the figure becomes much more cut up. This one I painted in the spring on a bright but not sunny day, so there's a lot of light reflecting off the figure.'

Sarah Allongée
Oil on canvas, 1990. 24 × 48ins (RA 1990, No 83).

The model is superbly drawn with broad, thin brushstrokes. It may be that her relaxation while posing has encouraged the artist to describe her form more clearly than some of his earlier nudes. The soft light catching her body also illuminates the red shirt and reflects on the glass table-top. Its unifying influence brings together the several strongly coloured shapes into a harmonious design.

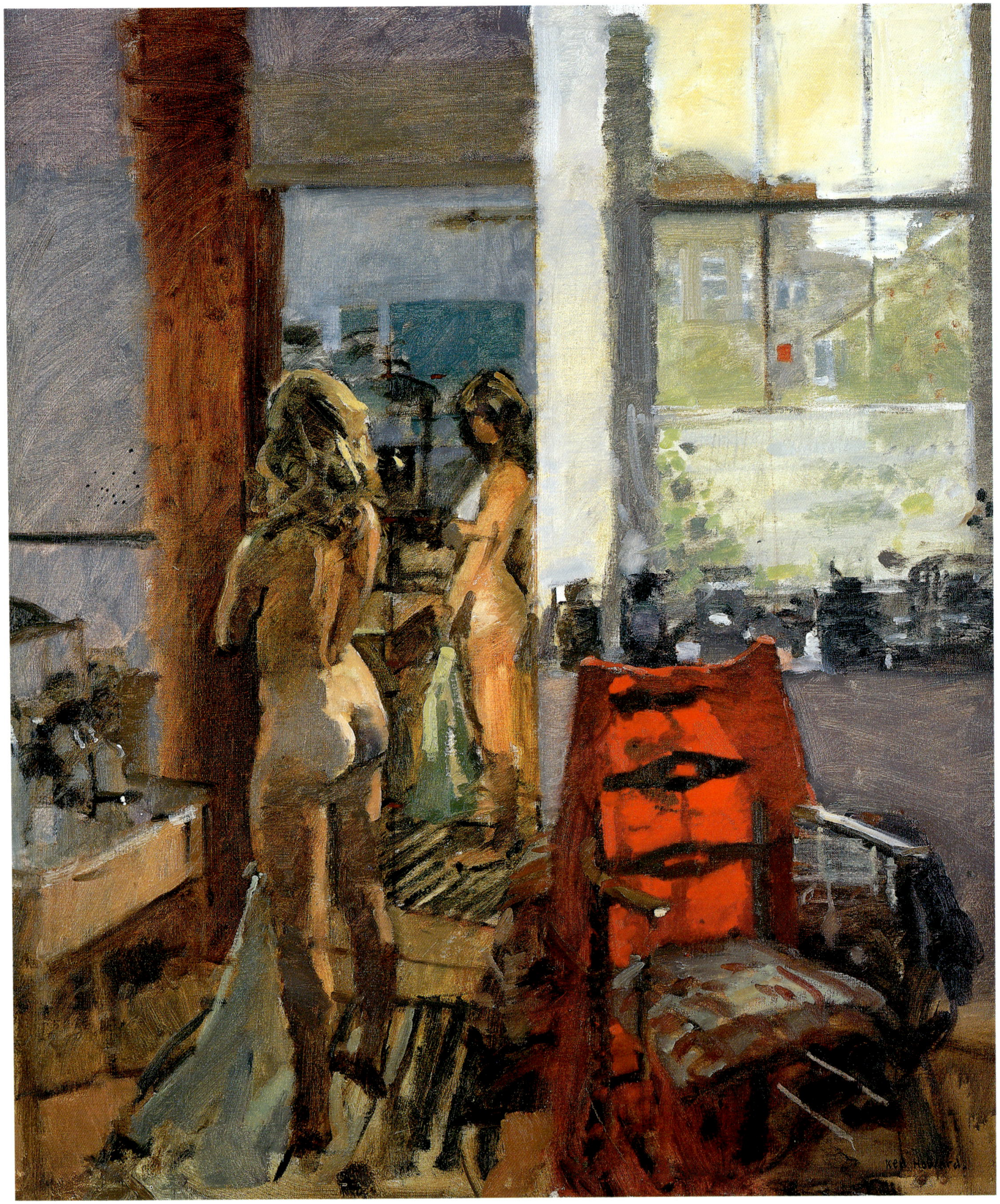

Charlotte Reflecting
'In 1990 I started a series of paintings of reflections in the studio. I've had two big mirrors put up here in Cornwall and I might yet get more put up. It harks back to an earlier period when I was doing a lot of reflecting subjects, whether they were reflections of cars in shop windows, or churches in marble walls. I wanted to get new space into the studio and also introduce a new theme.

'I've become very keen on back views of models. This is partly because the back presents a simple shape, but also to get the mirror image of her front. Mirror images have always excited me. There is a certain magic about them – the way that animals react to mirrors – the way that some animals aren't even able to see a reflection. I think even some humans aren't able to see a reflection. The whole issue of mirror pictures presents great possibilities in the next year or so.'

Within the familiar arrangement of motifs in St Clement's Studio, Howard has posed Charlotte against a subdued light, which brightens her mirror image sufficiently to draw our attention and gives some illumination to the shadows. Her back is, as it were, sculpted out of the air by the hazy light, which also catches a red kimono, glowing with deep resonance. If the light is restrained, the powerfully brushed passages of strong colour are not:

'You can see my palette is again lightened. When my 1990 exhibition was on, there was comment upon the fact the paintings were now so much lighter, so much brighter in colour. People said this must mean I was a much happier man. I never think consciously of things like that – in fact I've tended to deny such things, because I have believed very much in painting being an objective exercise, that should not really be dependent on the state of mind of the person who is doing it. But in fact I have been proved wrong on this, and I know it. In the three or four months after my mother died, for instance, I painted very dark, sombre pictures – not deliberately, not that I wanted to.

'Yes, I am happier. After that long wait I married Chrissie in 1990, and she continues to be a source of strength and constructive criticism. Although I still go through this business of pictures rarely satisfying me, I now feel a certain confidence in what I'm doing. This is also very much helped by the people who seem to want what I paint.'

Charlotte Reflecting
Oil on canvas, 1990. 36 × 30ins.

And Turner came to Mousehole
The title of this painting was suggested by a radio broadcast by the late Gerald Priestland, called *And Christ came to Ding Dong*. The programme concerned an old Sunday school – near a mine with this unusual name, between St Ives and Penzance – that Priestland had converted. Howard had met Priestland, and perhaps their similar experiences in building work meant the unusual title stuck in his mind. It resurfaced when he was asked to paint a homage to Turner for a National Trust Foundation for Art exhibition and auction, at which the resulting canvas obtained the second highest price.

'I thought that if I did a Turnerian landscape I would fall flat on my face. For some years I had believed that if Turner had actually come to St Clement's Studio early in the morning, he would have been absolutely knocked out. So I decided to do a painting of the studio interior, with Turner standing at the easel painting.

'Like *Ulster Crucifixion* and *Boat People* it is in a sense an imaginary picture – obviously not even I have ever seen Turner in Mousehole. But when I was in the Marines, I met a chap in Plymouth called Turner. He swore that he was a descendant of an illegitimate child of J.M.W. Turner, conceived on a West Country tour. This man was slightly mad, but he was convinced that his "ancestor" did come to Cornwall on one of these tours. Much later I remembered this and began to muse on the idea of Turner actually working in this studio.'

So here he is, *contre-jour* and rather mysterious, but unmistakably the dumpy figure of Turner. On his easel rests a canvas, on which he appears to be working. From what we can see it seems to be one of the late, personal works, in which radiant light fills the picture and dissolves all form. Around him are not his own trappings, but Ken Howard's silk shirt catching the light, and two of the same artist's beach canvases on nearby easels. We are seeing an apparition of the great man in the St Clement's Studio of today:

'I used a dress stand, on which I sometimes leave kimonos, as the figure. Then finally I got Charlotte – who is herself quite short – to pose, so that I knew I would get the scale right. I also used some funny little things like the model boat in the foreground, which I imagine was the kind of thing Turner might have used when painting his sea pieces. But I couldn't resist my silk shirt to sum up the whole feeling of light breaking through things.

'I managed to keep the picture very transparent, something I am aiming for more and more. In a sense I would like to break down the barriers between the use of oils and watercolour. Since the Impressionists and people like the Euston Road painters, Ginner and Gore, there has been such a tendency to paint thickly – *à la prima*. The whole history of using transparent colour and glazes seemed to be thrown away. Perhaps this was because it is a studio rather than an on-the-spot process.

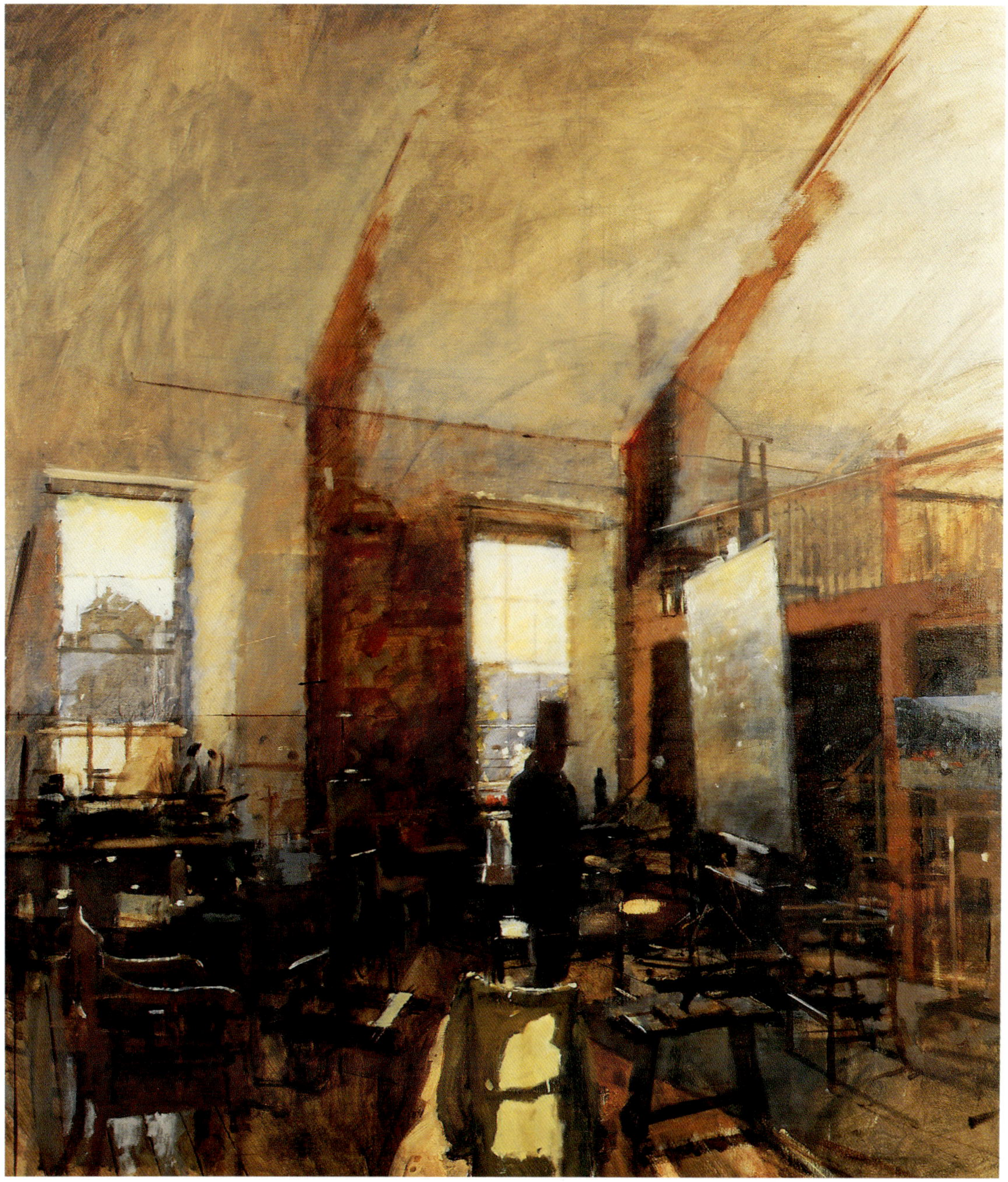

And Turner came to Mousehole
Oil on canvas, 1989. 60 × 50ins.

'For some while I have been trying to bring this process back into my work – not only glazing when the picture is finished, but keeping the paint itself transparent and open, and getting a difference in texture between the thick light paint and the thin darks. In this particular painting, I thought that came off. The darks in the lower part of the picture never became thick, heavy and bogged down. I got them by building up glaze after glaze when the painting was dry.'

The result is quite magical. The studio is bathed in the sparkling West Penwith sunlight, flooding through the windows. Howard has taken an unusual, and very successful, wide angle of vision, embracing two windows on this large canvas. Thus he has allowed more sunlight to flow over the picture and opened up the arrangement of furniture to more complex light and shade. This complexity he handles with breathtaking lucidity and breadth. His thin brush-strokes seem to absorb every last drop of the light. Although Turner's apparition in Ken Howard's studio was temporary, what both men will continue to share is that they have been drawn to such light as to a drug, and each in his own way has understood its qualities.

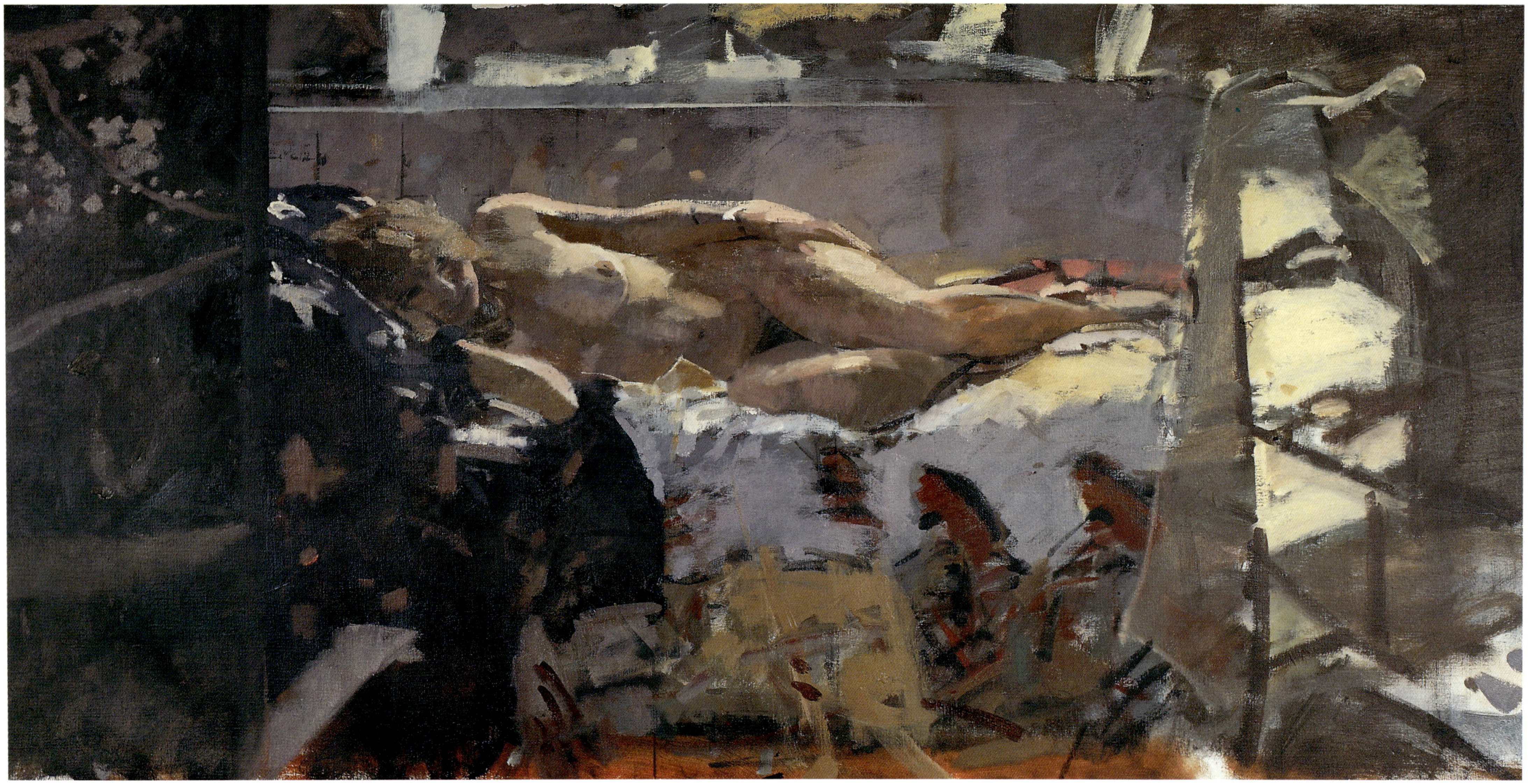

Charlotte and the Silk Shirt
This painting of Charlotte is typical of the double-square canvases, vertical as well as horizontal, that Howard has been working on in recent years. Lying the opposite way from *Sarah Allongée*, the model has again been posed behind a silk lightbreak on the right, and the rectangle of the screen to the left. The artist's deep-rooted interest in composing with horizontals and verticals is pivotal to these two works, in which the figures form T-squares with the rectangle of the screen.

'This long thin shape has often intrigued me, both for landscapes and interiors. I particularly liked to use it for the railway pictures, because somehow the shape of the subject seemed to suggest the shape of the canvas. So it is with the reclining figure. For me it is quite common for the subject itself to dictate the type of canvas that should be used. Having got the subject and having got the canvas, one then begins to compose relative to the two things. Often I've started a painting and just not been able to get the composition to work. I've then realised that in fact all the stresses and all the main movements in the picture are fighting against the shape of the canvas.

'This image was in fact painted over another picture. I quite like using an old picture as a base, because there are already colours and tones to which I can relate the start of the new painting. I don't always put a coloured ground on my canvas and indeed in the last year or so, while I've been concentrating on the possibilities of glazes, I have tended to keep the canvas white. Nevertheless, when I run into a real problem with a picture, I let it dry off for a couple of months and then use it as a base for another one. Often this does produce an effect which is quite different from the picture painted on fresh canvas. In fact sometimes I can leave quite a lot of the first painting showing, to work within the context of the new painting.'

Charlotte and the Silk Shirt
Oil on canvas, 1990. 48 × 24ins.

The light filling this scene is more diffused and hazy than that striking Sarah. The effect is achieved in part by the application of thin washes of paint over the textured surface of the existing picture. The tiny ridges of the brush-strokes underneath catch reflected light and give a soft sparkle to the picture surface. The light gently bathes the form of the reclining figure and settles in the artist's shirt. The atmosphere is nostalgic, almost mysterious, and the pastel colours reminiscent of Bonnard or Vuillard. The handling is exceptionally free, but no sharp brush-strokes jar the sleepy mood.

The Yellow Kimono II
As a final sentence to this chapter of studio paintings, this small canvas makes remarkable reading. So much so, that it suggests rather a beginning than a denouement. It is so thinly covered that, as a plastic substance, the paint has all but evaporated from the canvas. The texture of the canvas is visually the most reliably solid thing about the picture. The paint has in fact been worked and scraped and rescraped, paring the image down to the core, as Howard once saw and admired in the work of Giacometti and Pasmore.

Any sexuality his nudes might have possessed has also gone from this work. The artist is looking beyond the immediate physical presence of the woman, beyond even the shimmer of sunlight on his silk shirt, characteristically draped on a foreground chair. In this hard-won and summary image, Howard appears to be looking forward to a less physical way of painting. Perhaps the gesture will be less grand, the composition less complex, the light captured and drawn with less felicitous naturalism.

However Ken Howard's art matures, it will undoubtedly continue the purposeful evolution that we have seen from the early 1980s, when he decided to give up commissioned work and focus upon nurturing the painter within. Having made this important decision, he settled on a few subject themes. Through reworking these again and again, he drove himself hard in search of ever greater lucidity. Although he has never been one to cut corners, Howard was not now going to waste any more time in his urgent mission of discovery. In gradually but surely crystallising his painterly language, he now moves ever closer towards the source of all vision – the source of light.

'My idea of the way the artist develops is by refining and continuing to refine certain ideas and themes. I know this isn't the only way. Picasso obviously developed by inventing and trying new ideas all the time. He made big steps forward, then consolidated, then took another big step. But the people I most love – like Velázquez and Goya, Corot and Monet – are all men whose essential vision I think didn't change. It was their ways and means of expressing that vision, and the depth to which they could express it, that developed.

'I don't feel I have yet painted the picture I really want to paint. So far I have never got up in the morning and wondered what I was going to paint that day. I have always had an image in front of me of what I am striving for. As long as this lasts I shall feel that I have something to say. I still have a great desire to be able to paint more naturally, more directly, more freely, and to have an ever clearer idea in my mind of what I want to put down. I have realised in recent years that light has always been my principal concern. The question for the future is how that light will be expressed.'

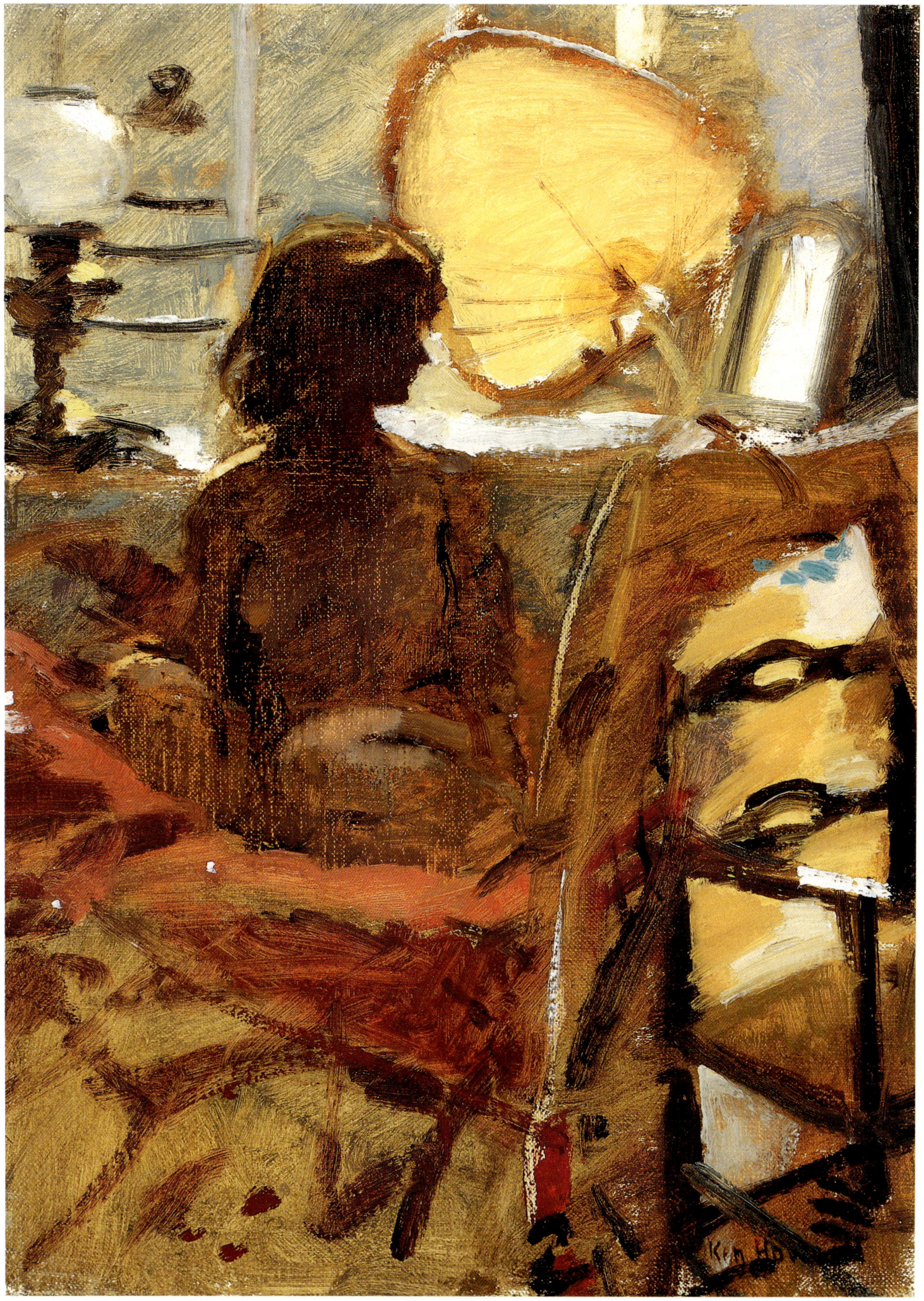

The Yellow Kimono II
Oil on canvas, 1990. 14 × 10ins.

Index of Illustrated Works

Photographic Acknowledgements

Belgrave Gallery
Chapman, Robert
Charing Cross Hospital, Department of Medical Illustration
Cooper, A. C., Ltd
Ellerslie, Max
Greenly, Richard
Imperial War Museum
Johnson, Oscar & Peter, Ltd
Macaré, Steve
Richardson, John
Royal Academy of Arts
Schnepf, Lothar
Slingsby, Miki
Spender, Michael
Times Photographic Service, Richmond
Todd-White, Rodney & Son
Wedgewood, Peter W.